Tinkercad™

A Wiley Brand

Tinkercad™

by Shaun C. Bryant
Autodesk Certified Professional

for
dummies®
A Wiley Brand

Tinkercad™ For Dummies®

Published by: **John Wiley & Sons, Inc.**, 111 River Street, Hoboken, NJ 07030-5774, www.wiley.com

Copyright © 2018 by John Wiley & Sons, Inc., Hoboken, New Jersey

Published simultaneously in Canada

For general information on our other products and services, please contact our Customer Care Department within the U.S. at 877-762-2974, outside the U.S. at 317-572-3993, or fax 317-572-4002. For technical support, please visit https://hub.wiley.com/community/support/dummies.

Wiley publishes in a variety of print and electronic formats and by print-on-demand. Some material included with standard print versions of this book may not be included in e-books or in print-on-demand. If this book refers to media such as a CD or DVD that is not included in the version you purchased, you may download this material at http://booksupport.wiley.com. For more information about Wiley products, visit www.wiley.com.

Library of Congress Control Number: 2018932639

ISBN 978-1-119-46441-9 (pbk); ISBN 978-1-119-46448-8 (ePub); 978-1-119-46447-1 (ePDF)

Manufactured in the United States of America

10 9 8 7 6 5 4 3 2 1

Contents at a Glance

Table of Contents

Introduction

Welcome to *Tinkercad For Dummies!*

This book has been written for you to get a head start with Autodesk's amazing entry-level 3D modeling app called Tinkercad. Tinkercad is cloud-based, so you don't need any expensive 3D modeling software to get started — just an Internet connection and a computer, such as a desktop PC or a suitable laptop.

You find out about basic 3D modeling concepts and how to use Tinkercad to model simple 3D designs, which in turn you can then 3D print, using the information and lessons provided.

Tinkercad is a great way to get started in the world of 3D modeling and 3D design, regardless of age, experience, and expertise, and this book is a perfect way to get your first step into that 3D world. Enjoy!

About This Book

So why do you need *Tinkercad For Dummies?* Well, this book gives you a great insight in to Tinkercad, world-class instruction that you find in *For Dummies* books, and easy-access organization.

Throughout this book, I follow several conventions:

>> **Bold text** means that you're meant to type the text just as it appears in the book. The exception is when you're working through a steps list: Because each step is bold, the text to type is not bold.

>> If you're reading a digital version of this book on a device connected to the Internet, note that you can click the web address to visit that website, like this: www.dummies.com.

>> Tinkercad is a browser-based app. Therefore, you may find that some of your regular keyboard shortcuts and the right-hand mouse button menu

are not available. You can, however, find a great list of keyboard shortcuts and commands on the Tinkercad blog at `https://blog.tinkercad.com/keyboard-shortcuts/`.

Foolish Assumptions

This book is aimed at the Tinkercad beginner who has general computer knowledge, such as the ability to use a PC/laptop/MacBook, a mouse, and a keyboard. I also use the Microsoft Windows operating system throughout this book, so you may see subtle differences when using Tinkercad on a browser when using a Mac with the Mac OSX operating system.

I also assume that you know how to use an Internet browser. (I use Google Chrome throughout this book as the host browser for Tinkercad).

As Tinkercad is browser-based, you can find a plethora of assistance available on the Tinkercad website at `https://blog.tinkercad.com/`, with numerous help screens and the Tinkercad blog.

Icons Used in This Book

Throughout the margins in this book are little pictures. Here's what those icons mean:

The Tip icon marks tips (duh!) and shortcuts that you can use to make using Tinkercad easier.

The Remember icon marks the information that's especially important to know. To siphon off the most important information in each chapter, just skim through these icons.

The Technical Stuff icon marks information of a highly technical nature that you can normally skip over.

The Warning icon tells you to watch out! It marks important information that may save you headaches when using Tinkercad.

Beyond the Book

Extra content is available beyond this book. If you go online, you can find the following:

>> **Sample 3D output files that you can use in conjunction with this book:** Output STL, OBJ, and SVG files from Chapters 17, 18, and 19 are available at www.dummies.com/go/tinkercadfd.

>> **The Tinkercad blog and gallery:** You can find a huge amount of useful information in the pages of the Tinkercad blog at https://blog.tinkercad.com/. Here, you find many uses of Tinkercad and user designs. You're also able to converse about Tinkercad with other users. Check out numerous user designs in the Tinkercad gallery as well at www.tinkercad.com/things.

>> **The Cheat Sheet for this book:** At www.dummies.com/cheatsheet/tinkercad, you'll find a roadmap to setting up your drawings and keyboard shortcuts.

>> **Updates to this book:** If we have any, you can find them at www.dummies.com/go/tinkercadfdupdates.

Where to Go from Here

So where do you go from here? Well, if you're like me, you'll follow this book all the way through from start to finish. But that's just how I roll. You may not want to work like that. That's the benefits of a *For Dummies* title, though. The book is not linear. You can start anywhere and then get going, using the book as a reference.

Here are a few suggestions if you want to get straight into designing with Tinkercad:

>> **Part 2, Chapter 6** gets you going with the beginnings of a 3D nameplate to design.

>> **Part 3, Chapter 10** gets you straight into designing a simple skyscraper, with its own helicopter landing pad.

Also, make sure to check out the Part of Tens. These chapters offer some great background information that will stand you in good stead as you start to involve yourself more deeply in 3D modeling.

1

Getting Started with Tinkercad

IN THIS PART . . .

Learn about 3D modeling, the modeling process, and various modeling techniques.

Get started with Tinkercad by creating a Tinkercad account, logging in and out of Tinkercad, and creating a Tinkercad design.

View recent designs, choose options and settings, find the help screens, and visit the Tinkercad Twitter page, gallery, and blog.

Explore the Tinkercad user interface and use the ViewCube, viewing tools, the Tinkercad grid, and keyboard shortcuts.

Explore the 3D tools in Tinkercad, including Copy and Paste, Duplicate, Hide, Show All, Group and Ungroup, Align, Flip, Workplane, Ruler, the Tinkercad Basic Shapes menu, and the Featured Shape Generators and Community Shape Generators.

Chapter **1**

Exploring 3D Design

n this chapter, you discover all things 3D so that you can understand the basic terminology and concepts of the 3D universe before you go rushing off to the world of Tinkercad.

What Is 3D Modeling?

3D is the abbreviation for 3-dimensional. In the world of *Computer Aided Design* (CAD), *3D modeling* (also known as three-dimensional modeling) is the process or workflow of developing a computer-based (mathematical) model of any surface of an object, regardless of whether it's inanimate (such as a gear wheel) or living (such as an animal or a human being).

3D modeling is done in three dimensions via specialized software and, in your case, Tinkercad. The end product is normally called a *3D model*. Someone who works with 3D models may often be referred to as a *3D artist*.

The 3D model has the advantage that it can be displayed on the computer screen as a two-dimensional image through a process called *3D rendering*. For example, these images are often the uber-cool pictures you see in an architect's slideshow of a new building or house he designed. They also may be used in a computer simulation of physical phenomena, such as virtual prototype testing to see whether the lighting makes a new product desirable to a given market.

The iPhone is a typical example where lighting is an important facet of the design to highlight all the lovely curves and bevels on the iPhone case. (Can you tell I'm an Apple fan?) The model can also be physically created using 3D printing devices, which is where Tinkercad comes into its own, with the ability to export 3D model files for 3D printing.

3D models may be created automatically or manually. The manual modeling process of preparing geometric data for 3D computer graphics is similar to plastic arts, such as sculpting. Now that does sound complicated, right? It's not. The Tinkercad interface simplifies the manual 3D workflow, allowing you, the Tinkercad user, to manually create your 3D designs and take them all the way to 3D printing.

TECHNICAL STUFF

Tinkercad is classed as *3D modeling software,* which is a class of 3D computer graphics software used to produce 3D models. Individual programs of this class are called *modeling applications* or *modelers.* Tinkercad is one of several 3D modeling applications or modelers that are provided by the San Francisco–based software company, Autodesk.

Figure 1-1 shows a typical example of 3D design.

FIGURE 1-1:
The ERIS
high-resolution
camera and
spectrograph
concept design
for ESO's Very
Large Telescope.

Credit: ESO/ERIS Phase A Team

3D MODELING IN THE REAL WORLD

As technology and computer hardware have moved forward and become much faster and much more capable, 3D models are now widely used anywhere in 3D graphics and CAD. Their use predates the widespread use of 3D graphics on personal computers nowadays, and many computer games used prerendered images of 3D models as sprites (not the soft drink) before computers could render them in real-time.

Today, 3D models are used in a diverse variety of fields:

- The **medical industry** uses detailed models of organs, which are created with multiple two-dimensional (2D) image slices from an MRI or CT scan.

- The **movie and television industry** uses them as characters and objects for animated and real-life motion pictures in film and television (think *Avatar*, *Star Wars*, and *Game of Thrones*).

- The **video game industry** uses them as assets for computer and video games. If you've used an Xbox, a PlayStation 4, or a Nintendo, you've used 3D assets in the games you've played, regardless of how cartoony or real-life they are.

- The **science industry sector** uses them as highly detailed models of chemical compounds, such as the human genome project.

- The **architecture and construction industry** uses them instead of traditional, physical architectural models to demonstrate proposed buildings and landscapes. However, some of those 3D models then become 3D printed models to show the new building or landscape in place in a city environment, for example.

- The **engineering community** uses them for the design of new devices, vehicles, and structures, as well as a host of other uses, such as nondestructive prototyping.

- In recent decades, the **earth science community** has started to construct 3D geological models as a standard practice. City modeling is now common practice within government departments in an effort to become more environmentally sustainable with the study of light and wind to create a more "green" world in which to live.

3D models can also be the basis for physical devices that are built with 3D printers or CNC machines.

Comparing 3D to 2D Methods

3D photorealistic effects achieved without wireframe modeling can be hard to distinguish when in their final form. Some of the software available has incredibly sophisticated filters that you can apply to 2D vector graphics or 2D raster graphics on transparent layers, making the finished image look remarkably realistic.

However, wireframe 3D modeling has several advantages over the 2D method:

>> **Flexibility:** The ability to change angles or animate images with quicker rendering, because a realistic 3D model is already there to be used.

>> **Easy rendering:** The automatic calculation and rendering is easier as the 3D modeler has built-in algorithms to render realistically rather than mentally visualizing or estimating the rendered image.

>> **Accurate photorealism:** You have less chance of overdoing, misplacing, or forgetting to include any visual effects.

So, what disadvantages are there to 3D?

>> **Software learning curve:** Learning 3D software can take longer as 3D modelers tend to be more sophisticated and have more "under the hood."

>> **Difficulty achieving certain photorealistic effects:** You can achieve some photorealistic effects with special rendering filters included in the modeling software and specific to a 3D modeler. 3D artists sometimes use a combination of 3D modelers, following that up with 2D editing of the 2D computer-rendered images from the 3D model.

3D modeling makes sense if you're going to fabricate or manufacture your design. It provides a real-world model that can be viewed from any angle, 3D printed in order for it to be visualized for real, and even submitted for nondestructive testing (such as the outer casing for a cell phone such as the iPhone, for example).

2D, on the other hand, is great for conceptual work. There is no need for full visualization because 2D is great for approximating what a model might look like with no need for a full 3D model to be created, thus saving on time, training, and costs.

Discovering Model Representation

A 3D model is represented either as a full solid or a shell of a solid. Imagine an old-fashioned wooden toy block as compared to a hollow Lego™ brick. Pretty much all 3D models fall into one of two categories:

>> **Solid:** These models define the volume of the object or entity they represent (like a cube, for example). Solid models are often used for engineering and medical applications and are usually built with constructive solid geometry.

In this book, I show you how Tinkercad utilizes solids to make your life easier as you design.

>> **Shell/boundary:** These models represent the surface of an object or entity. The boundary of the object is a bit like an eggshell and forms the object's shell, which is infinitesimally thin. Almost all visual models used in games and film are shell models, with surface properties applied.

Solid and shell modeling can create functionally identical objects, such as the Utah teapot, which is one of the most common models used in 3D graphics education (see Figure 1-2).

The differences between solid and shell modeling are the different methods in which they're created and edited in the various 3D modelers that are used, along with differing conventions of use in various fields.

Another difference is in the types of approximations between the model and reality, such as units of measurement and how the solids, shells, and boundaries are represented.

FIGURE 1-2:
A modern rendering of the iconic Utah teapot model developed by Martin Newell (1975).

Credit: Dhatfield/CC BY-SA 3.0.

Looking at the Modeling Process

Imagine a big, infinite space, such as a galaxy in *Star Wars*. Your 3D models represent a physical object, such as a building, a gear cog, or even a nut or a bolt, by using a collection of points in that infinite 3D space (galaxy). You can connect these points using various geometric entities, such as triangles, lines, and curved surfaces.

Because the 3D model is formed by a collection of data (points and other information), you can create these 3D models by hand (manually), algorithmically (procedural modeling), or scanned (using 3D scanning methods).

You can further define their surfaces with *texture mapping*, which adds physical material attributes, such as brick, metal, or glass.

Creation of a 3D model

You can create a 3D model in one of three popular ways:

» Polygonal modeling

» Curve modeling

» Digital sculpting

These methods, which are described in the following sections, allow for very artistic exploration of the model with topology created over it after the models form and details have been sculpted. The new mesh will usually have the original high-res mesh information transferred into displacement data or normal map data if it's for a game engine. *Meshes* are nets of interconnected triangles.

Due to the accuracy and artistry digital sculpting provides, the 3D modelers used are often installed on tablets using highly accurate styli. Check out the 3D fantasy fish in Figure 1-3 for a typical example of a 3D model. It was modeled using organic surfaces.

FIGURE 1-3:
A 3D fantasy fish composed of organic surfaces generated using LAI4D.

Credit: Jahurtado/CC BY-SA 4.0.

Polygonal modeling

The points used to create a 3D model are called *vertices* and are connected by line segments to form a polygon mesh. (Imagine a 3D spider web, where it forms a 3D shape, and each line from each interconnecting point forms a 3D edge, and each of these edges forms the 3D model.)

Many 3D models created are developed as textured polygonal models because they're flexible and can be rendered extremely quickly.

The downside, however, is that polygons are planar and can only approximate curved surfaces using many polygons.

Figure 1-4 gives you a good idea of how polygonal modeling breaks down an object — in this case, a human head — into polygons to allow it to be modeled and rendered quickly.

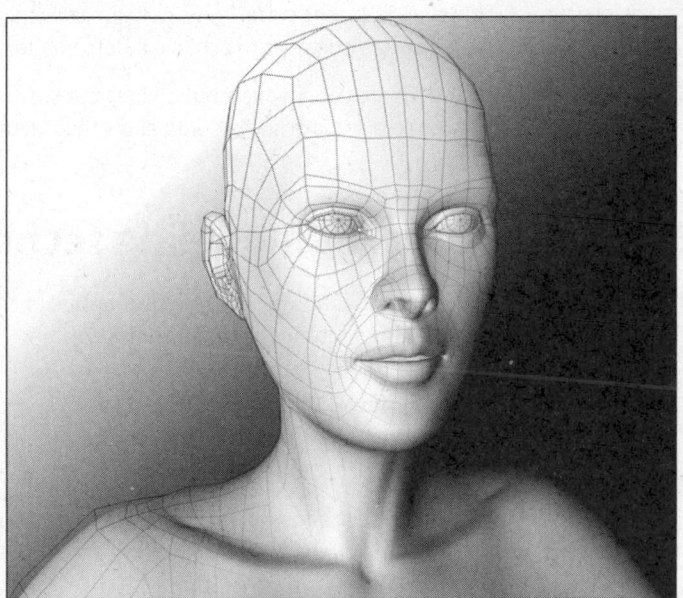

FIGURE 1-4:
Polygonal
modeling.

Curve modeling

Using curve modeling, the 3D surfaces are defined by curves, influenced by weighted control points, which pull the curves in the appropriate direction.

The curve then follows the points (but sometimes will not interpolate them). If the weighting for a point is increased, it will pull the curve closer to that point.

Curve types include Non-Uniform Rational B-Spline (NURBS), splines, patches, and geometric primitives. While they all sound complicated, the 3D modeler, such as Tinkercad, will do all the math.

Digital sculpting

Digital sculpting is a new modeling method, which has become popular on current tablet devices that use the highly accurate styli now available.

There are currently three types of digital sculpting:

- » **Displacement** is the most widely used among applications at this moment. Displacement uses a dense mesh model and stores locations for the vertex positions through use of a 32-bit image map.
- » **Volumetric** is loosely based on *voxels* (an array of elements of volume that form a notional three-dimensional space) and has similar capabilities as displacement. However, it doesn't suffer from polygon stretching when a region doesn't have enough polygons to achieve a deformation.
- » **Dynamic tessellation** is similar to voxels but divides the surface using triangulation to maintain a smooth surface and allow finer detail.

Exploring different modeling techniques

The modeling stage consists of shaping the individual objects that are used in the 3D scene. Numerous modeling techniques exist, including

- » **Constructive solid geometry:** This is where you create a complex 3D surface or 3D object using Boolean to combine simpler 3D objects together.
- » **Implicit surfaces:** An implicit model is formed by a continuous, volumetric model, where the volume of the model forms the 3D implicit surface, developed using numerous mathematical algorithms.
- » **Subdivision surfaces:** In this modeling technique for making high-res models, a lower resolution cage model is subdivided by the modeling software for a smoother 3D surface.

The modeling is performed by means of a dedicated application, such as Autodesk 3ds Max or Maya, or a plug-in component, such as Lofter in 3ds Max.

Sometimes, no defined boundaries exist between the modeling techniques, and they are often used in conjunction with each other as part of the scene-creation process.

Often, complex materials, such as blowing sand, clouds, and liquid sprays, are modeled with particle systems and are a mass of 3D coordinates, which have either points, polygons, texture splats, or sprites assigned to them.

In the mathematical sense, 3D modeling has been around for a long time, but *virtual models,* where the real world is represented in 3D for you to see on your screen, really kicked in during the late '90s:

» **Human models:** The first available application of human virtual models appeared in 1998 on the Lands' End clothing website. The models used on the website were created by the company My Virtual Mode, Inc., and enabled users to create a model of themselves and try on 3D clothing. You can use many 3D modeling software applications, such as Poser, to create virtual human models.

» **3D clothing:** Software that simulates cloth and textiles has allowed artists and fashion designers to model dynamic 3D clothing in modelers, such as MarvelousDesigner, CLO3D, and Optitex. Dynamic 3D clothing is often used for virtual fashion catalogs, realistically clothing 3D characters in video games, 3D animated movies, and digital doubles in movies. These 3D modelers are also used for making clothes for avatars in virtual worlds, such as Second Life.

Figure 1-5 shows a dynamic 3D clothing model made in MarvelousDesigner.

FIGURE 1-5:
3D clothing model made in Marvelous-Designer.

Credit: CGElves/CC by SA 4.0.

Recognizing the 3D Model Market

Did you know that 3D models are, quite literally, everywhere? Many consumer products you now buy and use are 3D printed verbatim from their 3D models and used at work, in the home, and in numerous industries. The technology behind 3D is moving fast, and you'll find that 3D "stuff" is affecting design and the human interface in ways you never thought existed.

Here's an example for you. Remember those old mice you used to use on your old PC? You know the ones, right? They were a very basic shape with a ball inside that you needed to get out once a month to clean crumbs, food, and dust off the contacts. You remember? Need I say more? I am sure that the mouse in Figure 1-6 will jog your memory!

FIGURE 1-6:
A typical 1980s Microsoft mouse. Check out those ergonomic curves!

Credit: PCWorld.

For one, new mice don't have that annoying ball inside anymore and use laser technology to work, but for two, they're designed so much better. They fit your hand both ergonomically and anthropometrically to alleviate things such as Repetitive Strain Injury (RSI). This transformation is due to the advent of 3D design, but also more importantly, 3D printing. Mouse manufacturers now use 3D prototypes developed by 3D design studios to test those ergonomic principles that alleviate RSI and other associated office-based injuries. (Bet you never knew the office was so dangerous, right?) The mouse in Figure 1-7 is similar to the mouse people now use every day for 3D modeling.

There are numerous uses for 3D models (way too many to mention here), but design software vendors, such as Autodesk, have realized that their software applications need to address this issue. The world has moved forward from just simple 3D designs in applications, such as AutoCAD. While AutoCAD is still a very relevant CAD application, Autodesk has continued to add to its toolbox of 3D CAD applications with products such as Inventor, Fusion 360, and, of course, Tinkercad.

3D models are now the norm. They're the benchmark for design. Computers are now powerful enough to manage large-scale 3D models easily. The Internet is now very powerful as well, with cable and fiber broadband Internet providing incredible speeds and bandwidth. The cloud is becoming all the more powerful, allowing complex design tasks to be done on the Internet remotely, taking away the need for large processing tasks on your computer on your desk.

These reasons are why Autodesk has invested so much time in Tinkercad. Being cloud-based, Tinkercad provides an entry-level 3D design product for everyone, processing your 3D designs quickly and easily in real-time, with no need for heavy local processing on your computer.

3D models in Tinkercad are easy, and this book shows you how easy it is and gets you out there into the 3D world, creating and even 3D printing your 3D models, just like those uber-cool mouse manufacturers do now with their new designs.

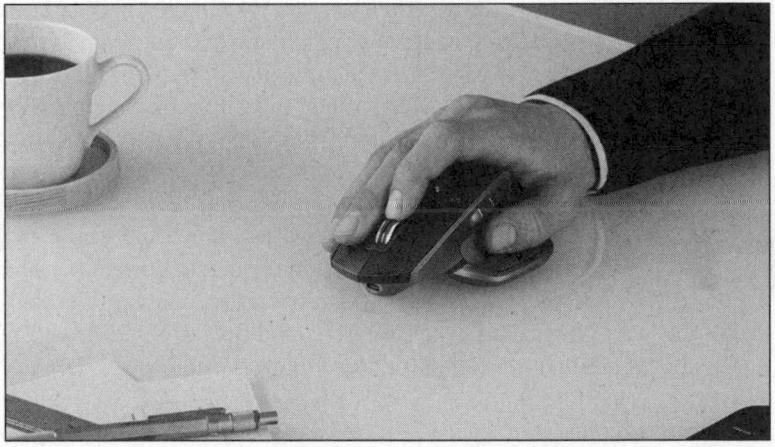

FIGURE 1-7:
A Logitech MX Master 2S mouse. It sure looks cool, right?

Credit: Logitech Europe/CC by SA.

TECHNICAL STUFF

Cloud computing (the cloud) is a software and infrastructure model based on the Internet. It allows access to shared pools of data via an Internet interface in an Internet browser, such as Google Chrome or Microsoft Edge. Networks and servers can be managed this way, as can applications, such as Tinkercad. Cloud computing allows users to store and process data either in a private cloud or on a third-party cloud server located in a data center in a remote location. When using Tinkercad, your 3D designs are processed, calculated, and stored on a cloud-based remote server.

Exploring 3D Printing

3D printing is often known as additive manufacturing (AM), the additives often being powdered materials fed into a 3D printer to form a 3D printed solid model. These materials are layered under computer control to create the 3D solid.

A typical file format used is a STereoLithography file (STL). STL is one of the most common file types that 3D printers can read. 3D printing is different than traditional production processes where material is removed from machine stock, such as metal sheets. 3D printing (AM) builds a 3D solid object from a CAD model (often in a STL file format) by adding material layer by layer, using multiple passes of the printer head, in the same way you now print onto paper using inkjet technology.

Historically, the term *3D printing* refers to a chemical process that deposits a binding material onto a powder bed with inkjet printer heads layer by layer. However, 3D printing is now used in much more general terms and is the popular terminology used to describe a wide variety of additive manufacturing (AM) techniques. For the real techie nerds amongst you, the United States and global technical standards use the official term *additive manufacturing* (AM) to encompass all of the manufacturing techniques out there, and the documented standard ISO/ASTM52900-15 defines seven categories of AM processes within the standard document: binder jetting, directed energy deposition, material extrusion, material jetting, powder bed fusion, sheet lamination, and vat photopolymerization. Now, these all sound somewhat complex, and they are, and if you're really interested, check them out on Google and/or Wikipedia.

At a simpler level, you'll be pleased to know that if you design your 3D models on Tinkercad, you can output them as 3D physical models using the STL file format, which in turn can allow you to 3D print to the Autodesk 3D printer and use the Autodesk Spark platform, for example. Figure 1-8 shows you the new Autodesk 3D printer that has adopted the Spark platform for 3D printing.

Using 3D Printed Models

Well, now that there is a process where the 3D conceptual design (inside your computer) can be made into something real (outside your computer, in the REAL world), it has revolutionized the world of design. Designers and manufacturers can now 3D print anything and everything they need to.

The following sections provide just a small overview of some of the uses of 3D printed models around the world right now.

Prosthetics

One of the more humanitarian and heartwarming uses of 3D printing is in the medical industry by way of 3D printing human prosthetics. Using nanotechnology for incredible accuracy for the fit to the human form, 3D-customized prosthetics that would normally cost in the region of $50,000 can now be replaced with their 3D printed equivalent, which will sometimes only cost in the region of $50.

This ability has led to a movement within companies, such as Autodesk, to work closely with individuals who need prosthetics and the companies that provide them, sharing the technology for the benefit of the person requiring a prosthetic.

An incredible organization called the Enable Community Foundation pairs volunteers in the e-NABLE community with designs and children needing prosthetic limbs, such as arms and hands, even giving the kids the choice of design and colors they want. In fact, a UK-based company called Open Bionics even offers low-cost, 3D printed hands with famous movie themes, such as Marvel's *Iron Man*, Disney's *Frozen*, and Disney's *Star Wars*, as shown in Figure 1-9. Open Bionics also offers free downloads of 3D designs that can be 3D printed, such as the Ada prosthetic hand shown in Figure 1-9.

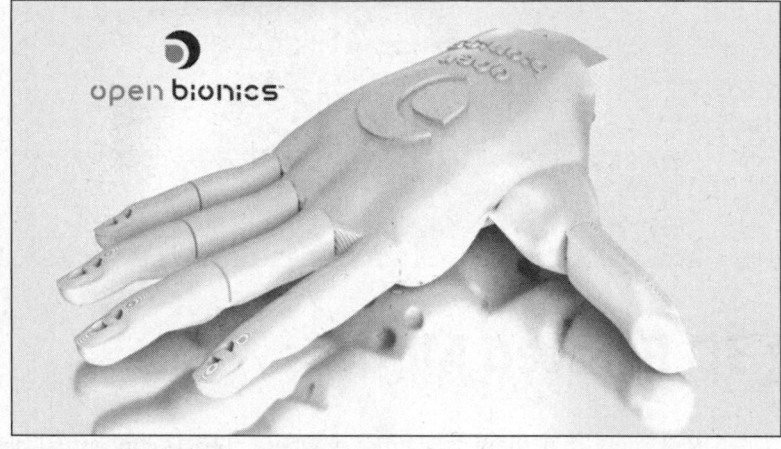

FIGURE 1-9:
The range of children's prosthetic hands available from UK-based company Open Bionics.

Credit: Open Bionics.

Rapid prototyping

Rapid prototyping is probably the most popular use of 3D printing. Manufacturers can now design and print on site, saving a lot of time and money on outsourcing this type (pardon the pun) of work to a third-party. 3D designers can then test and calculate whether their design fails and needs reworking much faster. 3D printing their design allows them to identify any design problems, fix them, and then reprint them.

In previous years, traditional prototyping was an expensive process, where (often) a full design was modeled, built, and then tested against specific project standards. This could take weeks, or even months, for more complex 3D models. The new rapid prototyping methodologies with the new, faster 3D printers allow companies to even 3D print in parallel, creating many variations on a theme so that they can compare each design to work out which one works best. This process is sometimes known as *iterative design*. This kind of rapid prototyping can be used in any industry, especially for nondestructive testing objects, such as eyeglasses, mobile phones, and even children's toys.

Education

3D printing is becoming extremely popular at all levels of education. It's not just being used for product design and engineering. 3D printing is also being used as an educational resource for the future. The world of 3D printing is growing rapidly, and schools, colleges, and universities are seeing that there will be a high demand for students with 3D printing and CAD skills. Figure 1-10 shows schoolchildren using a 3D printer in the classroom — a valuable resource for children learning technology and design in class.

Credit: Materialize.

FIGURE 1-10:
Schoolchildren using a 3D printer in the classroom.

Education has to prepare the workforce for the skills needed in the future, and 3D printing is right up there. There is, however, still the need for education funding to ensure that students have full access to the 3D printing equipment, and that momentum needs to be maintained. 3Ders Autodesk works closely with many schools promoting Tinkercad as an entry-level application that gives the children access to 3D modeling and 3D printing. Figure 1-11 shows the Tinkercad team at work.

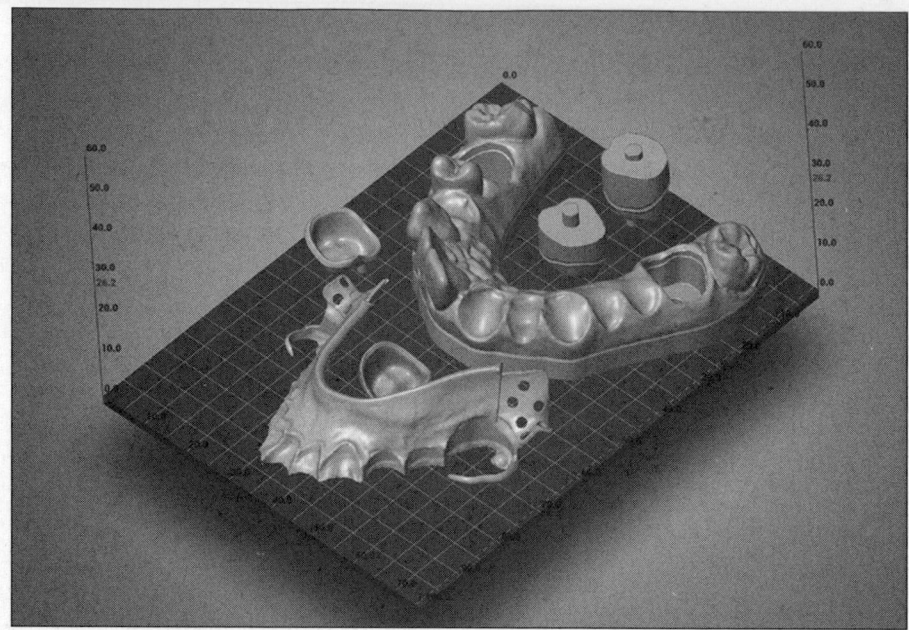

FIGURE 1-11:
A nesting of
partial dental
framework,
model, and
crowns waiting to
be 3D printed.

Credit: Dental Wings, Canada.

Low volume manufacturing

Many organizations and companies in the product design and manufacturing industries are moving from rapid prototyping to low volume manufacturing. There is often a need for only a small run on a specific part or product. If only, say, 50 copies of a part or product are needed for a low volume manufacturing run, it's likcly to be much more cost-effective to have them 3D printed than shipped to a large-volume third-party manufacturer.

Bespoke manufacturing

Sometimes a bespoke or customized product or part may be needed. In manufacturing, it's often much less expensive to quickly 3D print a unique product or part like this as the materials can be obtained for the 3D printer and it can be individually designed and 3D printed in-house, instead of having to go to an external design company.

An example could be the production of a box with a client's logo embedded or embossed in it. This would be a great Tinkercad project!

Dentistry

I can bet that when you have been to your dentist, she has, at least once, taken an impression of your teeth to create a copy (sometimes known as a stone) to store for dental and legal reasons. On a macabre note, should you die in suspicious circumstances, dental records have been used for identification purposes. On a much brighter note, 3D printing is now becoming used as the norm in dentistry, allowing dentists to use a 3D dental scanner. This process captures a 3D image of your mouth, which means that the stones can be printed on demand, negating the need for the dentist to store hundreds of thousands of stones in a warehouse for many years.

Dental labs can now use 3D impressions of your teeth to create perfect fitting crowns, bridges, and implants. This ability saves on the time taken for these dental items to be made, reduces the risk of error, and saves the dental lab (and you) money. Figure 1-11 shows a partial dental framework, model, and crowns waiting to be 3D printed. The dentist, with appropriate 3D modeling training, can do this in-house for his patients, saving valuable time and money.

Using Tinkercad in 3D Modeling

Tinkercad is a cloud-based 3D modeler provided by one of the biggest design software companies in the world, Autodesk.

This cloud-based approach removes the need for local 3D model storage (no need for huge hard drives or servers), utilizing the cloud for both model storage and processing of the 3D model design as you work through your design, refining the model to the required look and feel.

Tinkercad is a great entry-level to 3D modeling, and with its ease of access (all you need is an Autodesk ID), it can be used by designers of all ages, from young children all the way up to advanced adult designers. It even has links in it that allow you to create 3D models for the online game Minecraft, and you can convert your models into Lego bricks, too!

While Tinkercad is a great entry-level modeler, you may want to consider a more sophisticated 3D application should you wish to develop and manufacture your designs on the factory floor. Tinkercad is great, but it is more suited to the hobbyist/maker space rather than the corporate production line methods needed to get a fully fledged design out to market.

Saying that, though, who knows? You may design the next latest and greatest in Tinkercad and then take it to the next level. You just never know!

Chapter **2**

Introducing Tinkercad

I n this chapter, I introduce you to Tinkercad, the entry-level, cloud-based 3D design application from Autodesk. I also show you how to navigate to the Tinkercad website so that you can set up your own Tinkercad account and start your own Tinkercad design.

Visiting the Tinkercad Website

Tinkercad is really easy to find on the Internet. Simply head on over to www. tinkercad.com. The homepage, shown in Figure 2-1, is extremely colorful, and so is the Tinkercad logo.

As it says on the webpage, Tinkercad is a simple, online 3D design and 3D printing app for everyone. Tinkercad is used by designers, hobbyists, teachers, and kids to make toys, prototypes, home decor, Minecraft models, jewelry, and more — the list is truly endless!

TIP

If you want to see some examples of amazing 3D designs created by the Tinkercad community, click on the Gallery link at the top of the Tinkercad homepage.

On the webpage, you see loads of information about how Tinkercad works, the things you can do with it, and a number of how-to videos. It also contains links to some website locations, such as the Gallery, Features, and the Tinkercad Blog. The blog articles are really interesting and also give you all the latest Tinkercad news.

Creating a Tinkercad Account

When you sign up for a Tinkercad account, the login you create becomes your Autodesk ID, too, which means you can use the same login everywhere on all of the Autodesk websites. This is especially useful if you're using other Autodesk applications, such as AutoCAD or Inventor, because it gives you an identity on the Autodesk user forums (http://forums.autodesk.com) and on the Autodesk Knowledge Network, or AKN for short (http://knowledge.autodesk.com).

To create a Tinkercad account:

1. **Click Sign Up on the Tinkercad homepage.**

   The Create Account dialog box, shown in Figure 2-2, appears.

2. **Choose your country from the drop-down list.**

   In my case, that would be the United Kingdom. Yours may be different, such as the United States. The default country is the United States. That's purely because Autodesk is an American company, with its headquarters in San Francisco, California.

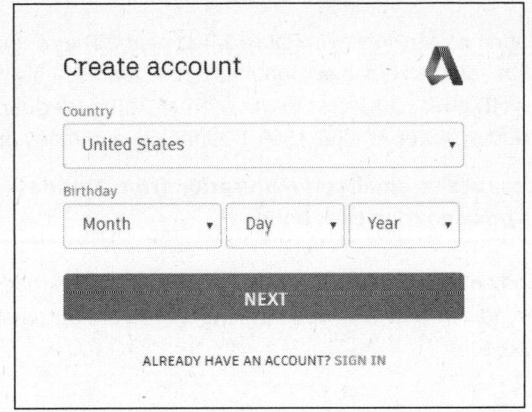

FIGURE 2-2:
The initial signup
page for
Tinkercad.

3. **Enter your birthday.**

   No, there's no big party or cake (sadly), but you have to put in your birthday so that Autodesk knows whether you're a child or an adult. Tinkercad is used by adults and children alike, and purely for precautionary purposes, they need to know your age.

4. **Click the Next button.**

   The next Create Account dialog box, shown in Figure 2-3, appears.

5. **Add your email address and a password, accept the Tinkercad terms of service, and click Create Account.**

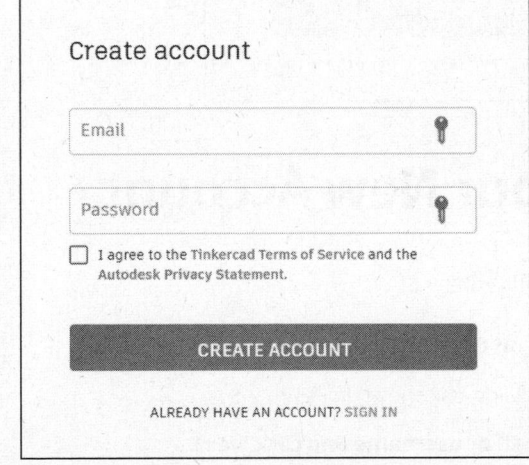

FIGURE 2-3:
The email and
password screen
as you set up
your Autodesk ID
to use your
Tinkercad
account.

The confirmation screen shown in Figure 2-4 appears. The confirmation screen shows you that your Tinkercad account has been created. It also tells you that your Autodesk ID gives you access to many other Autodesk cloud-based products, including AutoCAD 360, A360, Fusion 360, and many others.

6. **If you want to receive email communication from Autodesk, select the permissions box and then click Done.**

   A confirmation email is sent to the email you provided. And that's it! You now have a Tinkercad account. Also, upon signing up you are automatically logged in to Tinkercad, too.

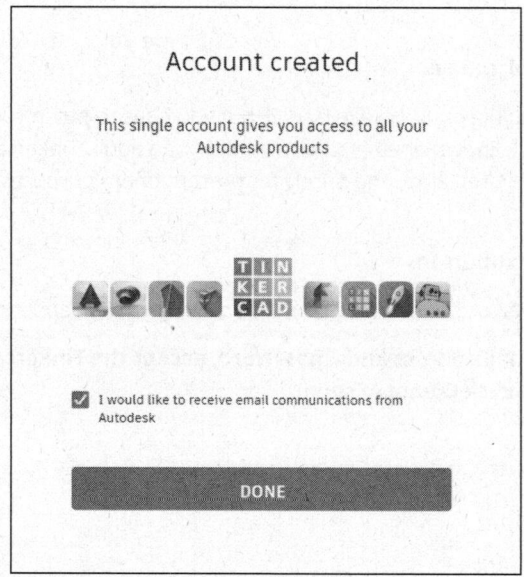

FIGURE 2-4:
The confirmation screen for Tinkercad.

Logging in to Your New Account

To log in to Tinkercad:

1. **Click Sign In on the Tinkercad home page.**

   You see the dialog box shown in Figure 2-5.

2. **Type the email or username and click Next.**

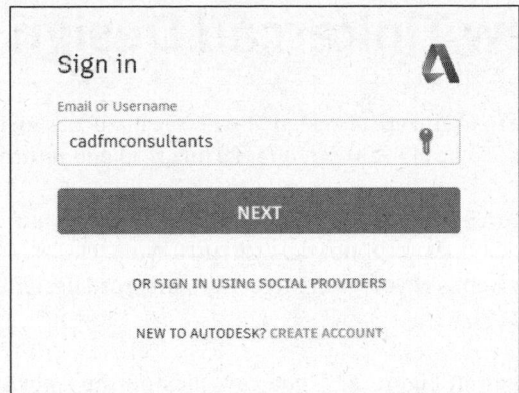

FIGURE 2-5:
The sign-in page
for Tinkercad
using your newly
created
Autodesk ID.

3. **In the next dialog box, shown in Figure 2-6, type your password and click Sign In.**

4. **(Optional) Check the option to stay signed in.**

   As with all Internet-related accounts, please ensure that you check this option if you're on a computer that only you use. You don't want anyone stealing your incredible Tinkercad designs or accessing your personal details.

FIGURE 2-6:
The second
sign-in page
dialog box.

You now see your Tinkercad account.

TIP

If you're logging in to Tinkercad for the first time, a set of simple training exercises kicks in. It is recommended that you make sure that you work your way through them to get a basic understanding of some of the simple tools and workflows in Tinkercad.

Launching a New Tinkercad Design

When you set up a new Tinkercad design, it will be a blank design initially, but you'll add to it as you go. You can even sign out of Tinkercad and return to finish it later.

When you log in to Tinkercad, your Tinkercad profile is top left, along with a profile picture if you set one up. (If not, you can go to your Tinkercad account settings to add one, if you want.) If you've created any Tinkercad designs, you see them as well (see Figure 2-7).

To get to the screen in Figure 2-7, you can click on the colorful Tinkercad logo. You don't have to log in and out to see it. Also, bear in mind that you won't have any Tinkercad designs showing as you haven't designed anything yet!

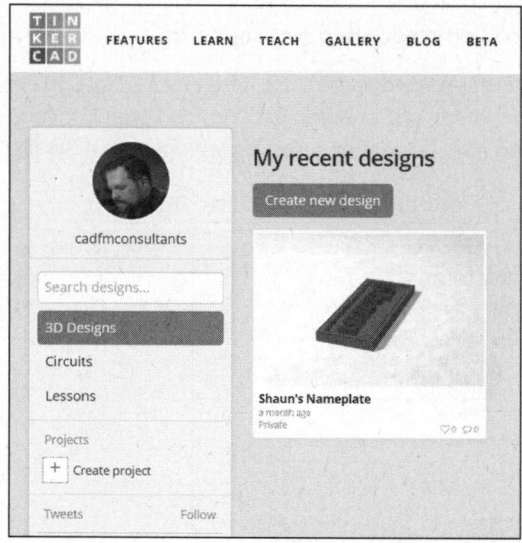

FIGURE 2-7:
The opening Tinkercad screen upon logging in.

To create a new design:

1. **Click the Create new design button.**

   A new design that is all set up and ready to go appears. Tinkercad gives each new design a weird and wacky new design name, some of which can be fun, but you'll want to change the design name so that it's relevant.

2. **Name your new design by clicking on the name, typing the new name, and pressing Enter.**

   Your new name appears in the top-left corner of the screen, as shown in Figure 2-8. I named my design Grand Rottis-Duup (see Figure 2-9).

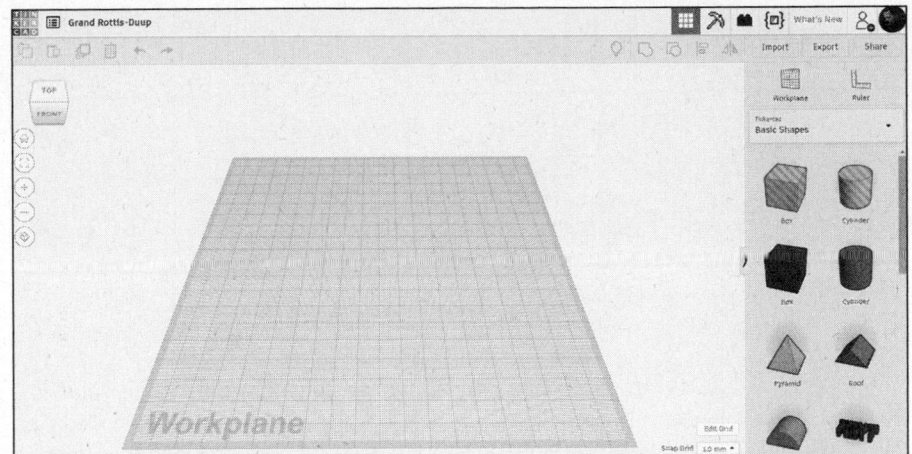

FIGURE 2-8:
A new Tinkercad design ready to go, with its weird and wacky design name.

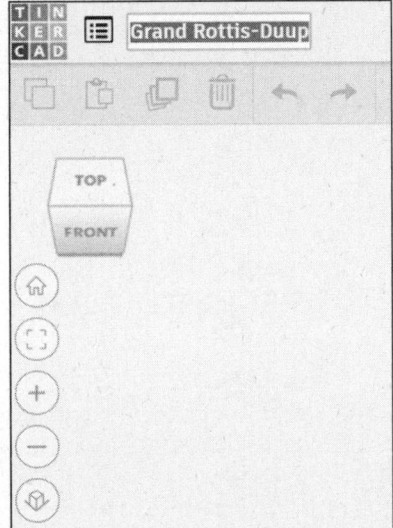

FIGURE 2-9:
My new Tinkercad design name.

Chapter **3**

Taking a Tour of Tinkercad

I n this chapter, you take a tour of the Tinkercad screens. You find out how to view your recent designs and tinker with Tinkercad. You discover how to use the Help screens to access the amazing knowledge base that is incorporated into Tinkercad. You also explore the Tinkercad community by visiting the Tinkercad Gallery and blog.

Viewing Recent Designs

Tinkercad provides great visual tools so that you can easily view and open your recent designs.

When you log in, your Tinkercad profile is on the left side of the screen (see Figure 3-1). Just to the right of your profile you see your recent designs. In the following example, my existing Tinkercad design is called Shaun's Nameplate. All your recent designs have a little preview box. If you move your mouse over it, you can even manipulate the mini design in the box. Also, note the Tinker This button that appears. That's what you click to open your design.

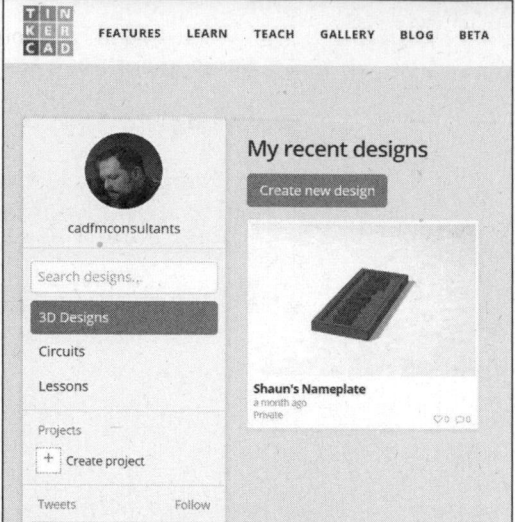

FIGURE 3-1:
A partial view of
the Tinkercad
screen, where
you can see your
Tinkercad profile
and your recent
Tinkercad
designs.

Choosing Options and Settings

When you hover over your recent designs, you see a gearwheel cog icon in the top right of the recent designs box. If you hover over it, an Options tooltip appears. Click it, and Tinkercad gives you four options, which are shown in Figure 3-2:

FIGURE 3-2:
The options
available in a
recent Tinkercad
design when
clicking the
Options
gearwheel cog
icon.

>> **Properties:** This option, shown in Figure 3-3, allows you to change your design's file properties, such as its name and description. You can add up to five tags to make your design more searchable, both on Tinkercad and on the

Internet in general. You can also decide on whether you want your Tinkercad design to be public or private and specify which creative license type applies to your design so that others give you credit should they use your Tinkercad design as a part of their designs elsewhere. After you make your changes, click Save changes.

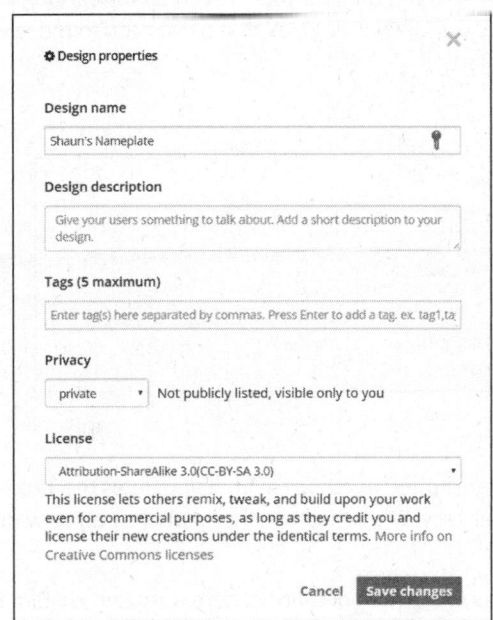

>> **Duplicate:** The Duplicate option, shown in Figure 3-4, does exactly what it says. It duplicates your Tinkercad design and adds it to your recent designs.

>> **Move to Project:** In your Tinkercad profile, you can set up projects. Just click Create project, and a new project appears on the screen. (It's normally called Project 1 or a similar name.) Click on the new project to see the project page.

Click the gearwheel cog on the project page for your new project to name it in your project properties. After you set up your project name and description, click the Tinkercad logo in the top left of the screen. You then return to your recent designs where you can add your design to any existing project. Figure 3-5 shows the Move dialog box that allows you to move your design to the relevant project.

FIGURE 3-5:
The Move dialog box, ready to move my Nameplate design in to my Nameplates project.

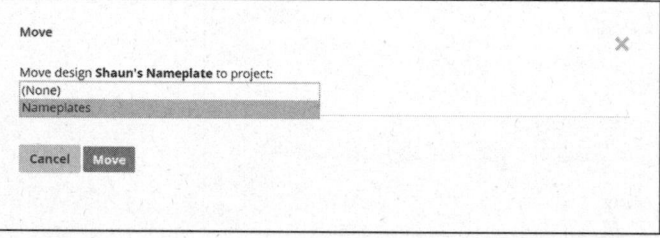

Move

Move design **Shaun's Nameplate** to project:
(None)
Nameplates

Cancel   Move

>> **Delete:** The Delete option does exactly that. It deletes the Tinkercad design. Upon clicking Delete, you're asked whether you're sure you want to delete the design.

WARNING

Tinkercad is a cloud-based application. There is no Recycle Bin! That means that you cannot recover any deleted files, so just make sure you want to delete that Tinkercad file before you click to delete!

'Tinkering' with Tinkercad

When you hover over any of your recent designs in Tinkercad, a small blue icon appears in the top-left corner of the small design preview box (see Figure 3-6). It says, quite simply, Tinker this.

A tinker is someone who can do a lot of different things — in other words, a jack-of-all-trades. Tinkercad allows you to tinker on any type of design in 3D.

When you click Tinker this, Tinkercad opens up a design for you so that you can tinker in Tinkercad.

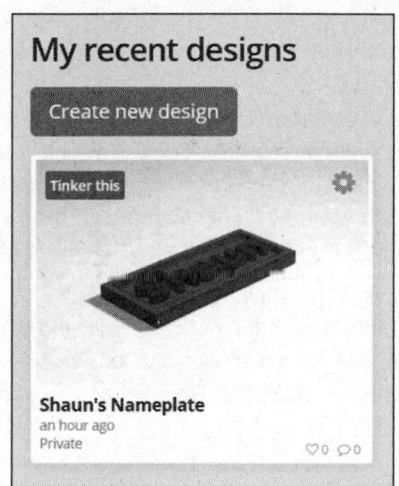

FIGURE 3-6:
A recent
Tinkercad design.

All of the Tinkercad design tools appear in the Tinkercad drawing screen, shown in Figure 3-7. The Snap Grid is also there to assist you with your 3D designing.

FIGURE 3-7:
The Tinkercad
drawing screen.

If you have used a CAD or 3D product before, some of the design tools will be familiar to you. In addition, some of the workflows and processes used in Tinkercad are virtually the same as other Autodesk applications, such as AutoCAD and Inventor.

Here are a few things you can tinker with:

- **Navigation – Mouse and ViewCube:** Navigation in Tinkercad is a combination of mouse control and keyboard control. It's up to you. If you're a mouse person, utilize the mouse wheel to zoom in and out by rolling the wheel and pan by holding down the wheel and moving the mouse. These standard Autodesk navigation methods are used in many of their applications.

  To get different preset views of your Tinkercad design, click on the faces of the ViewCube or the corners of the ViewCube. Click a corner, and you see an isometric view. Click a face, and you get an elevation or plan view. Click an edge, and you get an elevation or plan view. Figure 3-8 shows an isometric view of my design.

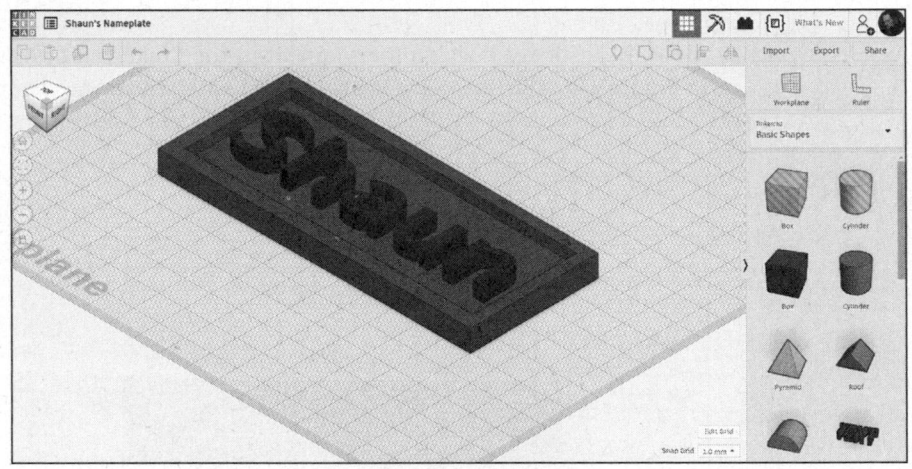

FIGURE 3-8: My Shaun's Nameplate design in an isometric view set by the corresponding view on the ViewCube. Note the highlighted corner of the ViewCube.

- **Drag and Drop:** If you haven't got any 3D solids or elements in your design yet, use the drag and drop functionality to drag a 3D basic shape from the Basic Shapes shown on the right side of the Tinkercad screen. Simply click the shape you want and drag it in to the drawing area, known as the Workplane. The Workplane is the pale blue grid that fills the drawing area of the Tinkercad screen.

- **Viewing tools:** The Tinkercad viewing tools appear below the ViewCube, on the left hand side of the Tinkercad screen. As you work down the icons, you can hover over them to see their names: Home view, Fit all in view, Zoom in, Zoom out, and Switch to Orthographic view. After you have a shape in your design on the Workplane, tinker with the viewing tools to familiarize yourself with them.

Tinker in Tinkercad to get used to the interface. You should find the interface easy to use, even if you haven't ever used a CAD product.

Finding the Right Help

As the saying goes, good help is hard to find these days. That is not so with Tinkercad. Because Tinkercad is cloud-based, you're always on the Internet. This constant connectivity means that the Help screens in Tinkercad are always up to date with the newest information that you need to help drive and tinker with your Tinkercad designs.

To access Tinkercad Help, go to `http://support.tinkercad.com`. You will need to use your Tinkercad login to log in to the page as well. Once logged in, type your topic in the search box (see Figure 3-9).

FIGURE 3-9:
The Tinkercad
Help page.

Credit: Autodesk, Inc.

TIP

If you want to keep the Tinkercad Help page open all the time, consider opening it in another instance of your browser. That way, you'll have two browsers open and can quickly jump between the two screens.

Tweeting on Twitter

If you tweet, you can find Tinkercad on Twitter using the Twitter name @tinkercad. This great Twitter page, shown in Figure 3-10, often has multiple posts on the same day. You can tweet your Tinkercad posts on Twitter and include the @tinkercad name to get your own Tinkercad tweets noticed. Maybe you have a new Tinkercad design you want to get noticed?

FIGURE 3-10:
The Tinkercad
Twitter account.

Browsing the Gallery

You can find the Tinkercad Gallery, shown in Figure 3-11, at www.tinkercad.com. You don't even have to be logged in to Tinkercad to peruse all the amazing designs in the Gallery. You can also upload your own designs, if you want to!

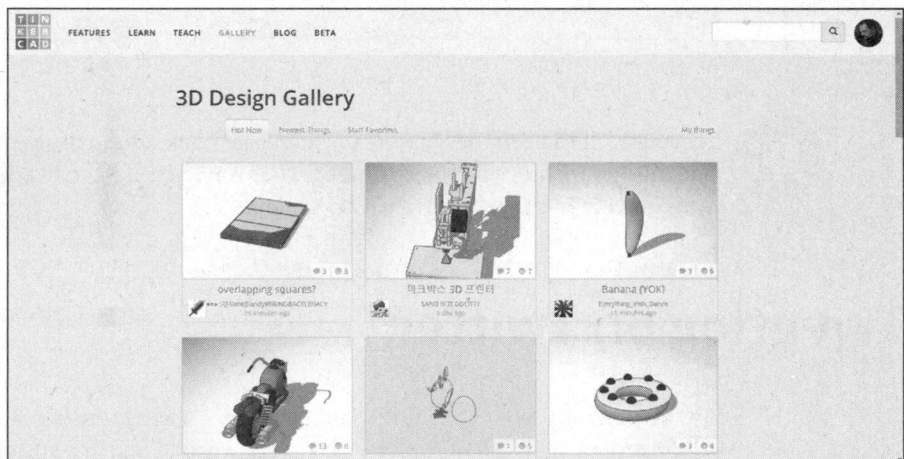

FIGURE 3-11:
The Tinkercad
Gallery in all its
splendor!

You can find the Gallery listed at the top left of the Tinkercad home page, just in case you weren't sure where to find it. It also has the webpage URL of www.tinkercad.com/things.

If your browser page is a bit *thin* (not maximized), you may find that the menu items are consolidated into a menu icon on the far right of the browser screen.

Reading the Tinkercad Blog

You can find the link to the Tinkercad blog at the top of the Tinkercad home page (www.tinkercad.com). It also has its own webpage at http://blog.tinkercad.com. When you click the link at the top of the Tinkercad home page, the blog opens in a separate tab in your Internet browser.

The Tinkercad blog, shown in Figure 3-12, is a great reference resource, providing Tinkercad users with items of interest and all things Tinkercad. The latest news on Tinkercad is always in there, as well as some great technical posts that can be really helpful.

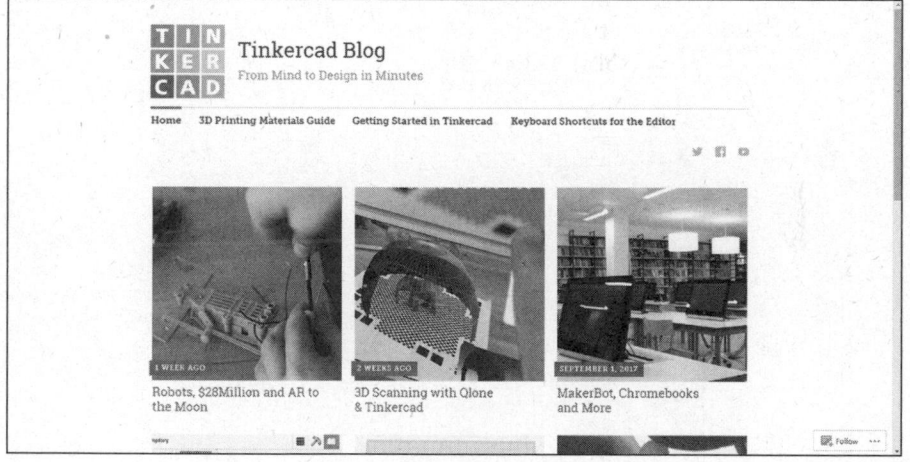

FIGURE 3-12: The Tinkercad blog.

Credit: Autodesk, Inc.

IN THIS CHAPTER

» Exploring the Tinkercad Start screen
and Dashboard

» Using the Tinkercad ViewCube to
your advantage

» Seeing how the Tinkercad viewing
tools work and how they make your
life easier!

» Using the Snap Grid in the Tinkercad
Workplane

» Applying some great Tinkercad
keyboard shortcuts

Chapter **4**

Exploring the User Interface

I n this chapter, you delve deeper into Tinkercad and its user interface. You explore the Start screen and Tinkercad Dashboard and discover how to use the ViewCube to your advantage when working on your Tinkercad designs. You also find out more about the viewing tools and Snap Grid and discover some great Tinkercad keyboard shortcuts!

Venturing Away from the Start screen

After you log in to Tinkercad, you see the Start screen.

The Start screen incorporates the Tinkercad Dashboard, but if you're not sure what to design, go abstract. Just click Create new design. Tinkercad takes you to a blank design where you can drop a basic shape into the Workplane and see what you can do with it (see Figure 4-1). Consider clicking the shape and using the Tinkercad tools to just tinker.

Tinkercad is great for abstract stuff. Sometimes designs will come to you in the strangest of ways. You'll be tweaking a basic 3D shape, and suddenly, a design will come in to your head. Try it. It sometimes works!

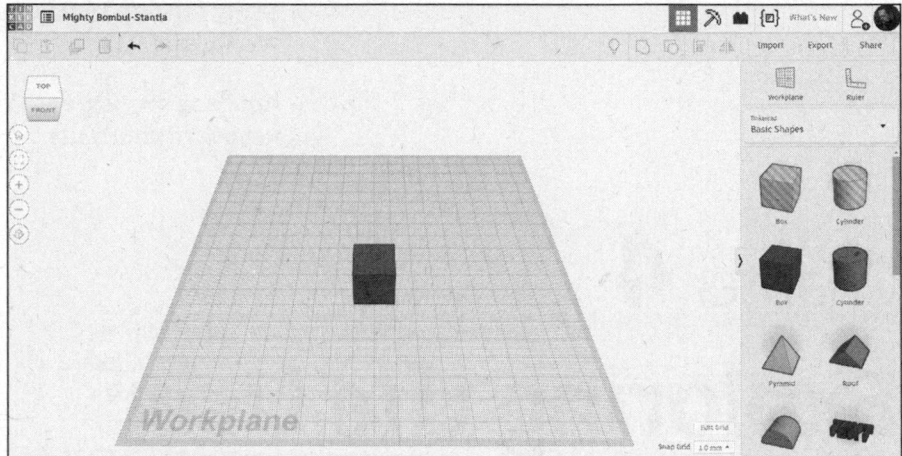

FIGURE 4-1:
The Tinkercad Workplane with a simple basic shape on the Snap Grid.

Viewing the Tinkercad ViewCube

The ViewCube in Tinkercad is an essential navigation tool. Because you're working in three dimensions (3D), you have to think about length, breadth (width), and depth of any design. You need to be able to see all sides of your design. The ViewCube gives you that ability to view any side (or face) of your design, any time.

To use ViewCube, set up a new design in Tinkercad and drag and drop one of the basic shapes onto the Snap Grid in the Workplane. Then, start clicking on the views on the ViewCube. Every time you select a design view on the ViewCube, the basic shape adopts that view, and the ViewCube displays the same view characteristics (see Figure 4-2). So, if you select a corner of the ViewCube to view from, the design also displays from that same corner view.

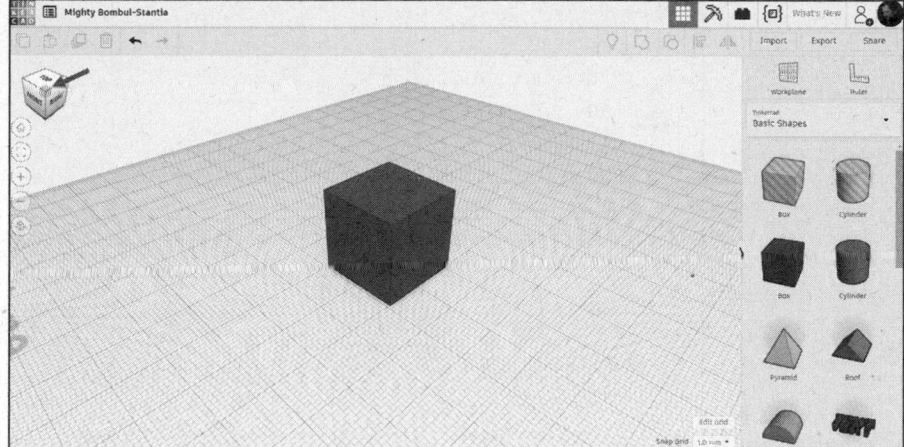

FIGURE 4-2:
An isometric
corner view of a
basic shape on
the Snap Grid in
the Workplane in
Tinkercad.

Using the Viewing Tools

The Tinkercad viewing tools are located on the left side of the Tinkercad screen underneath the ViewCube. They provide you with some great tools for navigating your designs, and when combined with the ViewCube and the mouse navigation, you have a great interface for working in 3D.

The viewing tools are

>> **Home view:** Allows you to reset your view of your Tinkercad to the default view you have when you first start your design on the Workplane. It also resets the ViewCube to the Top/Front view. Home view, shown in Figure 4-3, allows you to go back to square one, and it's a great sanity check to make sure that your Tinkercad design is looking good.

>> **Fit all in view:** Zooms you in to your design, up close and personal, filling the screen with your design (see Figure 4-4). This view is superb for when you need close-up, detail work on your Tinkercad design. Combined with the mouse zoom and pan navigation, it provides you with the necessary magnification to see smaller design details.

>> **Zoom in/Zoom out:** Gives you a default magnification both in and out when you're looking at your Tinkercad design. When used one after another, they cancel each other out. So, if you zoom in using Zoom in and then zoom out using Zoom out, you're back to the original magnification. Zoom in and out are great for viewing designs because they give you a quick, measured zoom with one click.

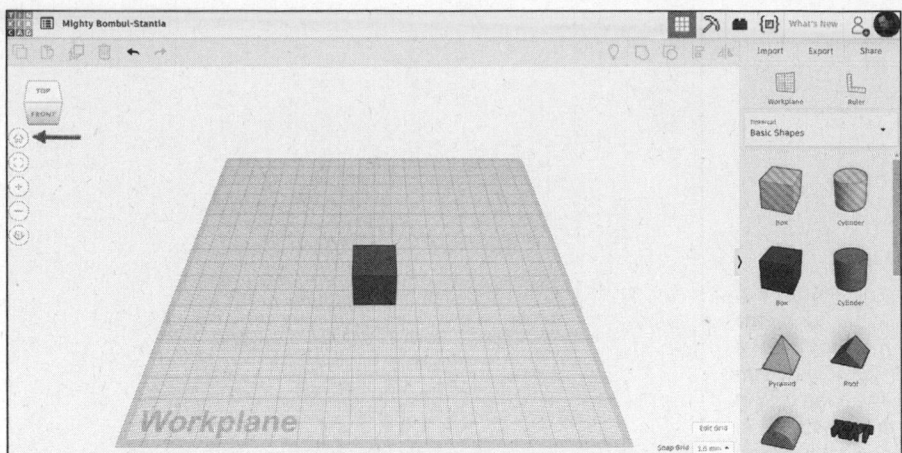

FIGURE 4-3:
The Home view.

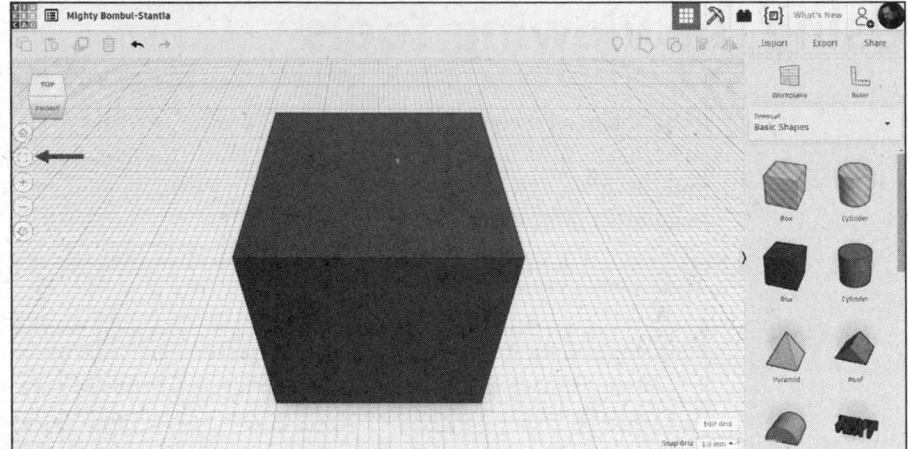

FIGURE 4-4:
A basic shape on
the Workplane
after Fit all in view
has been used.

>> **Switch to Orthographic view:** Switches off perspective view. Tinkercad is a
3D application. For that reason, all 3D views are set, by default, to show
perspective, as shown in Figure 4-5. *Perspective* means that all views will have
a perspective point on an artificial horizon, so it will look like faces and straight
edges are sloping like they do in real life, even though they're straight or
perpendicular. If you click on Switch to Orthographic view, the perspective is
switched off, thus giving you dead straight lines, both in plan and elevation.
You can switch this viewing tool either way. If you switch to the orthographic
setting (see Figure 4-6), you can click on the tool again, and it will switch back
to a perspective view. These view settings allow you to see your design in a
real-life perspective (pardon the pun).

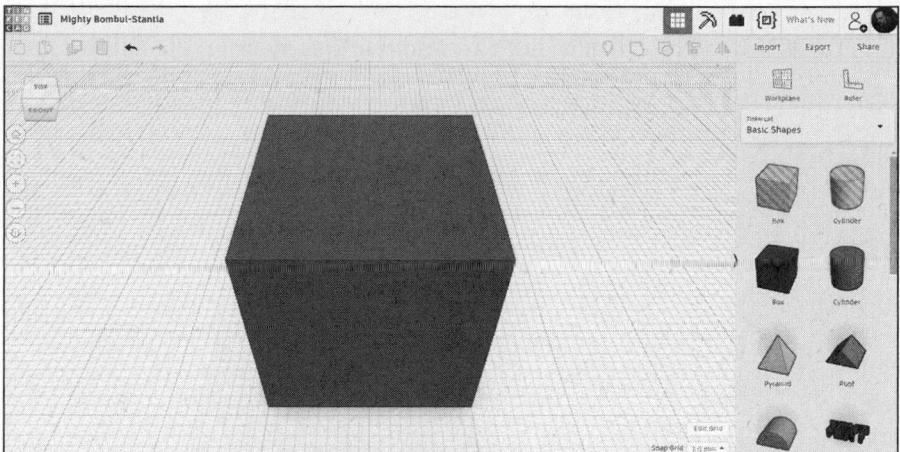

FIGURE 4-5:
The perspective
view setting.

FIGURE 4-6:
An orthographic
view. Spot the
difference!

Working with the Tinkercad Grid

The Workplane in Tinkercad has a grid you can use for reference when working on your designs. This Snap Grid is similar to sketching on graph paper with a pencil when you need datum lines or reference lines to keep things straight or in the same working plane. The Snap Grid is placed in the Workplane at a zero (0) level and is your datum level when you place shapes onto the Workplane to work with in your Tinkercad designs.

When you place any Tinkercad shape onto the Workplane, it automatically snaps to the grid. When you move shapes, they also snap to the grid lines on the Snap Grid for easy positioning as you design.

You can edit the Snap Grid spacings by using the Edit Grid tool and the accuracy drop-down menu in the bottom-right corner of the Workplane area of the Tinkercad screen (see Figure 4-7).

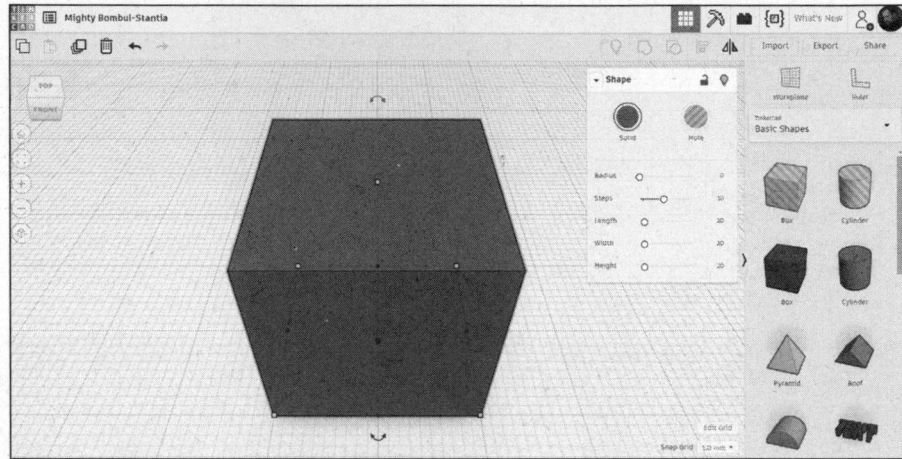

FIGURE 4-7:
A basic shape whose corners on the bottom face of the cube have been snapped to the Snap Grid.

Speeding Things Up by Using Keyboard Shortcuts

You may not be a keyboard person, but some users prefer keystrokes to clicks on a mouse. Tinkercad caters to all preferences. Fortunately, Tinkercad has numerous standard keyboard shortcuts.

You can find all the keyboard shortcuts on the Tinkercad blog at `https://blog.tinkercad.com/keyboard-shortcuts`. It gives you a comprehensive list of all the standard keyboard shortcuts in Tinkercad, and it even has a short video that explains the shortcuts in a visual style.

Figure 4-8 shows the typical keyboard shortcuts (Apple keyboard in parentheses):

>> **Workplane:** Type **W** to place a workplane

>> **Ruler:** Type **R** to place ruler

>> **Fit view to selection:** Type **F** to fit the view on the selected object

- » **Copy:** CTRL(CMD) + C to copy selected object/objects

- » **Paste:** CTRL(CMD) + V to paste object/objects

- » **Paste in place:** CTRL(CMD) + SHIFT + V to paste object/objects in place

- » **Undo:** CTRL(CMD) + Z to undo

- » **Redo:** CTRL(CMD) + SHIFT + Z to redo

- » **Group:** CTRL(CMD) + G to group objects

- » **Ungroup:** CTRL(CMD) + SHIFT + G to ungroup objects

- » **Duplicate in place:** CTRL(CMD) + D to duplicate selection in the same place

- » **Lock:** CTRL(CMD) + L to lock selection

- » **Select all:** CTRL(CMD) + A to select all objects

- » **Delete:** BACKSPACE to delete object

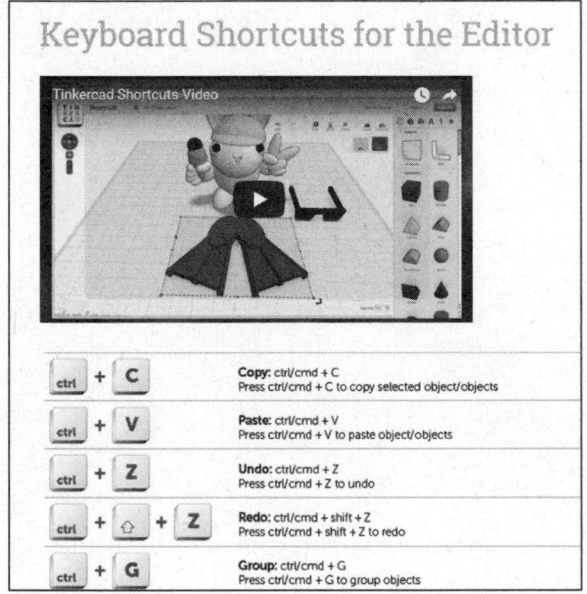

FIGURE 4-8:
Numerous
keyboard
shortcuts, plus a
short video on
how to use them.

Credit: Autodesk, Inc.

Chapter 5

Exploring 3D Tools in Tinkercad

I n this chapter, you find out about the great 3D tools you can use in Tinkercad to develop your 3D designs. You discover the fundamental 3D creation and editing tools that you can use on a day-to-day basis in Tinkercad. You also pick up some great tips and tricks for creating and editing along the way.

Copy and Paste

Copy and Paste are located at the top left of the Tinkercad screen in the toolbar above the ViewCube (see Figure 5-1). You can also use the usual Ctrl + C and Ctrl + V keyboard shortcuts as you would in any other application.

These two extremely useful editing commands, quite simply, provide you with the ability to copy and paste any parts (or the whole) of your design in Tinkercad. If you've used other CAD products or even just Microsoft Word, then you know that these two commands, in any application, are a lifesaver.

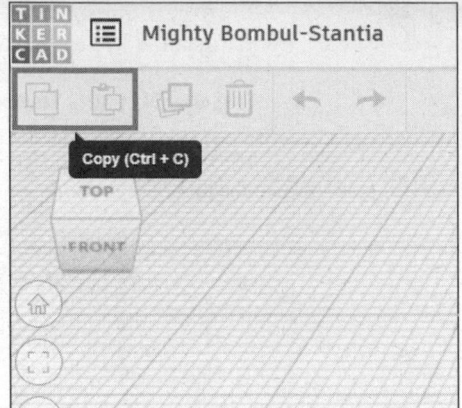

FIGURE 5-1:
Copy and Paste
on the Tinkercad
screen.

Duplicate

Duplicate is a wonderful command in Tinkercad. It, quite literally, duplicates anything in a Tinkercad design on the screen on top of the original object. It is located in the top left of the Tinkercad screen but is only activated when you select an object in Tinkercad. You can also use the keyboard shortcut of Ctrl + D.

After you select the object, Duplicate is active in the top-left toolbar (see Figure 5-2). Click on Duplicate, and Tinkercad duplicates your object exactly on top of the existing object. If you click, select, and drag the newly duplicated object away from the existing object, you now have two of the same object (see Figure 5-3). Pretty neat, huh?

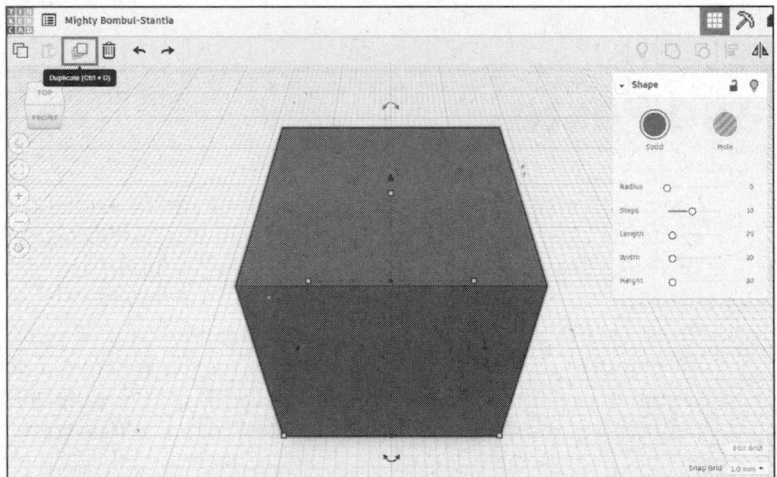

FIGURE 5-2:
The Duplicate
command on the
Tinkercad screen.

FIGURE 5-3:
Two simple cubes in a Tinkercad design, thanks to the Duplicate command.

Hide

You can hide any object in your Tinkercad design using the Hide command. Simply select an object and use the keyboard shortcut Ctrl + H. Hide is especially useful when you have a complex Tinkercad design and need to see the wood for the trees. Sometimes you just need to hide a few objects so that you can see the object you need to work on.

You can also find the Hide command on the top right of the Shape window in Tinkercad, as shown in Figure 5-4. The command appears as a lightbulb icon. When you select an object in Tinkercad, the Shape window always appears, offering you contextual commands for that particular shape. Simply click the lightbulb icon, and the shape is hidden.

Show All

If you hide an object in Tinkercad (see preceding section), it stands to reason that you will need to unhide it at some point, too. Showing all your objects is especially important when displaying your final Tinkercad design when you need to display the final design in its entirety.

You can find Show All in the top-right toolbar in the Tinkercad screen, as shown in Figure 5-5. It is represented by a lightbulb icon. When the Show All lightbulb icon is active and highlighted in bold (black) in the toolbar, it indicates that your design contains hidden objects. You can also use the keyboard shortcut Ctrl + Shift + H.

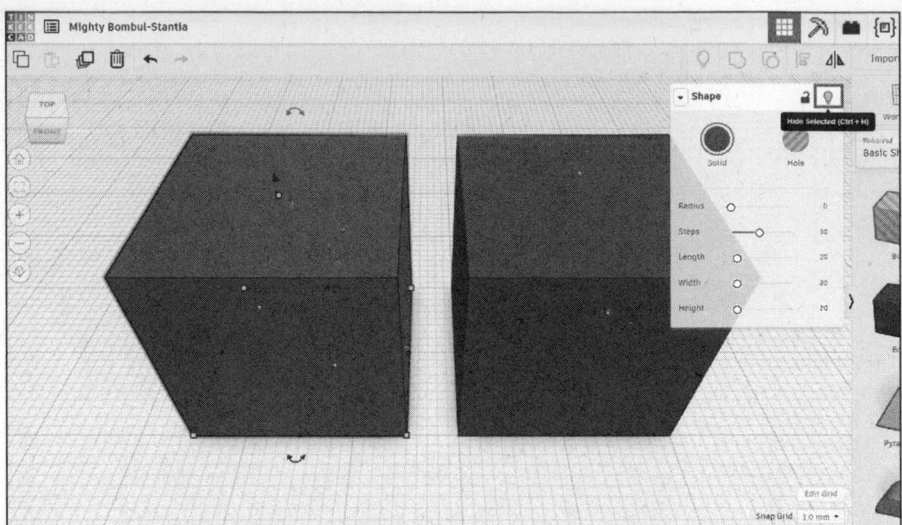

FIGURE 5-4:
The Hide
command.

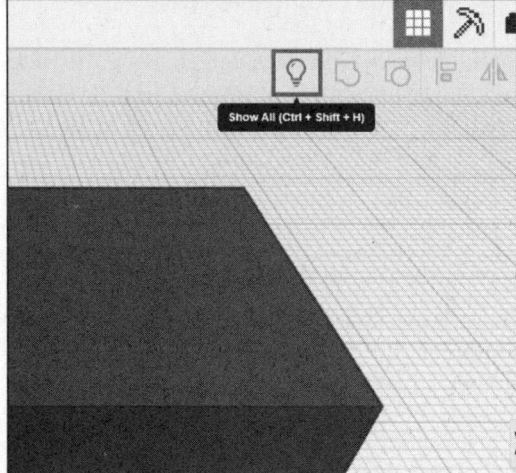

FIGURE 5-5:
The Show All
lightbulb icon
(highlighted) in
the top-right
toolbar of the
Tinkercad screen.

Group

When you're working in Tinkercad, you'll often place objects within objects or objects on objects to build complex shapes in your Tinkercad designs.

To convert the objects into one complex object, you use the Group command, which is located on the top-right toolbar on the Tinkercad screen (see Figure 5-6). You can also use the keyboard shortcut Ctrl + G.

Figure 5-6 shows you two Tinkercad objects selected and the Shape window.

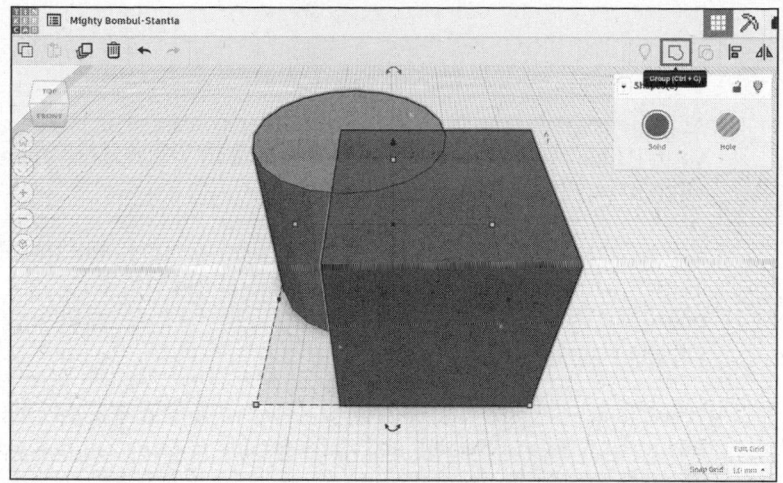

FIGURE 5-6:
The Group icon.

Ungroup

Ungroup is the opposite of Group. It appears to the right of the Group command icon on the top-right toolbar in Tinkercad. You can also use the keyboard shortcut Ctrl + Shift + G.

You can use Ungroup to break down a complex Tinkercad object back to its original component objects.

Figure 5-7 shows you a selected complex Tinkercad object that is made up of two Tinkercad component objects, and you can see the highlighted Ungroup icon in the top-right toolbar.

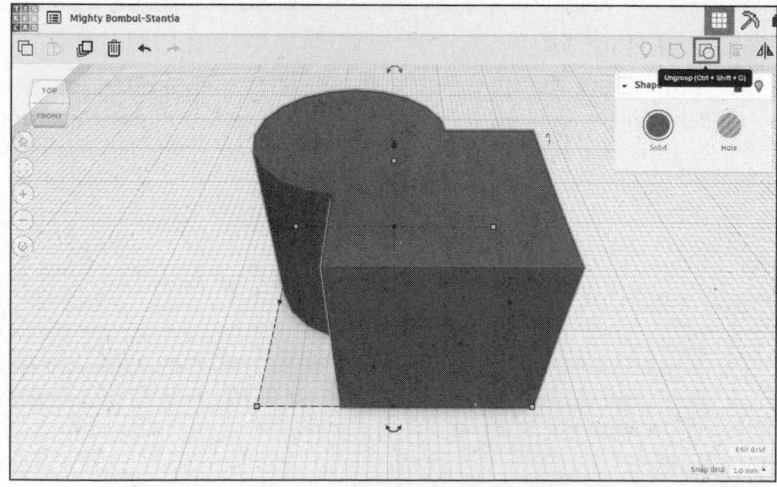

FIGURE 5-7:
The Ungroup
icon.

Align

Align is a great tool for making sure that you have accurate, aligned objects in your Tinkercad designs. As you're working in 3D, this command means you can align in any plane and in any direction.

You need to select both the object you want to align and the object you want to align it with. Then select the Align command from the top-right toolbar. The keyboard shortcut is just the letter L on the keyboard, assuming that you have the objects selected.

If you look at Figure 5-8, you can see the two objects selected. The Align command has already been selected, and the left cube is to be aligned with the right cube along the lower horizontal plane.

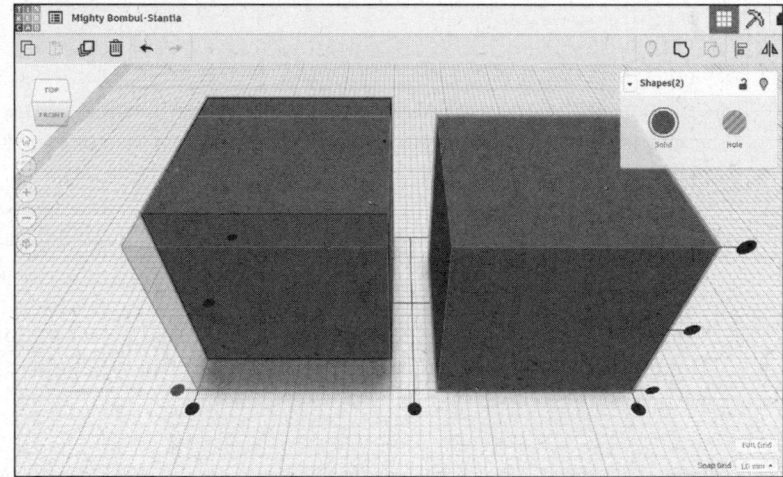

FIGURE 5-8: Two cubes ready to be aligned.

You can see the alignment guide planes shown on the screen as black lines with large black dots at each end and the proposed aligned position of the left cube highlighted in position, after the appropriate guide has been selected.

Flip

When you're working in 3D in Tinkercad, you may need to reverse the positioning of an object along one of the 3D planes in the Tinkercad 3D space. You can use the Flip command to do so.

The Flip command is in the top-right toolbar, and it is highlighted after you select the object you want to flip. It also has a simple keyboard shortcut of the key M after you select the object to be flipped.

After you click on Flip, you're presented with three arrow symbols around the selected object. These arrows represent the three 3D planes in which you can flip your object.

In Figure 5-9, the simple roof object is selected, and the Flip command is activated. Hovering over any of the three arrow symbols gives you a preview of how the flipped object will look.

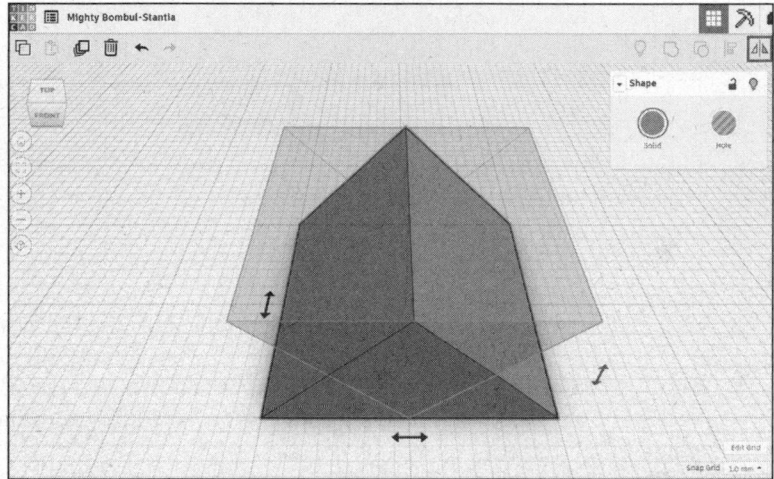

FIGURE 5-9:
A preview of the roof object being flipped.

Workplane

In a 3D environment in Tinkercad, you can define where you want your workplane to be. The workplane can be on the default snap grid provided when you first start designing in a Tinkercad design, or it can be on one of the faces you have on an existing Tinkercad design.

The Workplane command allows you to change your workplane at your leisure. It is located at the top of the right panel on your Tinkercad screen and is labeled Workplane. You can also access it by using the keyboard shortcut W.

After the command is active, you simply hover over the chosen Workplane, which is highlighted as you move over it, and click on the highlighted workplane you want to be on, as shown in Figure 5-10.

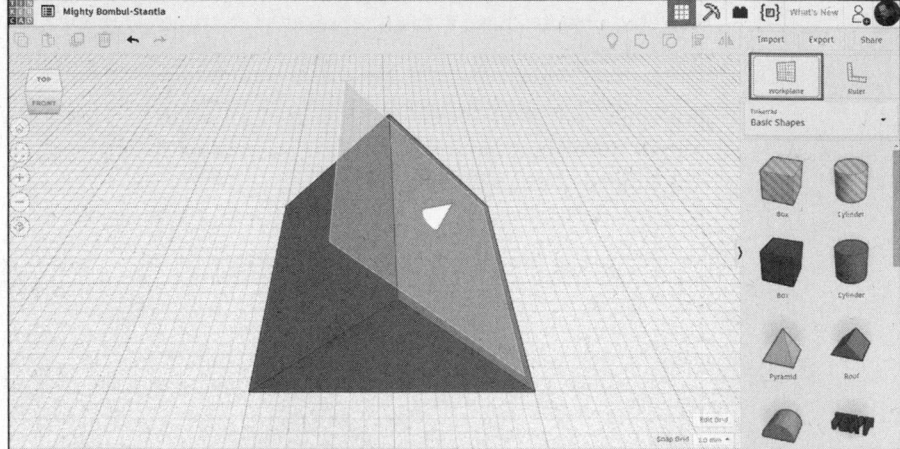

Ruler

You'll often need to measure exact distances so that you can place objects accurately and precisely as you create your design. The Ruler command offers a visual guide for placement.

To access the Ruler command, click on Ruler in the panel on the right of the Tinkercad screen or press the R key.

An L-shaped graphic appears on your pointer on the screen. Move the red circle so that its center is over the appropriate point you want to measure from (known as a datum) and click. The ruler markings appear on your current workplane (see Figure 5-11).

After you place the ruler and the ruler graduations are displayed in the appropriate workplane, select the object you used for the datum point. You are then able to see all the measurements of the selected object and measure them accordingly, against the ruler graduations.

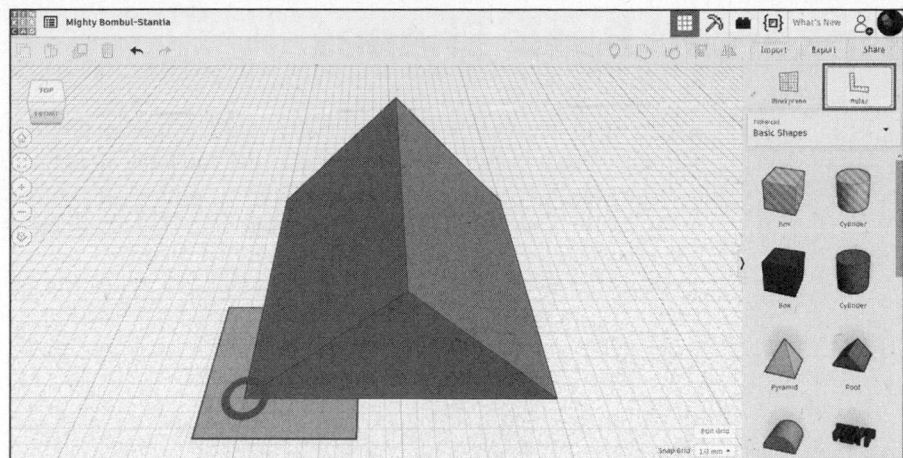

FIGURE 5-11:
The Ruler.

Figure 5-12 shows you the selected object and all its associated dimensions, with the ruler displayed.

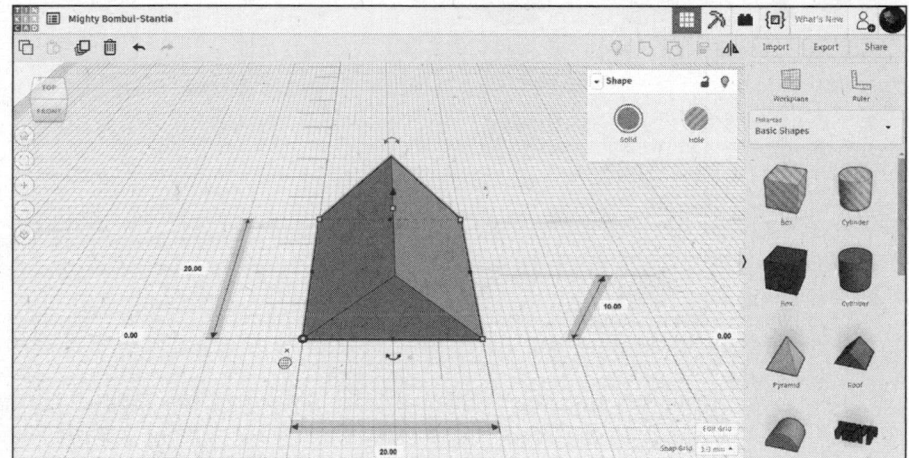

FIGURE 5-12:
A selected object used for the ruler datum, with the ruler graduations displayed.

If you want to turn off the ruler, simply click on the small X symbol next to the small circle with the three lines inside it.

Tinkercad Basic Shapes

Rather than expect you to create every shape you want to use in Tinkercad from scratch, Autodesk has kindly made sure that you have an extensive library of standard shapes to use. The Basics Shapes library, shown in Figure 5-13, allows you to build complex objects from simple, component objects, such as boxes, cylinders, and pyramids.

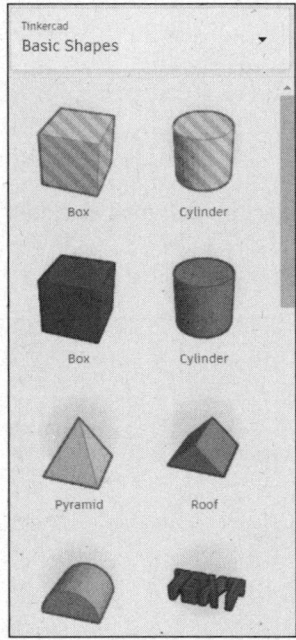

FIGURE 5-13:
Tinkercad Basic
Shapes.

You can find the Tinkercad Basic Shapes in the drop-down menu in the right panel on the Tinkercad screen. The default setting is Basic Shapes. In there, you will find standard boxes, cylinders, pyramids, and many other standard object elements, such as text, symbols, and connectors. Just click on the drop-down menu to find many different standard objects that are useful!

Community Shapes

On the Tinkercad Basic Shapes drop-down menu, shown in Figure 5-14, is a Community section. This section of shapes is provided by the Tinkercad community itself. When Tinkercad users create shapes that they think other Tinkercad users will find useful, they can submit them for use in either Featured Shape Generators or Community Shape Generators.

Click on either of the generator options to see the many shape generators created by Tinkercad users all over the world.

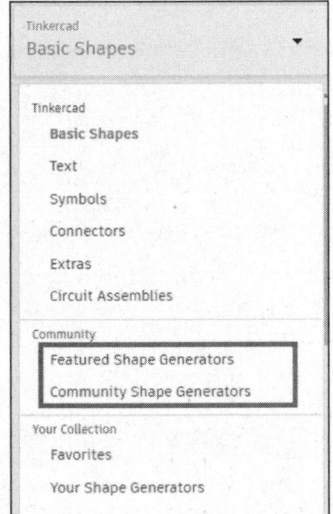

FIGURE 5-14:
The Community shape generator options.

2

Creating a Simple Nameplate for Your Office

IN THIS PART . . .

Use the Workplane, grid, and Basic Shapes to develop the nameplate's baseplate.

Give the nameplate's baseplate depth. Use the ViewCube to work on different faces, choose a shape for the indent in the baseplate, use the grid to check object positioning, pick a face to work on, and add depth.

Add your name as text. Get back to the view you need and choose your nameplate text.

Cut holes to mount the nameplate. Choose a shape for the hole in the nameplate, get the hole placement right, and use Grouping and Ungrouping to make the hole part of the nameplate.

Chapter **6**

Creating the Baseplate

I n this chapter, you discover how you can create a nameplate that you print later in 3D and mount on your office door, thus promoting your entry into Tinkercad geekdom.

Working with the Tinkercad basic shapes, you develop the baseplate of the nameplate and find out how to use the 3D workplanes in Tinkercad to your advantage.

Starting and Saving a New Project

You need to set up a new project that you can use to create your nameplate. You can call Tinkercad projects anything you like. I named my new project My Nameplate.

In this chapter, you discover what you need to do to create your nameplate:

1. Set up a new project.

2. Create a blank Tinkercad design.

3. Decide on public or private access to your design.

4. Decide on design properties and licensing.

You can also find out about basic Tinkercad tasks, such as using the Workplane, grid, and basic shapes.

You may have done some of these steps already, and if you have, you may want to jump ahead a little.

Setting Up Your Project

If you have a project set up already, refer to the Creating a Blank Design section. Otherwise, follow these steps to set up your project:

1. **Click on the Create project button in the Projects panel, shown in Figure 6-1.**

   A new unnamed project appears. In Figure 6-1, my new unnamed project is Project 2.

FIGURE 6-1: The Projects panel and the Create project button.

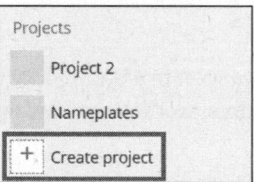

2. **Click on your new project in the Projects panel.**

   The project opens, but it has no Tinkercad designs. You see the Tinkercad screen, shown in Figure 6-2.

3. **Click on Add a description.**

4. **In the dialog box that appears, name your project, give it a description, and click on Save changes.**

   In this example, I called my project My Nameplate and gave it a description of My new office nameplate.

   Figure 6-3 shows you the dialog box with the completed project name and description.

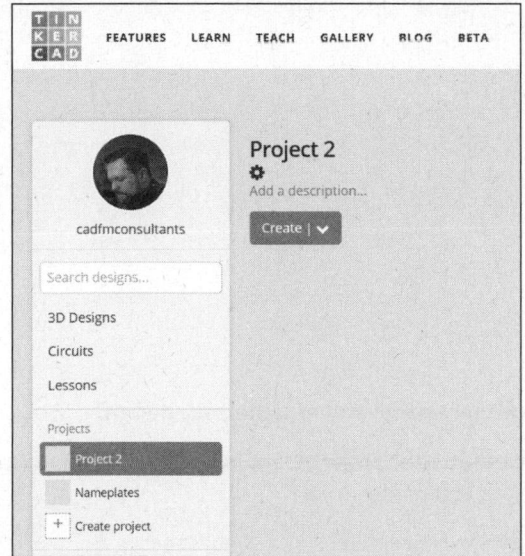

FIGURE 6-2:
A Tinkercad
project, ready for
naming.

FIGURE 6-3:
The Project
properties dialog
box, complete
with project
name and project
description.

Creating a Blank Design

After you create a project, you need to create a new blank design that will be in your project. Select your project from the list on the left side of the screen and follow these steps:

1. **Click on the Create drop-down list, shown in Figure 6-4, and choose 3D Design.**

   After clicking on the 3D Design option, Tinkercad takes you to a new default blank Tinkercad design. Notice the random, default name for the project at the top left of the Tinkercad screen.

FIGURE 6-4:
The 3D Design
option.

2. **Click on the project name and rename your design.**

In this example, name the project to *Yourname's* Office Nameplate, where *Yourname* is your first name.

Figure 6-5 shows my new project with its new name.

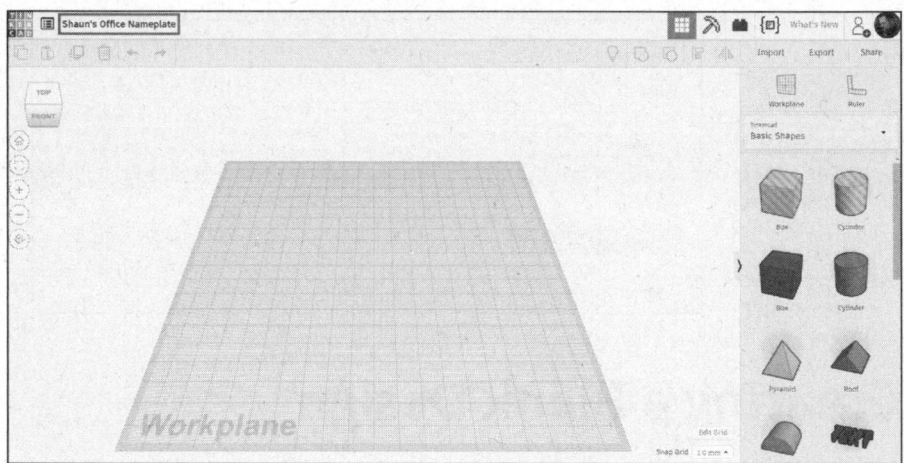

FIGURE 6-5:
My newly named
Tinkercad project.

3. **Click on the Tinkercad logo icon.**

You return to the Tinkercad home page where you're still logged in.

Your new project appears in the Projects panel, and your new project appears in My recent designs, as shown in Figure 6-6.

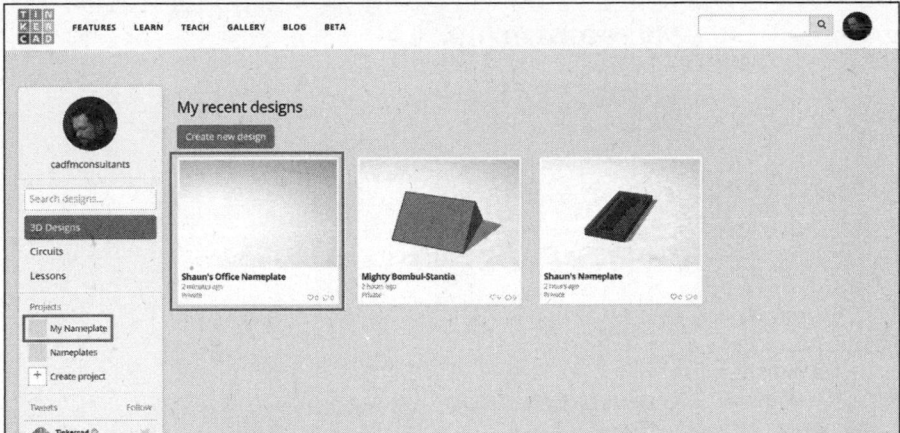

FIGURE 6-6:
The Tinkercad
home page with
your newly
created name-
plate design.

Choosing Public or Private Access

As Tinkercad is open and on the Internet in the public domain, you can decide whether to make your designs public or private. If your designs are private, they remain solely available to you to view when you log in to your Tinkercad account.

If you make them public, however, you can get feedback on your designs with Likes in a similar way to liking a picture or a post on social media.

To make your design public, you need to change its properties. You can do so by hovering over the gearwheel icon in your nameplate design in the My recent designs area. The gearwheel icon is your individual options for your Tinkercad design.

Figure 6-7 shows the nameplate design, with the Options gearwheel highlighted in orange.

When you click on the Options gearwheel, a small drop-down menu appears. Choose Properties from the menu, and the Design properties dialog box appears.

This dialog box has two sections:

» Design properties

» Licenses

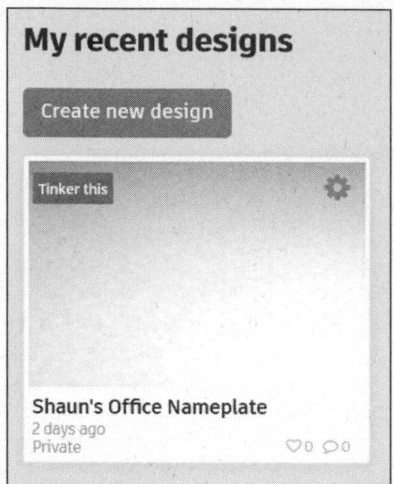

FIGURE 6-7:
The nameplate
design with the
Options
gearwheel
highlighted in
orange.

Choosing Design Properties

In the Design properties dialog box, you can change your design name, give your design a more detailed description, add tags to it so that it can be found more easily on the Internet, and set the design to public or private. These properties, shown in Figure 6-8, are simple and easy to set.

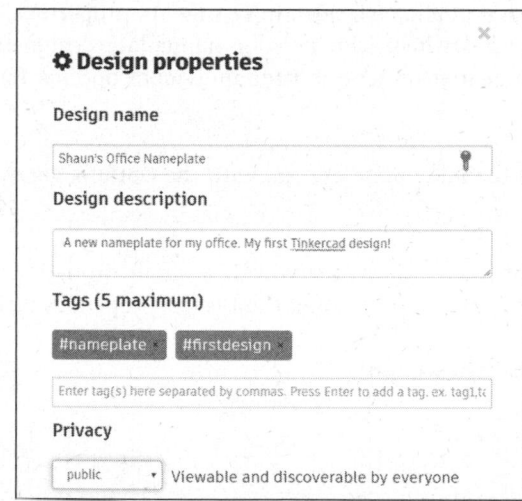

FIGURE 6-8:
The Design
properties
dialog box.

Deciding on Licensing

If your nameplate design is public, it's a legal requirement that it has to be licensed. Without going in to deep legal stuff, a Creative Commons license protects your design and your intellectual property.

Basically, this license protects your design by way of allowing others to use it, but not for commercial gain. In other words, they can't copy it and sell it without your say so.

Numerous Creative Commons license models are out there, and they're listed in the drop-down menu for licensing in the Design properties dialog box.

TIP

The Design properties dialog box also has a link to the Creative Commons website. Use this link and investigate which Creative Commons license is best for you and your design.

Figure 6-9 shows you the various Creative Commons licenses you can use for your Tinkercad design.

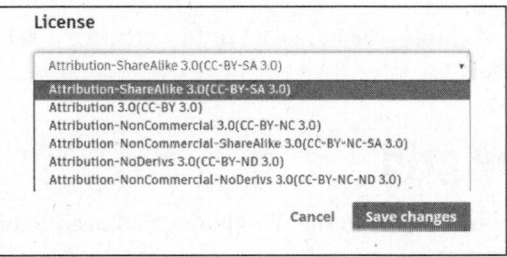

FIGURE 6-9:
The License
drop-down menu
in the Design
properties
dialog box.

After you set all your properties in the Design properties dialog box, click on Save changes.

Using the Workplane

After you set up all your properties in your design, you're ready to add some content to your design.

Hover over your nameplate design in My recent designs on the Tinkercad home page, and you see the Tinker this button highlighted. Click on it, and Tinkercad loads up your new blank design.

Setting up your dimensions

You now need to get all your Workplane settings up and running.

To give you an idea of how big you need your nameplate to be, the suggested metric dimensions are 200 mm x 80 mm. If you want to go imperial, the suggested dimensions are 8 inches x 3 ¼ inches.

These metric dimensions will fit nicely on the default grid in the Tinkercad Workplane (which is metric, you will notice). They have been set up this way to give you an example in Tinkercad that is workable within default settings to allow you to get started straight away, so to speak.

Bear in mind though, that these sizes are only suggestions. You can go bigger or smaller, if you like. You may also prefer to set your dimensions as imperial (feet and inches).

For the purposes of clarity, the baseplate in this chapter is set to the metric millimeters dimensions.

Editing the grid

After you have enough space on the Workplane, you need to use Edit grid to give yourself enough space:

1. **Click on the Edit grid button, which is located on the bottom right of the Tinkercad design screen.**

   You see the Grid properties dialog box, shown in Figure 6-10.

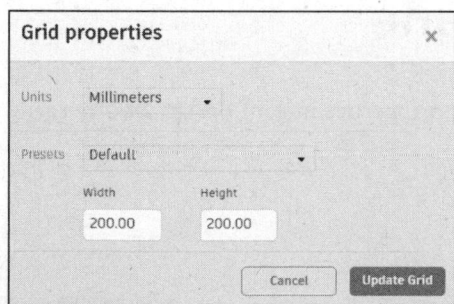

FIGURE 6-10: The Grid properties dialog box.

2. **Set the following settings for metric millimeters.**

- **Units:** Millimeters (inches)

- **Presets:** Default

- **Width:** 350 (14)

- **Height:** 200 (8)

If you're using alternate units of measurement, such as imperial, set the settings accordingly.

3. **Click on Update Grid.**

You see the grid on the Workplane change.

4. **Zoom accordingly using your mouse wheel to ensure the newly sized grid fits on your Tinkercad screen.**

TIP

Notice that the presets in the Grid properties dialog box have been left at the default setting. If you want to use a specific 3D printer grid setting, a variety of 3D printers are listed in the Presets drop-down menu. Simply select the printer you want to use to 3D print your design, and the preset automatically sets the width and height of the grid for you.

Using Basic Shapes

Tinkercad gives you an extensive library of component shapes you can use to develop your 3D designs. By adding these component shapes and using the 3D editing tools in Tinkercad, you can develop many complex objects.

As you progress with Tinkercad, you'll discover that your Tinkercad Basic Shapes are just the tip of the iceberg. You can archive your own libraries of component and complex shapes for re-use for your designs.

You can find the Tinkercad Basic Shapes menu in the panel to the right of the Tinkercad design screen.

Adding a box to the Workplane

The most basic of basic Tinkercad shapes is the box. The Box shape has two iterations in the Tinkercad Basic Shapes menu:

» The **transparent box** is denoted by a 3D box icon with gray hatched lines. You use this box to create box-shaped voids in other solid 3D shapes in Tinkercad.

>> The **solid box** is denoted by a 3D box icon colored in red. You use this box to create box-shaped solids in Tinkercad.

To create the baseplate of your nameplate, you need to add a solid 3D box to the Tinkercad Workplane. If your panel is set to Tinkercad Basic Shapes, you see the 3D box icons, which are both gray hatched and red in color.

To place your box on the Workplane, click on the red box and simply drag it on to the Workplane. It adapts to the Workplane grid and sits on top of the grid (see Figure 6-11).

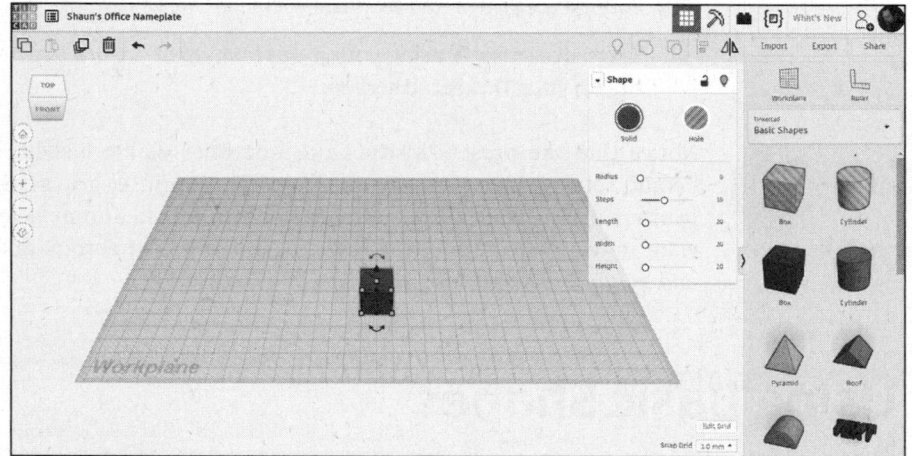

FIGURE 6-11:
A solid red box placed on the grid in the Tinkercad Workplane.

Sizing your box

After you place your box on the Workplane, you need to size it appropriately. If the box you placed is currently selected, its displays its grips on its corners (the small white squares) and the Shape window is displayed.

You can adjust the size of the box shape in the Shape window. I used the following settings, which are shown in Figure 6-12:

>> **Width:** 200

>> **Length:** 80

>> **Height:** 10

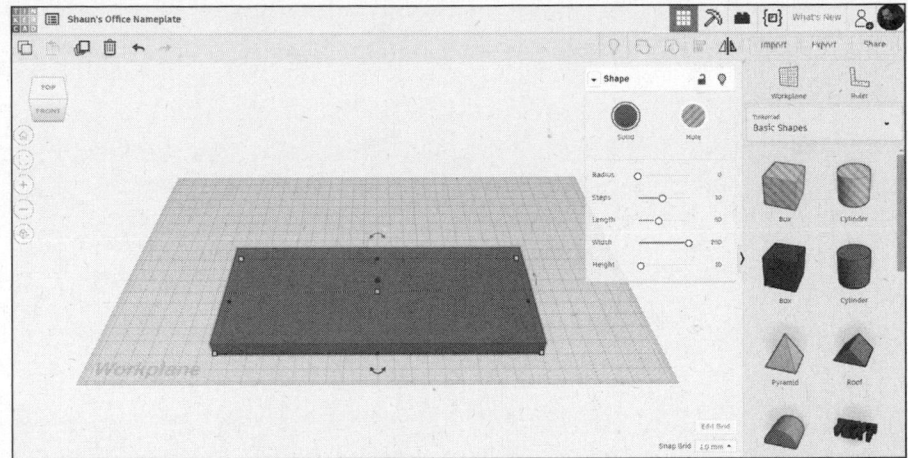

FIGURE 6-12:
The Tinkercad design screen with the baseplate sizes set.

The baseplate will adjust accordingly, and you now have your baseplate ready to go!

TIP

If you're using imperial inches for your baseplate, change the width and length to 8 inches x 3 ¼ inches and the height to 0.5. Also, using the sliders to get exact dimensions can be annoying, but you can adjust your dimensions by clicking on the required dimension and typing the dimension value in directly.

TIP

Using the grid on the Workplane, make sure you have your baseplate set nice and neatly on a grid intersection on the Workplane. Simply select the baseplate and drag it to a suitable intersection so that it sits exactly on the grid. This makes things much easier when working on your design because the Workplane grid can then be used as a point of reference.

Chapter 7

Giving the Baseplate Depth

In this chapter, you find out how to give your baseplate depth. (If you haven't formed the baseplate of your nameplate, see Chapter 6.) You also use the ViewCube and the Workplane together to navigate your design more effectively and then use the Group and Ungroup commands to develop your complex object from component objects.

Using the ViewCube

The ViewCube is a standard interface tool in all Autodesk applications, and Tinkercad is no exception.

The ViewCube gives you a full 360 degree view. It lets you view your design in its numerous preset views and gives you the ability to view your design from many different angles so that you can see views of your design that you may not see otherwise.

To use the ViewCube, simply hover over it and highlight which face, corner, or edge you want to view your design from.

The ViewCube provides the following views:

>> **Corners:** Click any corner of the ViewCube to view your 3D design from that corner in an isometric view, as shown in Figure 7-1.

>> **Edges:** Click any edge of the ViewCube to view your 3D design from that edge in an isometric view.

>> **Faces (sides):** Click any side of the ViewCube to view your 3D design in elevation.

>> **Faces (top/bottom):** Click the top or bottom view of the ViewCube to view your 3D design in plan.

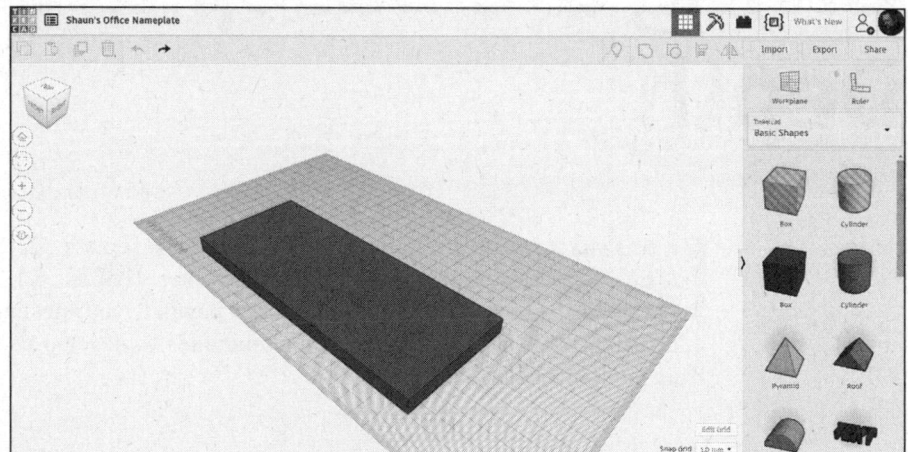

FIGURE 7-1:
The baseplate view in an isometric view from the top-right corner of the ViewCube.

TIP

You can also orbit your design manually instead of using the preset ViewCube angles. Simply hold down your mouse button and move the mouse. You then orbit your design view. Take care, though! It's pretty fast! Move the mouse slowly and purposefully. If you need to get back to a preset view, just use the ViewCube.

You can also click and hold the left mouse button on the ViewCube to move it around. And if you get lost, just click on the Home icon on the left side of the screen to get back to the normal view.

Working on Different Faces

As you develop your Tinkercad nameplate design, you need to work on different faces and thus need to alter or change your Workplane to a face on the nameplate baseplate.

The baseplate needs an indent in which to place the text for the name in the nameplate design. To do this, you need to be looking down at the baseplate in plan from the top:

1. **Ensure that you have a full view of the baseplate on the screen.**

   Use the zoom tools to do this, if you haven't already. Using the top/front edge preset view on the ViewCube makes selecting the top face of the baseplate easier.

2. **Click on the Workplane button at the top of the right-hand menu.**

   You can also type W on the keyboard to start the Workplane command.

3. **Using the Workplane command, hover over the top face of the nameplate; when it highlights, click on the top face.**

   A yellowish grid appears to distinguish it from the default Workplane. Your Workplane is now on the top face of the baseplate, as shown in Figure 7-2.

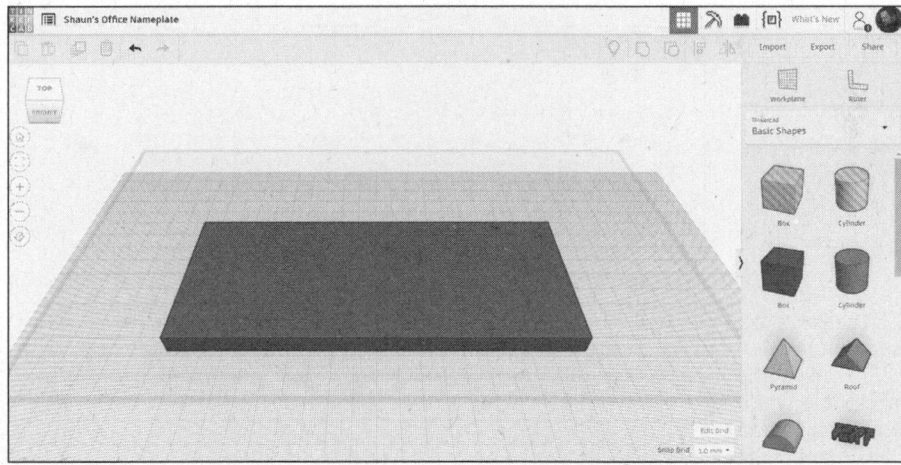

FIGURE 7-2: The baseplate with the top face set to the current Workplane.

Choosing a Shape for the Indent

You can place a Tinkercad shape to help you create the indent in the baseplate.

If you're working in metric units, your baseplate of your nameplate will be 10 mm deep (or ½ inch if using imperial). You want the indent to be half of that (5 mm or ¼ inch), cut out of the baseplate.

These measurements are purely a guide, and you may want to use other sizes. Just bear in mind that the metric measurements I mention are what are being used in the example in this section of the book.

To create the indent accurately and effectively, follow these steps:

1. **Make sure that you're in the Top view of the design.**

   Use the ViewCube to set this preset view.

2. **Drag and drop a Box shape to roughly the center of the Workplane.**

   Note that the Shape window denotes this box as a Hole.

Figure 7-3 shows you the baseplate in the Top view, with the Workplane set to the top face of the baseplate, with the Box (hole) shape sitting on top of the Workplane, roughly in the center.

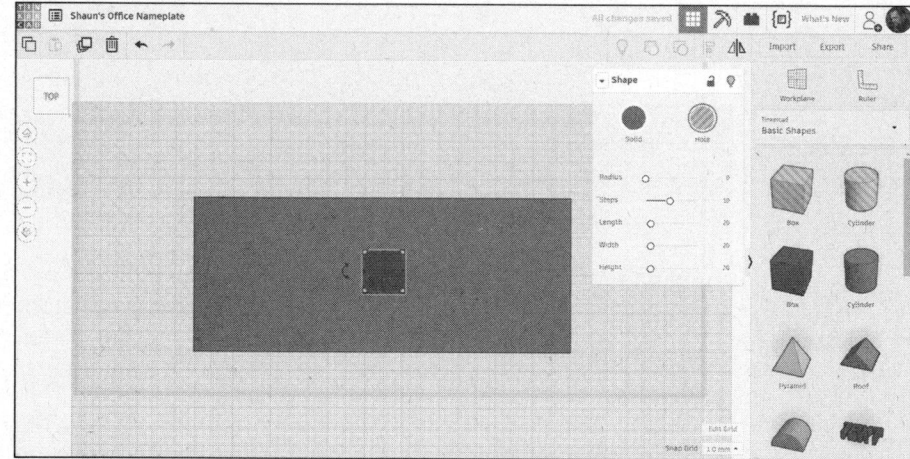

FIGURE 7-3:
The Box (hole) shape in place on top of the Workplane, which is set to the top face of the baseplate.

Checking Object Position Using the Grid

With the Box (hole) shape selected, you can now size it and then place it accurately using the grid on the Workplane:

1. **Use the Shape window to size the Box (hole) shape to the following dimensions:**

   - **Length** = 70 mm (2 ¾ inches)
   - **Width** = 190 mm (7 ½ inches)
   - **Height** = 10 mm (25/64 ins = 0.4 inches)

2. **If the box positions itself weirdly, use the grid to place it accurately.**

   Your baseplate should already be placed neatly on a grid intersection so as to utilize the grid for object placement. (If it isn't, select both shapes with a crossing window and drag them to a grid intersection on the Workplane.)

3. **Click on a free space somewhere to deselect both shapes and then select only the Box (hole) shape.**

4. **With only the Box (hole) shape selected, drag it so that the top-left corner is placed toward the top-left corner of the baseplate.**

   If you zoom in, it is easier to view.

   If you're using a metric millimeters grid, you want the top-left corner of the Box (hole) shape to be 5 grid increments (mm) inside the baseplate edges in both directions (if using imperial, it should be ¼ inches). Again, use the zoom tools if you need to.

5. **Use the ViewCube and the mouse (right-click and hold) to change your view if required for the preceding step.**

   You want to ensure that the bottom grips of the Box (hole) shape are aligned with the top of the baseplate, where the Workplace is at the moment.

TIP

Remember to utilize your mouse wheel. Rolling up and down allows you to zoom in and out on your Tinkercad design screen. If you hold down the wheel as a button and move your mouse, you can pan around the Tinkercad design screen as well. This feature is incredibly useful for close-up work in Tinkercad.

Figure 7-4 shows you the actual positioning of the Box (hole) shape on the baseplate, using the millimeter increments in the Workplane grid.

6. **If the perspective view looks a little weird, use the Switch to Orthographic view setting in the viewing tools on the left of the Tinkercad screen.**

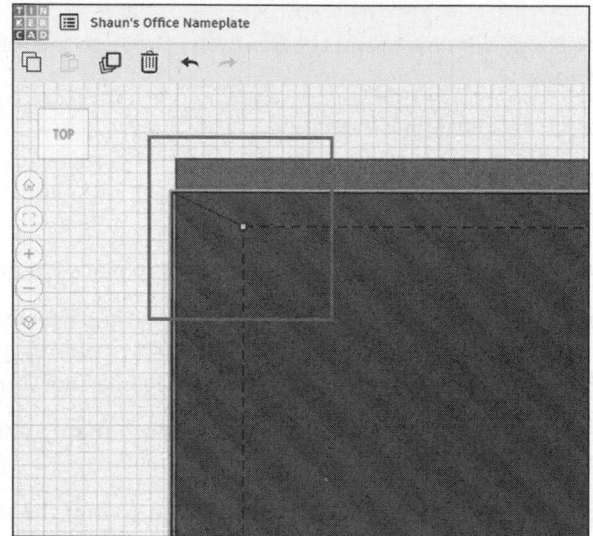

FIGURE 7-4:
The Box (hole) shape accurately positioned in the top-left corner of the baseplate.

Picking a Face to Work

The Box (hole) shape needs to be set to the correct depth so that it's flush to the top face of the baseplate and cuts the indent in the baseplate to the correct depth also.

To do this, you need to pick either the left or right face of the baseplate as a face to work with. For the purposes of clarity, use the Right view on the ViewCube.

After you select the Right view, it may look a bit strange. You may be zoomed in too close or perhaps zoomed out too far. Use your zoom tools that your mouse provides with the mouse wheel and also use a bit of manual orbit with the right mouse button, too.

After you're happy with the view, you are ready to make the Box (hole) shape do its work. Figure 7-5 shows you a typical view where you can work with the Right side of the baseplate effectively. Aim to have a view like that on your screen. Take note of the ViewCube alignment, too.

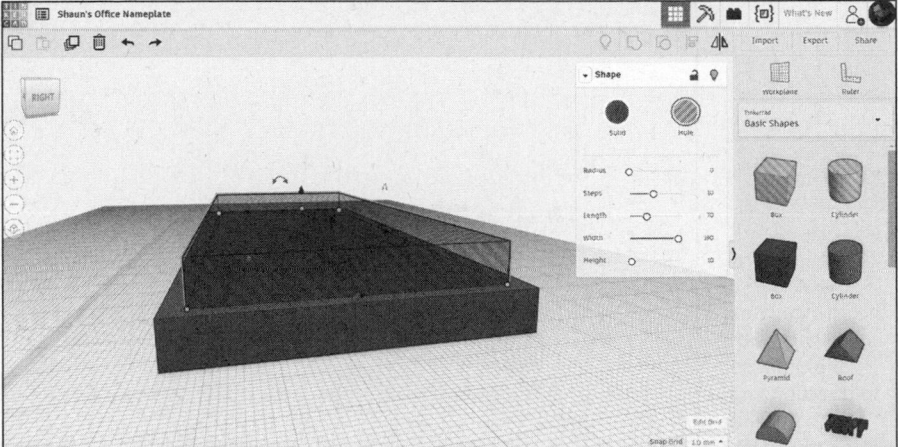

FIGURE 7-5:
A typical Right side view, after some adjustment with a manual orbit, with the Box (hole) shape selected.

Setting the Depth

You need to get the depth of the indent in your baseplate right. This is where that Box (hole) shape comes in to its own right by allowing you to form a hole in the basic solid shape the baseplate has right now.

You can use Right view to alter the depth (height) of the Box (hole) shape:

1. **Select the Box (hole) shape, if you haven't done so already.**

You see a little arrow in the center, pointing either up or down (it doesn't matter which).

2. **Hover over the arrowhead, and when it goes red, click and drag it vertically down using your mouse.**

You see the direction and depth (height) values go negative on your Tinkercad screen.

3. **Make sure the metric values both read –5.**

In imperial, it should be ¼ or 0.25 inches.

4. **When they read the appropriate values, click once to set them at those values.**

WARNING

If you let go of the arrowhead when you are working with the dimensions and start moving it again, it resets to 0. For example, if you move it down to, say, –2, and then let go, and then move it to, say, –5, you would then be at –7, not –5 as you may have thought. Be careful with that one!

The Box (hole) shape cut into the baseplate is solid, as shown in Figure 7-6.

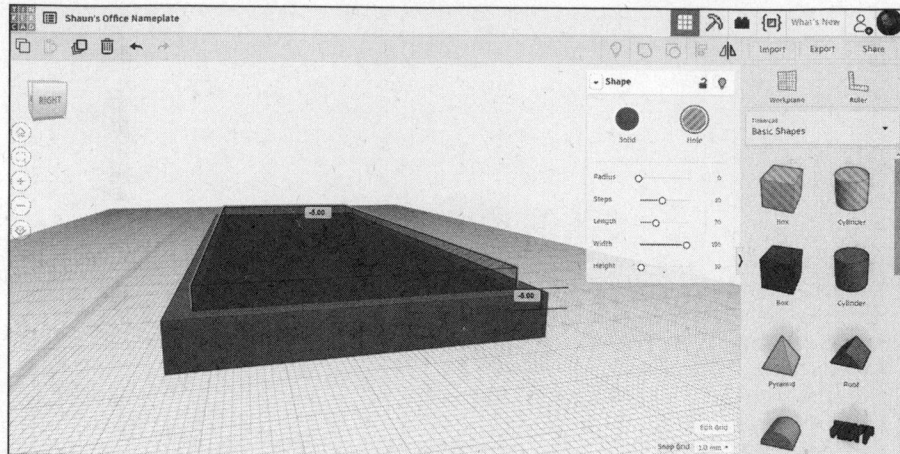

FIGURE 7-6:
The adjusted Box (hole) shape with the changed direction and depth (height) values displayed.

Grouping and Ungrouping

Grouping and ungrouping in Tinkercad is a repetitive task that you do often in order to build complex shapes from the component basic shapes Tinkercad provides.

To make the indent effective, you need to group both the solid baseplate with the Box (hole) shape indent. The Box (hole) shape then cuts the indent out of the baseplate.

You need to be in a sensible preset view of your design using the ViewCube. Make sure you have no objects selected and select the Top/Front/Right corner of the ViewCube (see Figure 7-7).

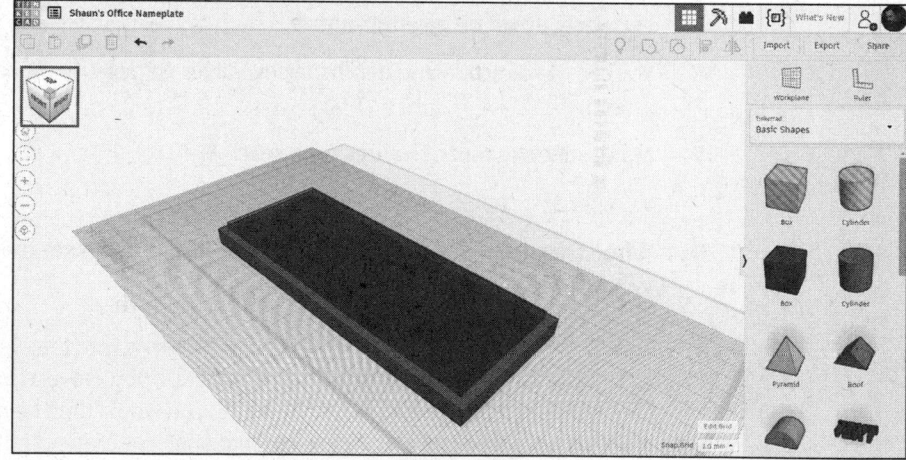

FIGURE 7-7:
The Top/Front/ Right isometric view of the baseplate in the Tinkercad design screen.

To group both the solid baseplate with the Box (hole) shape indent:

1. **Select both the baseplate solid and the Box (hole) shape by clicking in a free space near them and dragging a crossing window (dotted box) over both shapes.**

   The Shapes window displays Shapes(2), and the Group icon is active in the right toolbar (see Figure 7-8). The Group icon becomes active only when more than one shape is selected in the Tinkercad design screen.

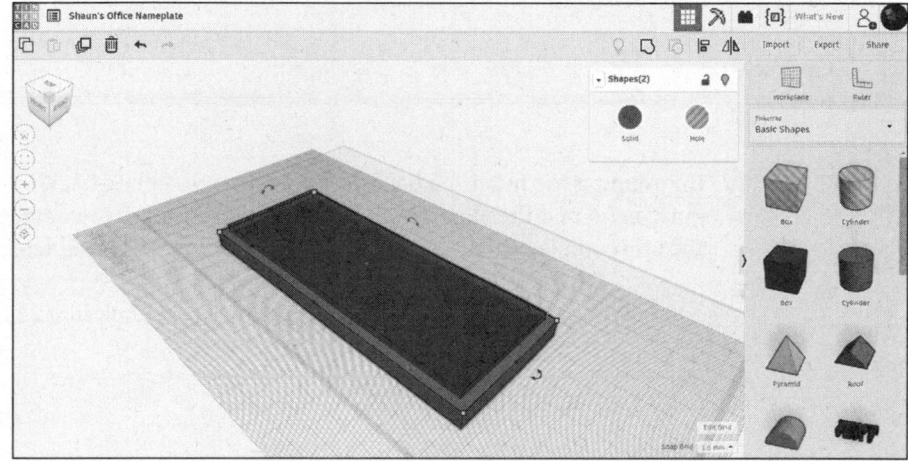

FIGURE 7-8:
The baseplate and the Box (hole) shape selected, with the Group icon active.

2. **Group the two shapes together.**

   You can click the Group icon or use the keyboard shortcut Ctrl + G.

   You now see your indent appear in the baseplate, where the Box (hole) shape has cut the indent from the baseplate solid (see Figure 7-9).

3. **Click away from the indented baseplate to deselect it to see the full detail of the indent created.**

If you want to ever ungroup your indent from the basic baseplate solid object, simply select the indented baseplate and use the Ungroup command R. Select the indented baseplate, and you see the Ungroup icon active. You can also use the keyboard shortcut Ctrl + Shift + G.

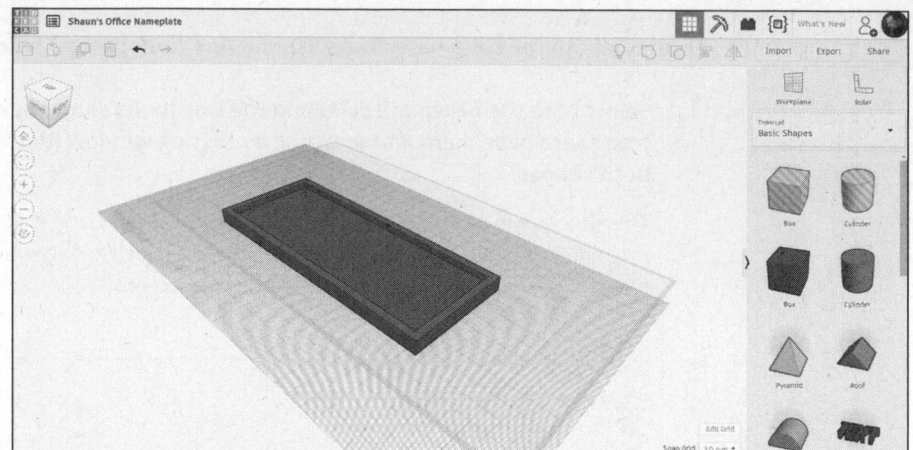

FIGURE 7-9:
The baseplate
with its new
indent.

Ungrouping the indented baseplate takes the baseplate back to its simple rectangular solid and the Box (hole) shape, thus creating two component objects from the one complex object — in this case, your indented baseplate.

You now have your indent all set. It's beginning to look like a nameplate now.

Chapter **8**

Adding Your Name as Text

I n this chapter, you find out how to add a text object inside the indent in your baseplate. (If you haven't created an indent in the baseplate, see Chapter 7.)

You also discover how to use text objects from the Tinkercad Basic Shapes menu and how to size them and give them specific fonts and colors so as to highlight them in your design.

Getting to the Right View

More often than not, you will end up in a view in Tinkercad where you don't want to be. You may have used your manual orbit or zoomed in too close or too far out perhaps.

TIP

The best way to get back to the right view in Tinkercad is to use the preset views on the ViewCube. These preset views provide you with full 360 degree viewing of your Tinkercad design.

Figure 8-1 shows you a typical view of your design that you may not want to be in.

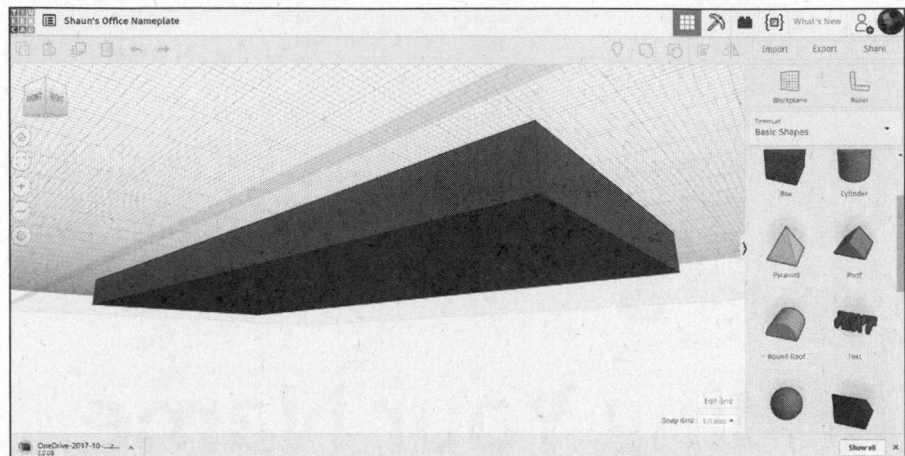

FIGURE 8-1:
A typical difficult
view of the
baseplate in
Tinkercad.

Take a closer look at the ViewCube in Figure 8-1. It is aligned to the view, and you can orient yourself in the 3D space in Tinkercad by working out which way is up, quite literally.

You can select a preset view in the ViewCube and work your way back to a view you do want to be in, such as an elevation (side view on the ViewCube) or an isometric view (corner view on the ViewCube).

Always make sure that you watch your ViewCube. That way, getting back to the right view is often so much easier!

TIP

Getting to the best view for placing text

The easiest view to use when placing your text in the indent on the baseplate is the Top view on the ViewCube, but with the Workplane set to the inside top face of the indent.

So how do you get to that view and get the Workplane in the correct position as well?

Click the Front view on the ViewCube first. Then, select the top edge, between the Front view and the Top view on the ViewCube. You may need to zoom in or out to make sure that you can see all the baseplate with the indent.

For reference, you see the view you need in Figure 8-2, which shows you the edge you need to select on the ViewCube and the baseplate set to that view as well.

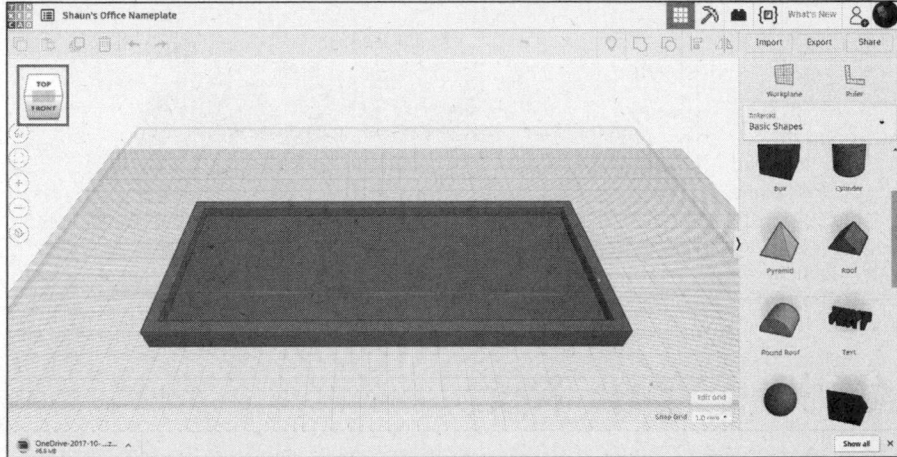

FIGURE 8-2:
The correctly aligned view in the Tinkercad design screen.

Positioning the Workplane

You also need to set the Workplane to the inside top face of the indent in the baseplate:

1. **Click the Workplace command in the right panel on the Tinkercad design screen.**

2. **Hover over the top face of the indent in the baseplate and click it.**

   You see the Workplane position itself. It looks as though the Workplane goes through the edges of the baseplate, level with the top face of the indent (see Figure 8-3).

TIP

Sometimes, the Workplane may not look as though it is where it should be. If you need to perform a sanity check, simply use a manual orbit using the right mouse button to orbit the view of your design to check. Then, just go back to your preset view using the ViewCube! Easy!

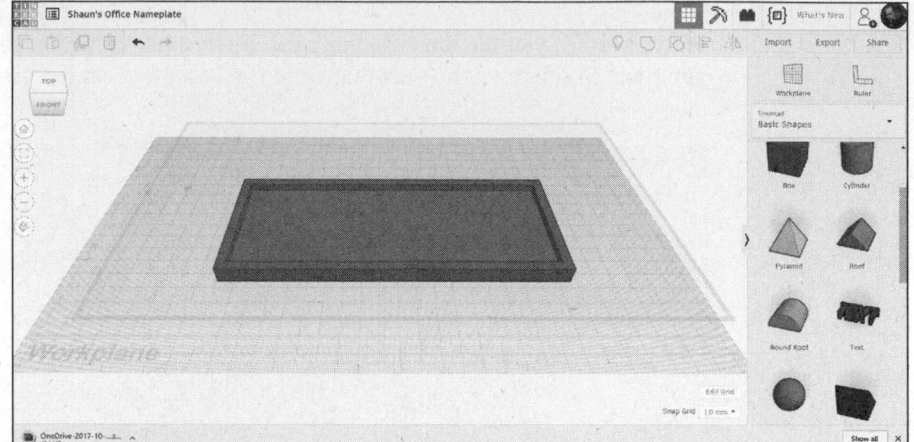

FIGURE 8-3:
The Tinkercad Workplane aligned with the top face of the indent in the baseplate.

Adding Your Text

Text is an important part of design. Not only does text enhance a design, but you can use it to annotate a design to communicate your design intent.

To add your text:.

1. **Click the Text object and drag it to the center of the indent on the Workplane.**

You can find a Text object in the Tinkercad Basic Shapes menu. You now have a piece of default text that says "TEXT" in your design (see Figure 8-4). The Text object auto-snaps to the center as you do so.

If your text does not auto-snap, use the grid and the temporary dimensions to position it.

2. **In the Shape window, set your height.**

The Height setting sets the depth of the text object. As your Workplane is set to the top face of the indent, you need the text to be the height (depth) of the indent. Set it to 5 mm if you're using metric millimeters or ¼ inches (0.25 inches) if you're working in imperial inches. The text object updates accordingly.

3. **To change your text object to the required text, type what you want to be shown in the Text field in the Shape window.**

In your case, it will be something like *Yourname's* Office, where *Yourname* is your name.

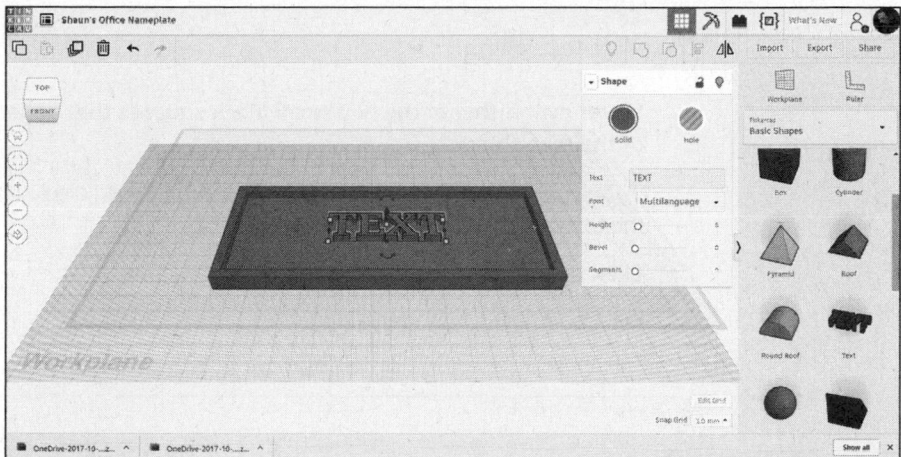

FIGURE 8-4:
The default text
object set to a
height of 5 mm.

4. **(Optional) Change your text color by clicking the Solid color dot in the Shape window.**

   You can find many colors there. Pick yourself a suitable contrasting color.

Changing the length of your text

The length of your name may also affect the text as well. You may well find that your text goes out past the edges of the indent, even the edges of the baseplate! Fortunately, that issue is easy to fix.

Figure 8-5 shows you the text, with its content and color changed, but extending out past the edges of the indent in the baseplate.

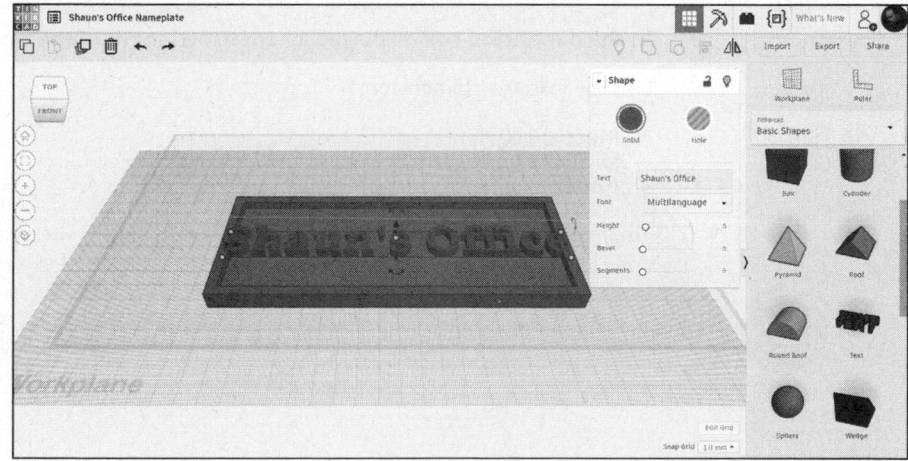

FIGURE 8-5:
Text extending
past the edges of
the indent in the
baseplate.

To update text length:

1. Hover over either of the two small black squares that appear at each end of the text object.

If you hover over either one, it goes red, and Tinkercad displays the length of the text object on the screen (see Figure 8-6).

2. Click the red highlighted square.

You can then edit the length of the text, and it updates accordingly.

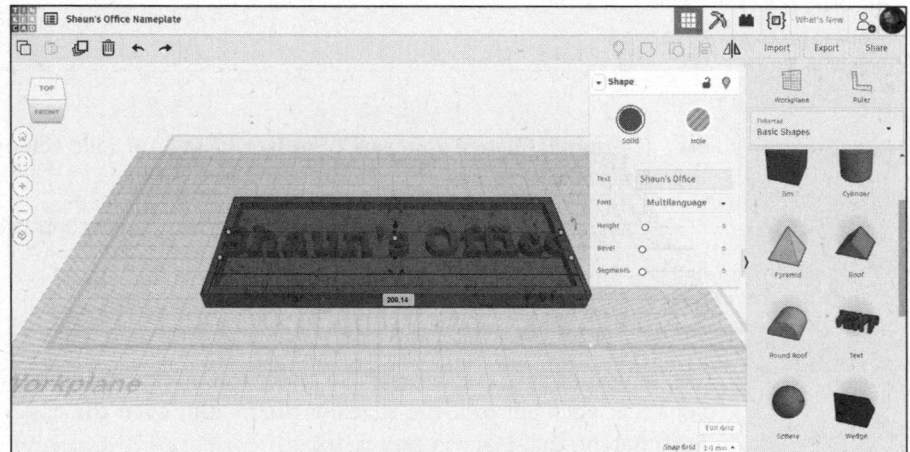

FIGURE 8-6:
The text object length.

TIP

The square you select depends on which end of the text Tinkercad updates from. So, if you select the left square, Tinkercad updates the length from the left side of the text and vice versa for the right end of the text.

3. In the dimension box displayed, change the length of the text object.

Use the following dimensions:

- **Metric:** 150 mm

- **Imperial:** 6 inches

The text object length changes from the right end, and the text sizes accordingly as well (see Figure 8-7).

TIP

You can change the width of the text, too, using this process.

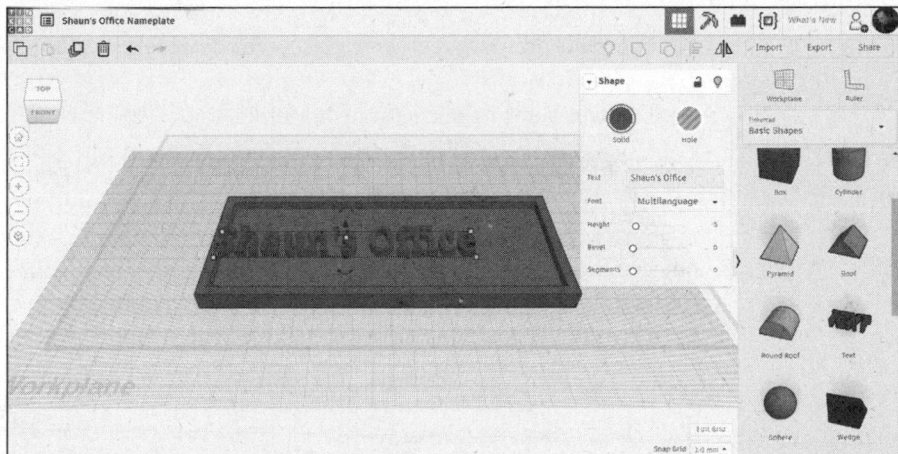

FIGURE 8-7:
The text object
with its length
updated from
the right end
of the text.

Centering your text

You can center the text object freehand by selecting the text object and dragging it. Use the Workplane grid for reference.

You can also use the placement dimensions that appear as you drag the text object. These dimensions are based on the original insertion point of the text object (see Figure 8-8).

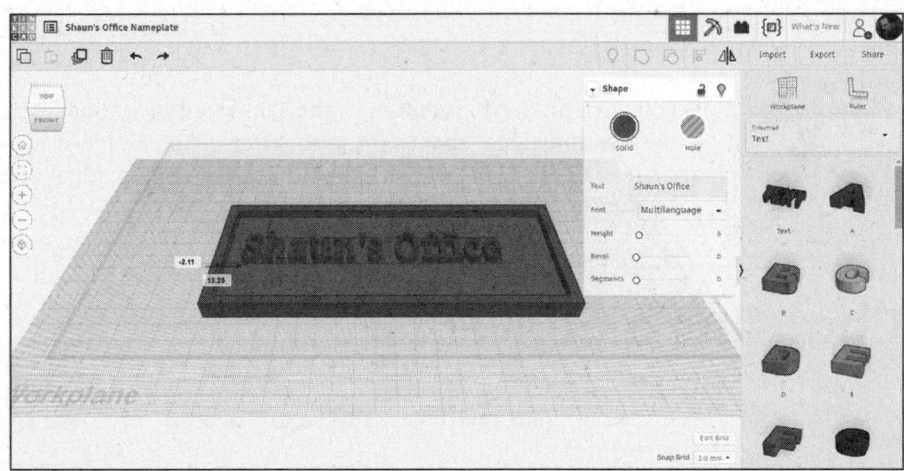

FIGURE 8-8:
The placement
dimensions.

For complete accuracy, set your placement dimensions to the following values:

>> **Metric:** Vertical value = 0 mm; horizontal value = 25 mm

>> **Imperial:** Vertical value = 0 inches; horizontal value = 1 inch

If your text auto-snapped to the center when you began this process, your text object centers nicely, and your text appears on your nameplate (see Figure 8-9). If you did not have that happen or you have moved the text in error, you will need to fine-tune its position using the grid and the temporary dimensions.

FIGURE 8-9: The resized text object repositioned accurately with the placement dimensions.

TIP

If you click on the Text option in the Tinkercad Basic Shapes menu, a text object as well as individual shapes for each letter of the alphabet appear. These shapes are great to use, but bear in mind that they're individual letters and numbers placed as shapes in your Tinkercad design.

Choosing a Cool Font

You can set your text object to use a cool font. You have several choices (see Figure 8-10):

>> Multilanguage

>> Sans

» Sans Mono

» Serif

You can play around with these fonts and choose the one you want to see on your nameplate for your office. Hey, it's your office, right? So you get to choose!

In my example, which is shown in Figure 8-11, the nameplate text is in the Sans font.

REMEMBER

If you change your font in Tinkercad, it also changes the size of the text. Remember this because you may need to change the font type before changing the text size or vice versa. You may need to reposition your text after changing the font type, too.

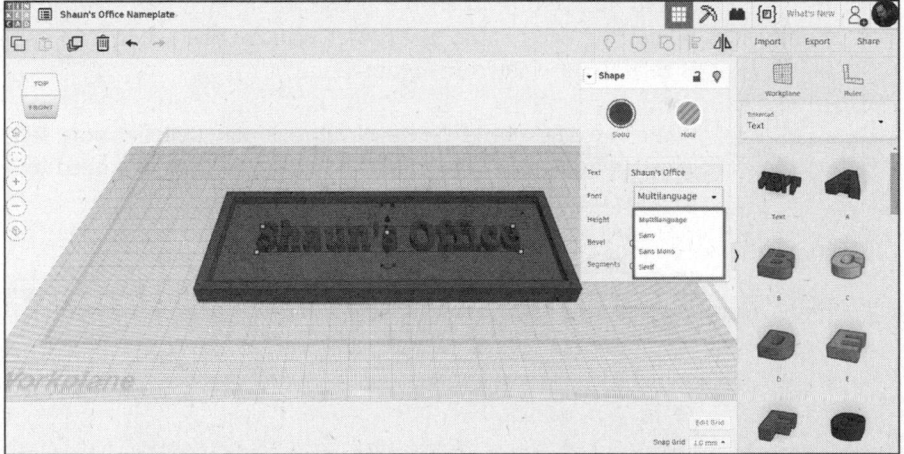

FIGURE 8-10: Available text fonts available.

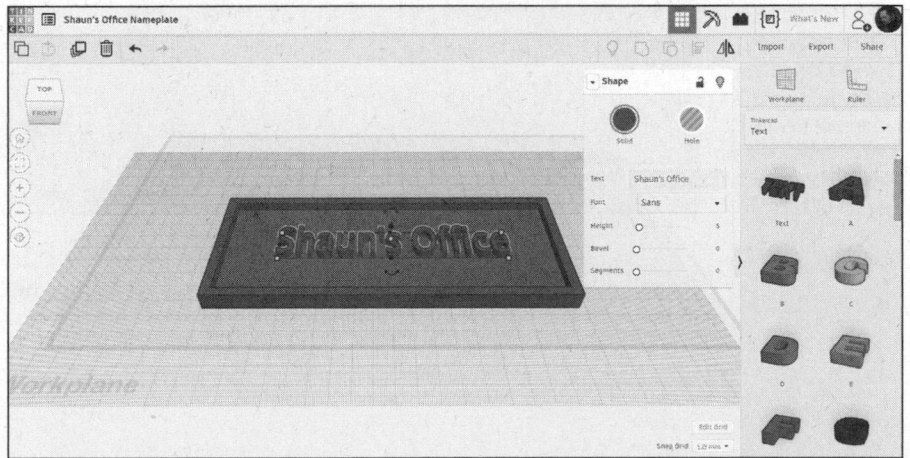

FIGURE 8-11: The text object on the nameplate, using the Sans font.

Smoothing the Edges with Bevels and Segments

The text has very sharp edges. If you 3D printed it as it is, the edges of the text would be sharp enough to cut paper!

So, from a safety standpoint and also an aesthetic standpoint, it would be good to round off those text edges. You can round off the edges by using the Bevel and Segments setting in the Shape window when your text object is selected.

Bevel

Setting a Bevel value in the Shape window bolds your text as if you were selecting a bold text setting in a word processor application, such as Microsoft Word. The higher the Bevel value, the bolder your text becomes. The default value for Bevel is zero (0), as shown in Figure 8-12.

When you adjust only the Bevel value, it may look like your letters in your text are overlapping. To change this, the Segments value will need to be updated (see the next section).

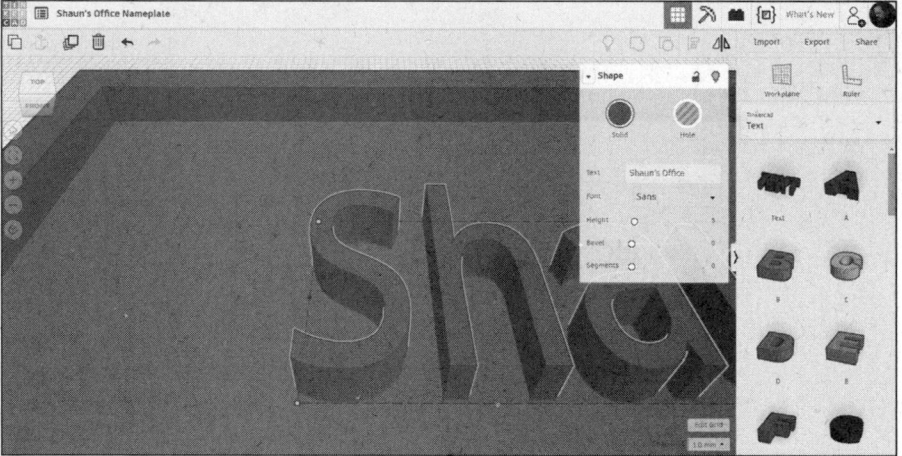

FIGURE 8-12: A close-up view (zoomed in) of the text on the nameplate, with the Bevel value set to the default value of zero (0).

If you look at Figure 8-13, you see in the close-up view that the text is bolder than in Figure 8-12, where the Bevel value is set to zero (0).

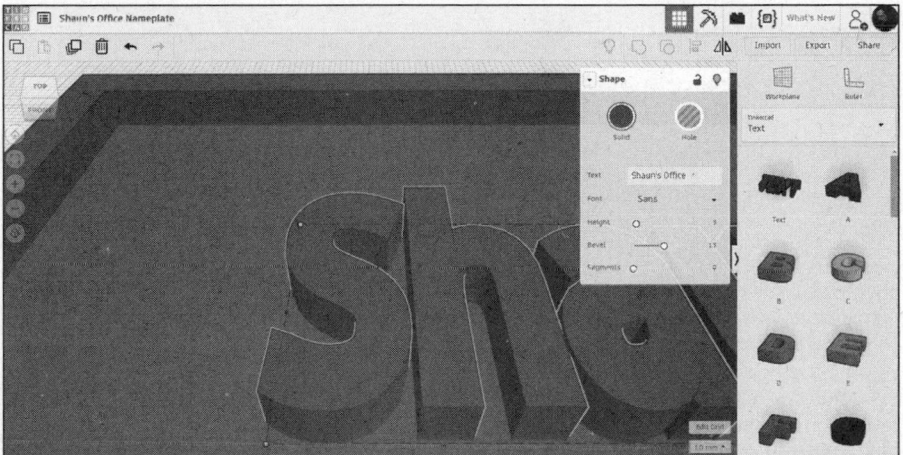

FIGURE 8-13:
A close-up view (zoomed in) of the text on the nameplate, with the Bevel value set to 1.5, showing the bolding of the text.

Segments

The Segments value in the Shape window changes the number of segments, or *slices*, your text object is made from. The default value is zero (0), giving you just one segment/slice.

If you increase the Segment value and increase the slices that your text is made up of, the effect of changing the Bevel value also becomes more apparent. When the Segments value is zero (default), you can't really see the full effect of changing the Bevel value, so it is best to work with both values to get a desired effect on the text that you prefer for your design.

If you refer to Figure 8-14, you can see that by combining a Bevel value of 1.5 and a Segments value of 5, you get bold text on your nameplate with curved edges, enhancing the effect of the text on the eye, giving it an aesthetic appeal.

You can work with these values and increase the Segments value of your text and change the Bevel value to get other enhanced text effects on your nameplate.

You can also change the text object from a Solid to a Hole in the Shape window and use it to engrave a Tinkercad solid as well, if you want.

FIGURE 8-14:
The text object with a Bevel value of 1.5 and the Segments value set to 5, enhancing the bevel effect.

IN THIS CHAPTER

» **Adding objects to an existing Tinkercad design**

» **Using objects to create holes in a Tinkercad solid**

» **Making holes part of the Tinkercad solid**

» **Grouping objects to make a complex object**

Chapter **9**

Cutting Holes to Mount the Nameplate

I n this chapter, you find out how you can add objects to create holes in your nameplate so that you can hang it (should you 3D print it) on your office door.

You also discover additional grouping objects in Tinkercad so that you can make your nameplate one complex solid object.

Choosing a Shape for the Hole

To hang your nameplate, if you do decide to 3D print it, you need some holes in it. Period.

It does not matter what you hang your nameplate with — screws, string, ribbon — some holes are required.

You need to choose a hole that is suitable to the method of hanging you need. More often than not, that hole will tend to be circular.

Getting into Position

The Workplane needs to be set to its original (default) position where the base of the nameplate is sitting on the Workplane. Simply select the Workplane command and then select a point in space behind your nameplate.

The Workplane returns to its default blue color, and you see that your nameplate is now sitting on the Workplane.

So, why reset the Workplane? Well, you need your holes in your nameplate to go all the way through the nameplate so that when you do 3D print it, the holes can then be used to hang the nameplate. They're no use if they don't go all the way through, right?

Figure 9-1 shows you the Tinkercad screen with the Workplane in its default position and color (blue), with the nameplate sitting on the Workplane.

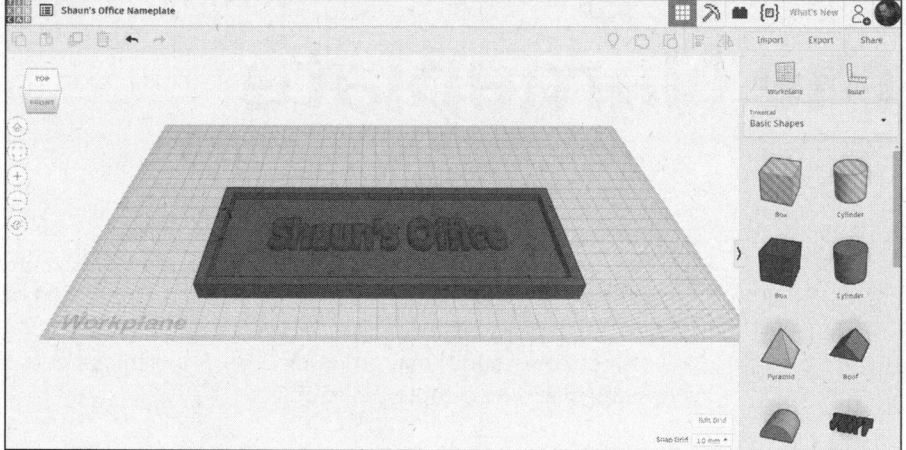

FIGURE 9-1: The Workplane in its default position, ready to be used to create holes in the nameplate.

Getting in the Right View

You need to get an object with depth in place to create a hole. The perfect object for this, initially, is a box.

Before you do, though, you need to be in the correct preset view. In this case, a plan view looking down on the nameplate. That's right. You need the Top view on the ViewCube.

Select the Top view so that you're looking directly down onto the nameplate and then zoom on the top-left corner of the nameplate.

Figure 9-2 shows you (approximately) where you should be zoomed in to on the nameplate, after selecting the Top preset view.

FIGURE 9-2:
A zoomed view of the top-left corner of the nameplate in the Top preset view on the ViewCube.

If you can't get that kind of view, go back to the Home view using the Home icon on the menu on the left, select the Top view on the ViewCube, and then use the mouse to zoom in. Sometimes, going back to the Home view helps with this!

Notice that the corner of the nameplate looks a little weird. That's because the view is using the perspective setting. Ideally, you need to be using an orthographic (flat) view for accuracy. That way, you can also use the grid on the Workplane more effectively as well.

Click Switch to Orthographic view to change the view. Although it looks like the nameplate has been made flat, it hasn't. You are now just seeing it without perspective being applied. The icon changes to show the orthographic setting, too.

Figure 9-3 shows you the nameplate Top view in its orthographic setting and also has the icon highlighted, showing you that it is now in an orthographic view.

Moving the Nameplate to a Grid Intersection

You need to move the whole nameplate to a grid intersection on the Workplane. Doing so will make life much easier when you place the cylinder object to start making the holes in the nameplate.

To move the nameplate to an intersection:

1. **Drag a crossing window over both the nameplate and the nameplate text.**

   You see the Shapes window appear reading Shapes (2) and they will both be highlighted also. It reads like that with a value in brackets (2) because two shapes are selected.

2. **Click and drag the nameplate and the nameplate text so that the top-left corner of the nameplate aligns with a grid intersection.**

   Figure 9-4 shows the nameplate aligned with a grid intersection and also shows the Shapes window.

3. **Using the Tinkercad Basic Shapes menu, drag the Box shape so that its center point aligns with the newly aligned top-left corner of the nameplate (see Figure 9-5).**

   You see it line up nicely with the grid with its default size, too.

   You're using a box shape here to form the outer part of the hole on the outer edge of the baseplate. You will add the holes to these outer boxes later on.

FIGURE 9-4:
The nameplate
aligned
with a grid
intersection on
the Workplane.

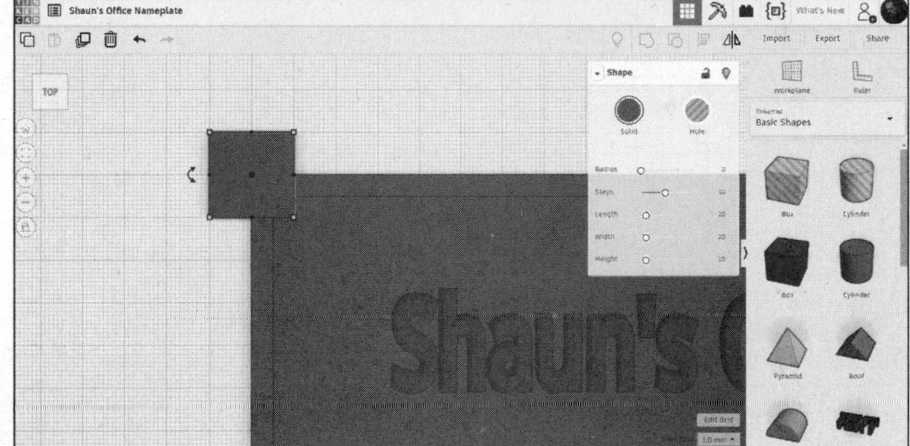

FIGURE 9-5:
The box placed
on the top-left
corner of the
nameplate.

4. **Making sure that only the box is selected, drag it to a suitable point along the nameplate so that the holes can later be placed in a sensible position along the top of the nameplate.**

Positioning the Box Accurately

If you're using metric millimeters, the box has a default size of 20 mm along each edge (go on, count the grid squares). If you're using imperial inches, you ideally want the box to have a default size of 1 inch along each edge, as your raised edge of your nameplate should be ¼ inch in size.

The offsets for the box from the top-left corner of the nameplate are

>> **Metric:** 40 mm horizontally to the right

>> **Imperial:** 1 ½ inches horizontally to the right

The metric measurement here is only true if your new Box shape was exactly aligned with the left side of the nameplate edge. You can also align the top-left corner of the new Box shape with the top-left corner of the nameplate and then move it right by 30 mm and up by 10 mm.

As you drag along to the right, Tinkercad gives you a dimension readout of how far you're dragging the box shape. As long as you drag exactly horizontally, the vertical dimension remains at zero (0), while the horizontal dimension increases. Figure 9-6 shows you the box in place at 40 mm with the dimension readout displayed.

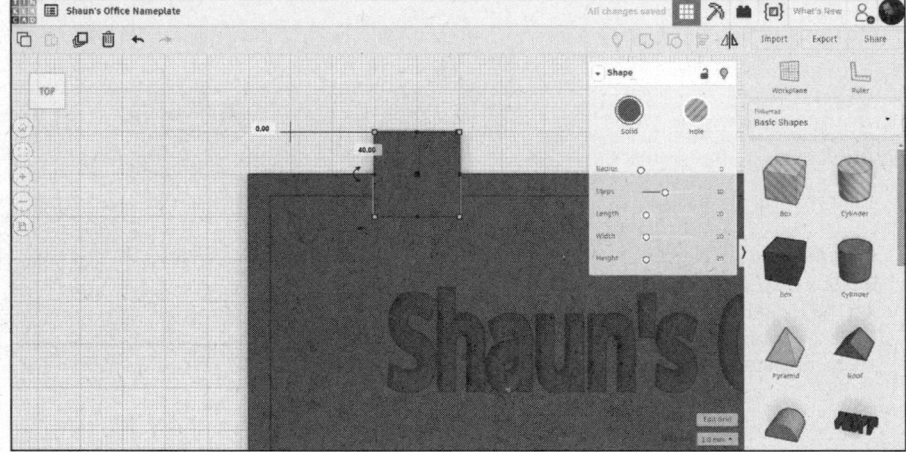

FIGURE 9-6:
The box shape in place at 40 mm from the top-left corner of the nameplate. Note the dimensions displayed.

Changing Your View to Assess Height

You need to change your view in order to assess the height of the new box shape.

To change your view:

1. **Use the ViewCube to select the Top/Front/Right corner of the ViewCube.**

You see an isometric view of the nameplate from that corner of the ViewCube.

2. **If you're in Top view, click the bottom-right corner of the ViewCube.**

The nameplate rotates into the new isometric view.

The new box shape looks very different in that view, as compared to the preset Top view.

Altering the Box to Suit the Nameplate

With the box shape selected, you can utilize the grips on it and the Shape window to alter it to suit the nameplate, as shown in Figure 9-7.

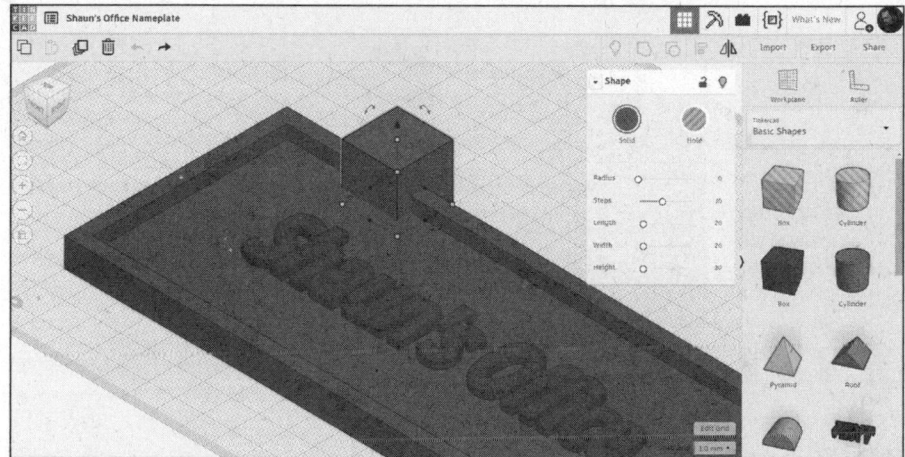

Using the grips on the box shape, you can now resize it to suit the nameplate.

Using the grip that is selected in Figure 9-8, change the dimension value to 10 mm (metric) or, if using imperial units, set it to half of the box size used originally. For example, if you're using a box of 1 ½ inches in size, set the new dimension to ¾ inches.

After typing the new dimension (or clicking and dragging in the appropriate direction), the shape of the box changes to align to the raised edge of the nameplate. Figure 9-9 displays this with the box shape still selected.

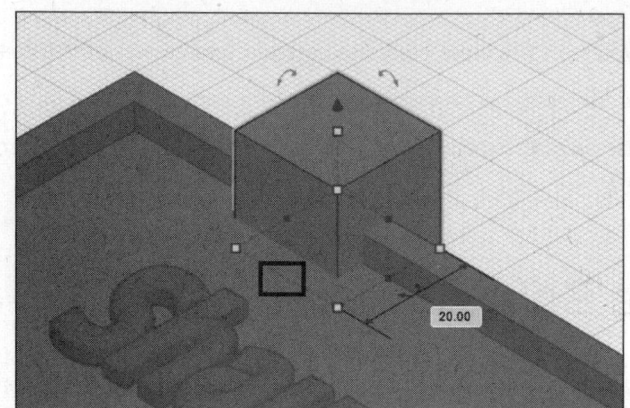

FIGURE 9-8:
The box shape selected, and the selected grip highlighted, with the original metric measurement displayed.

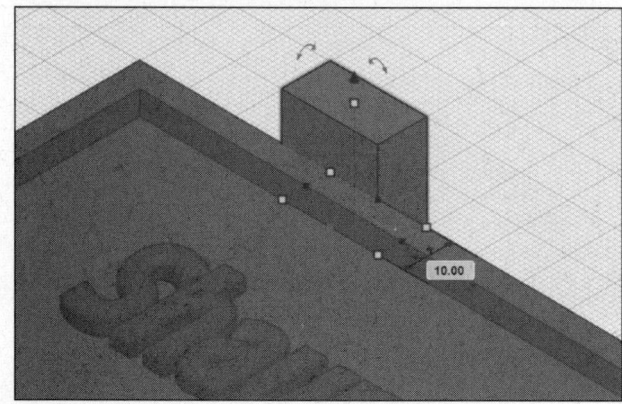

FIGURE 9-9:
The newly sized box shape still selected, with the new dimension value still displayed.

Adjusting the Height

The new box shape needs to be adjusted in height to suit the height of the raised edge of the nameplate.

With the box shape still selected, check the height of the box shape in the Shape dialog box. If using metric, it will read 20 mm. Change it to 10 mm.

If using imperial units, this value will be different. If it was using a size of 1 ½ inches, change it to ¾ inches.

Figure 9-10 shows the box shape with its new height value of 10 mm, set in the Shape window.

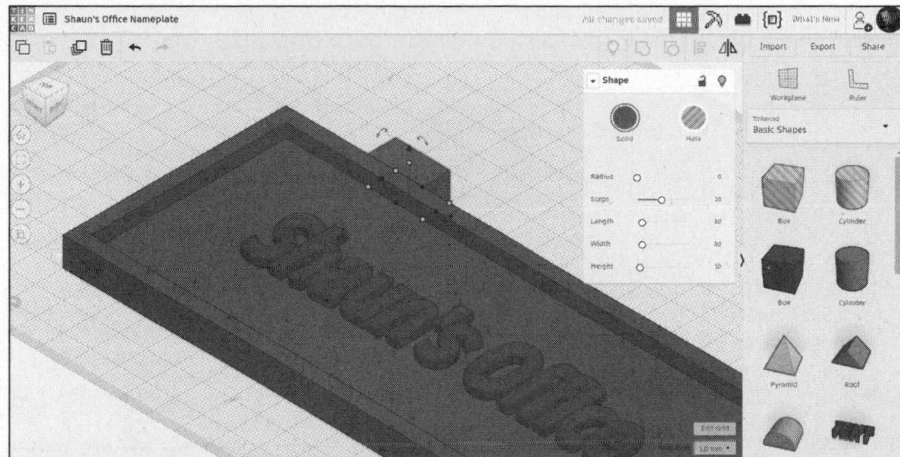

FIGURE 9-10:
The box shape,
with its revised
height value
displayed in the
Shape window.

Bear in mind here that you can adjust the size of any object in Tinkercad, by typing in the dimension values using the temporary dimensions, or you can just click and drag the black squares (grips). It is up to you which method you use or prefer. You can also select a shape and change its parameters in the Shapes window, too, if you want.

Adding the Hole

One of the major benefits of Tinkercad is that the Tinkercad Basic Shapes menu contains numerous basic shapes that are already in that menu as holes, and not solids. One of these shapes is the cylinder, which you can use to make a hanging hole for the nameplate.

Before you use the cylinder (hole) shape, though, you need to change your preset view, just to make things a bit easier. You need to be in the Top view on the View-Cube. Then zoom in to a suitable magnification to see the top-left corner of the nameplate, including the new box shape recently added and resized.

To add the hole:

1. **Drag and drop the cylinder (hole) shape from the Basic Shapes menu and place it near the nameplate (see Figure 9-11).**

2. **Resize the cylinder (hole) shape.**

   To do so, select the shape selected and use the grips on the shape to make the cylinder (hole) shape diameter smaller.

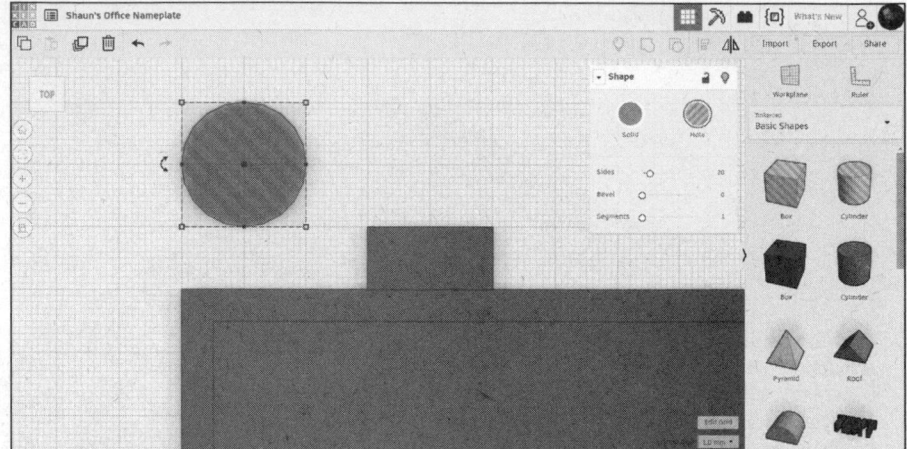

FIGURE 9-11:
The cylinder
(hole) shape
placed close
to the nameplate
in the Top
preset view.

3. **Select one of the midpoint grips on either side of the shape, as shown in Figure 9-12.**

   The grip turns red (letting you know it is active), and the dimension readout appears. If you're using metric millimeters, this dimension appears as 20. If you're using imperial inches, it may display as 1, for example.

4. **Apply the following sizes to the cylinder (hole) shape:**

   - **Metric:** 6 mm diameter

   - **Imperial:** ¼ inches diameter

WARNING

   This has to be applied to both sides of the cylinder (hole) shape to maintain its shape. Otherwise, it will become an elliptical cylinder.

   After you apply the sizes to both sides, you have a smaller diameter cylinder (hole) shape, ready to be used (see Figure 9-13.)

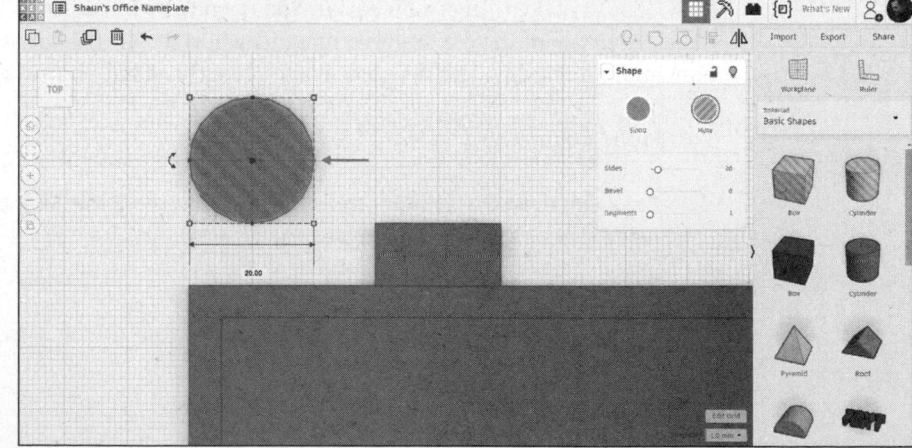

FIGURE 9-12:
The cylinder
(hole) shape
selected, with one
of the grips
selected, ready to
be resized. Note
the dimension
display.

FIGURE 9-13:
The cylinder (hole) shape, resized and ready to be placed on the nameplate.

5. **Zoom in as close as you need to and place the cylinder (hole) shape centrally over the area provided by the raised edge of the nameplate and the additional box shape on the edge of the nameplate.**

That's why you're using the Top preset view, as it allows you to use the Workplane grid to place the shape accurately.

Figure 9-14 shows you where the cylinder (hole) shape should be placed.

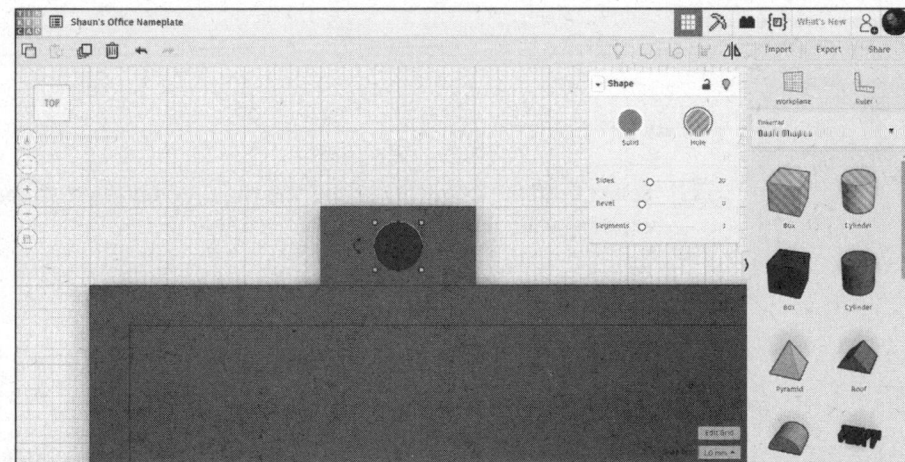

FIGURE 9-14:
The proper location of the cylinder (hole) shape on the nameplate.

Copying the Hole

If you followed the steps in the preceding section, you have a hole in your nameplate on the top-left corner. You also need a hanging hole on the top-right corner. Without that second hole, your nameplate will hang at an odd angle, raising concerns about your Tinkercad skills.

In the Top preset view on the ViewCube, zoom out so that you can see all of your nameplate in plan, as shown in Figure 9-15.

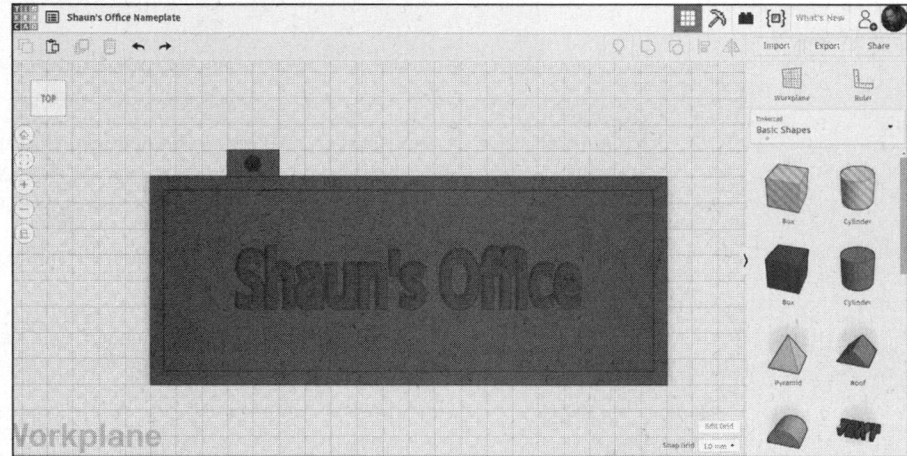

FIGURE 9-15:
All of the nameplate in plan in the Top preset view on the ViewCube.

To copy the hole:

1. **Select both the extra box shape and the cylinder (hole) shape by using a crossing window, as shown in Figure 9-16.**

   Do not select any part of the nameplate or its edge at this point. The Shapes (2) window tells you that you only have two shapes selected.

2. **Select the Copy command.**

3. **Paste the copied objects using the Paste command.**

   The copied and pasted versions of the box shape and the cylinder (hole) shape appear, and they are now the selected objects (see Figure 9-17). They sit just on top of the copied shapes and need to be moved to their appropriate location on the top-right corner of the nameplate.

4. **With the copied and pasted shapes selected, drag them horizontally to their appropriate location on the top-right corner of the nameplate (see Figure 9-18.)**

   So, in plan, you now have your hanging holes on your nameplate.

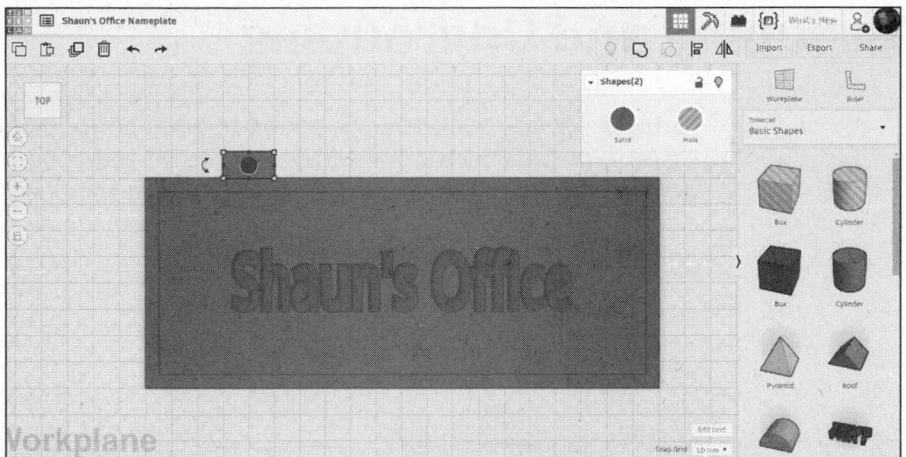

FIGURE 9-16:
The extra box shape and the cylinder (hole) shape selected. Note the Shapes (2) window.

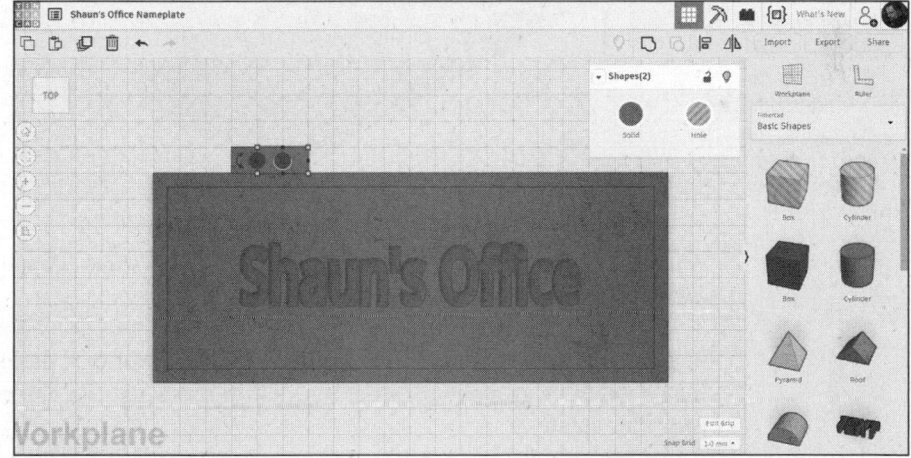

FIGURE 9-17:
The copied and pasted shapes selected, just on top of the original shapes.

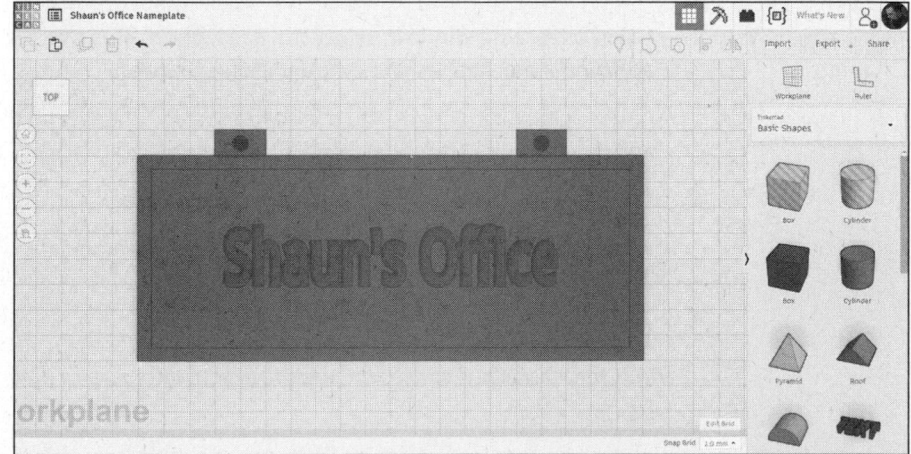

FIGURE 9-18:
The copied and pasted shapes in their new location on the top-right of the nameplate.

Grouping and Ungrouping

To finish off your nameplate, you need to be in an isometric view, shown in Figure 9-19. An isometric view often shows details that you may not see in other views, so if you can't see the detail you need, change the view!

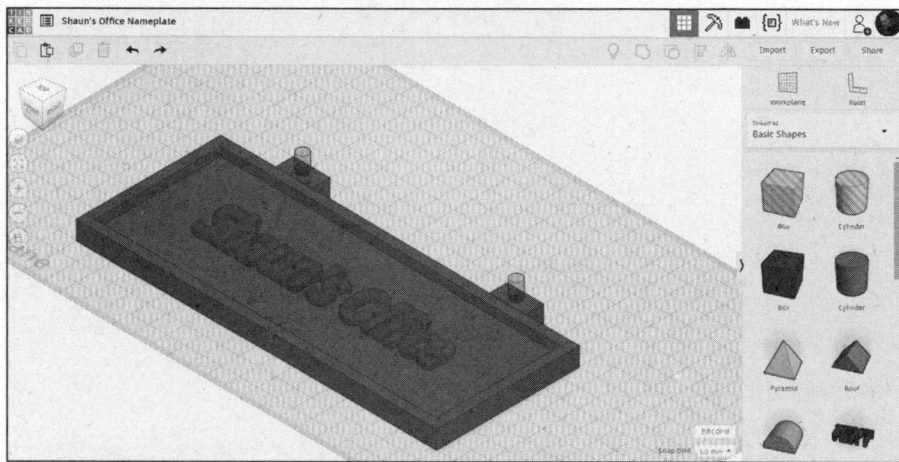

FIGURE 9-19:
The nameplate
and the
additional
shapes in the
Top/Front/Right
isometric view.

You can see the additional box shapes and cylinder (hole) shapes in Figure 9-19, with the holes protruding up above the nameplate.

Right now, these shapes are extra shapes. They're not part of your nameplate, so they need to be grouped together in order to form just the one complex object — your nameplate.

To group these shapes together:

1. **Using a crossing window, select the nameplate, plus one set of the additional box shapes and cylinder (hole) shapes.**

   Choose either left or right. You don't need to select the text on the nameplate, and your Shapes (3) window appears (see Figure 9-20).

2. **Click the Group command on the top-right toolbar.**

   You see the box and cylinder (hole) shapes join the nameplate, becoming a complex shape.

3. **Click away from the shapes to deselect them.**

   You see it all as one shape. You now have your left hanging hole, as shown in Figure 9-21.

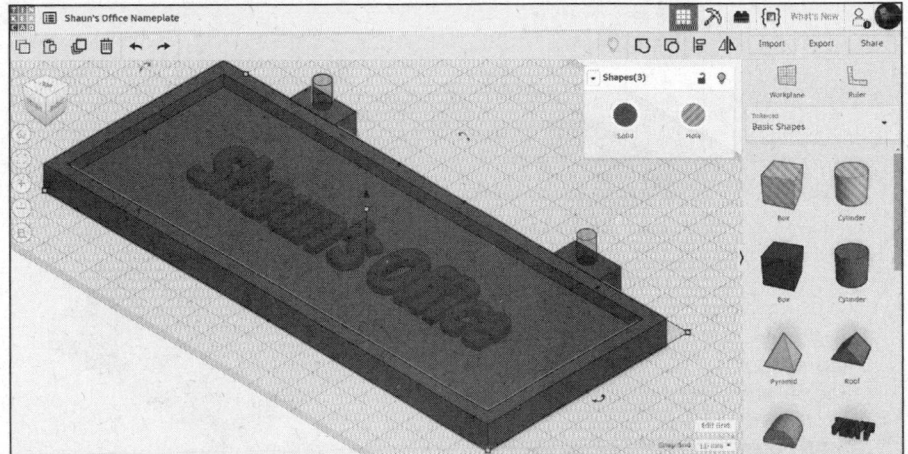

FIGURE 9-20:
The nameplate with the Shapes (3) window displayed.

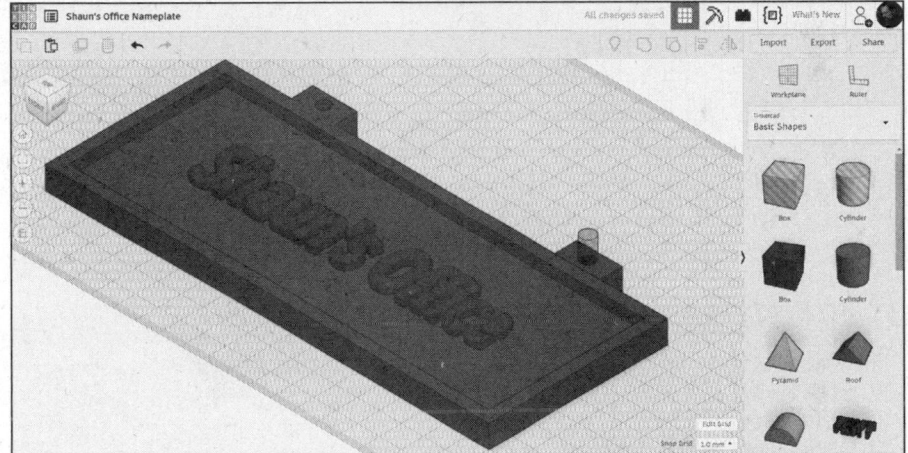

FIGURE 9-21:
The left hanging hole complete as part of the nameplate.

4. **Repeat Steps 1 to 3 for the right hanging hole.**

Figure 9-22 shows you the completed nameplate with hanging holes.

You now have a completed, albeit relatively simple, 3D nameplate that you can 3D print if you want to and hang on your office door (see Figure 9-23).

Take note that this nameplate is a very simple 3D model. You can enhance it and change it dramatically should you wish to do so.

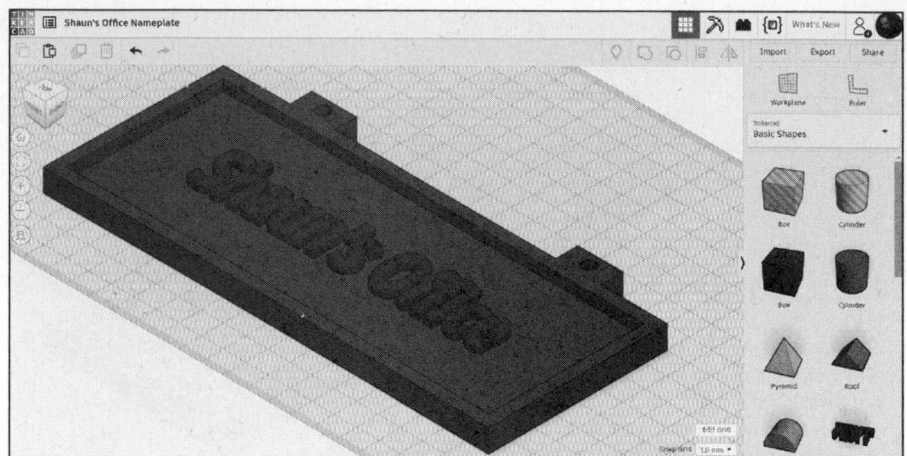

FIGURE 9-22:
The completed nameplate, with hanging holes.

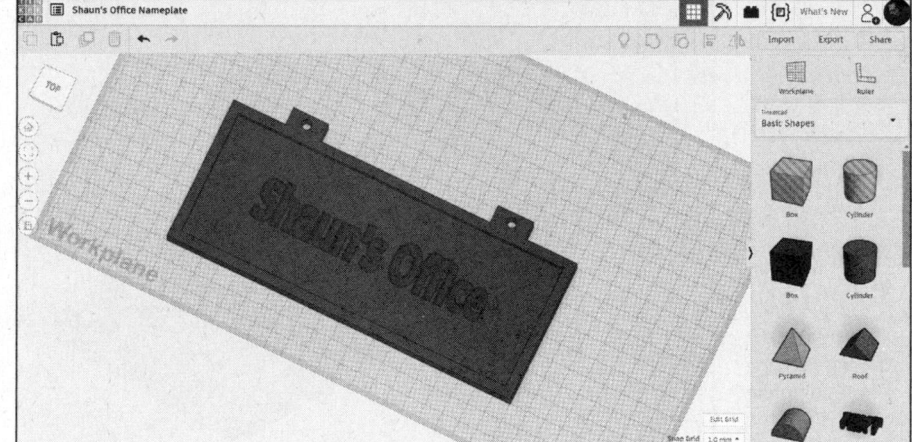

FIGURE 9-23:
The completed nameplate in a orbited view, highlighting the hanging holes.

3

Building Your First Skyscraper, in Miniature

Develop the ground floor. Start with the walls of your ground floor and then add windows and a ceiling.

Copy the floors as you build. Make sure that you get the grid placement right to add all the floors that you need.

Add the skyscraper roof. Choose the right Tinkercad shape and give it depth. Add a curved roof edge to allow the rain to drain off the roof.

Add the helipad to your skyscraper roof.

Chapter **10**

Creating the Building Footprint

n this chapter, you start the initial development of a new 3D design: a small 3D skyscraper. If you've ever seen those small plastic replicas of the Eiffel Tower from Paris, France, then you have a general idea of what you're aiming for, but with the added sophistication of Tinkercad.

In this chapter, you find out how to use Tinkercad to develop a simple floor plan, which you then refine to the required shape.

You also find out how to extrude the floor plan to the required depth.

The Basic Floor Plan: Keeping It Simple

To create your skyscraper (albeit in miniature), you need to start at the bottom and keep it simple.

You need a simple outline shape that initially outlines the floor plan, which you can then develop, ready to extrude to the required floor slab depth.

You can then develop the rest of the skyscraper, floor by floor.

TIP

The floor plan is fundamental to the shape of those floors as you go up the building. For this example in the book, keep the basic outline shape simple — say, square or rectangular. That way, it is easier for you to grasp the concepts first. Then, create another more complex design later to see how you go!

Getting (Your Floor Plan) in Shape

After you have a basic idea of your floor plan, you're ready to get it going in Tinkercad.

To follow along with this project:

1. **Log in to Tinkercad, create your new 3D design in Tinkercad, and save it to a known name that you prefer.**

2. **On the Tinkercad home page, click on the Tinker This button on your new design.**

   You see the Tinkercad design screen.

3. **Bring in a Tinkercad shape from the Basic Shapes menu.**

   For simplicity, I use the Box shape from the menu and drop it on to the Tinkercad Workplane (see Figure 10-1).

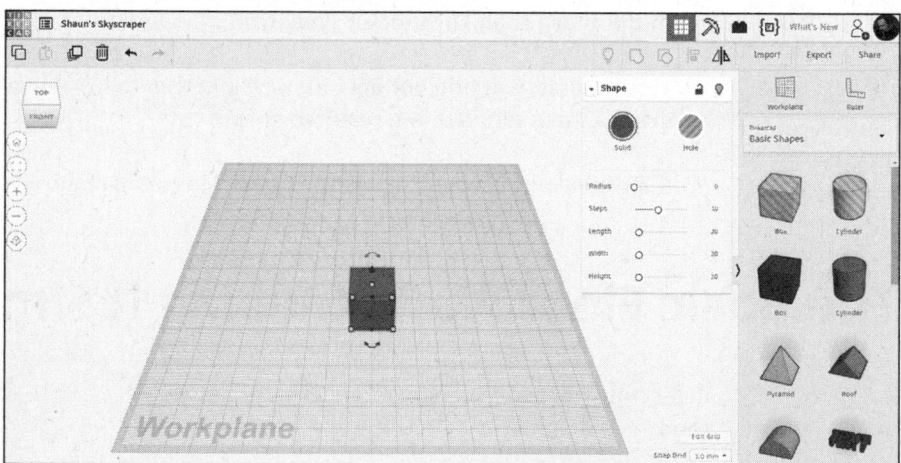

FIGURE 10-1: The basic Box shape on the Workplane ready to be used to develop the floor slab of the skyscraper.

4. **Change the size, dimensions, and color of your shape so that it bears some resemblance to a concrete floor slab.**

TIP

If you want to use imperial inches instead of metric millimeters, adjust the grid accordingly. You can use the Edit Grid button on the bottom right of the Tinkercad design screen to do this. Adjust the Snap Grid settings, too, if you're using imperial units for your design.

The basic shape of the floor slab defines the rest of the skyscraper, so you need to ensure that you have everything ready and working before you commit to adding floors to the building that sit on top of the floor slab.

5. **Select the Box shape and then click the default red Solid button in the Shape dialog box.**

A color palette appears, allowing you to change the color of not just this solid shape but any solid shape you use in Tinkercad when you select it. Cool, huh?

6. **Change the color to a gray to resemble concrete.**

The color of the basic Box shape changes accordingly.

7. **Set the dimensions for the floor slab:**

I suggest using the following dimensions:

- **Length:** 100 (mm)
- **Width:** 100 (mm)
- **Height:** 5 (mm)

As you change these values, the floor slab changes, too.

TIP

If you're working in imperial units (inches), consider using these imperial dimension settings as a guide:

- **Length:** 4 (in)
- **Width:** 4 (in)
- **Height:** 0.2 (in)

Bear in mind that the imperial conversion of the metric millimeters is approximate. You may want to be more accurate.

You now have a floor slab, ready as the foundation of your skyscraper (see Figure 10-2).

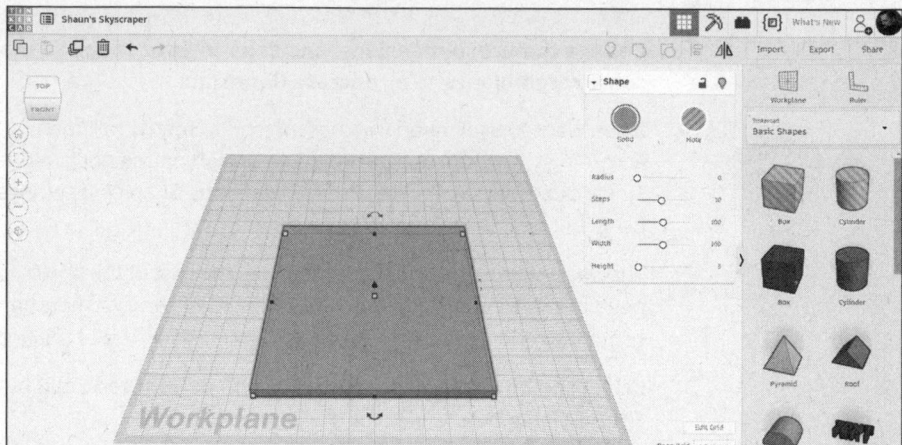

FIGURE 10-2:
The floor slab shape with its new gray color and new dimensions.

The next few chapters show you how to build the skyscraper, floor by floor, until you reach the roof and add the helipad.

Chapter **11**

Developing the Ground Floor

I n this chapter, you develop the foundation of your skyscraper. (If you haven't created a floor slab, see Chapter 10.) You find out how you can utilize the workflows of Tinkercad to create a complex design, discover the advantages of the basic shapes available in Tinkercad, and learn how you can use the ViewCube and the Workplane to your advantage well.

Preparing to Add Your Wallls

After you have a foundation slab (see Chapter 10), you can add walls to sit on the slab and form the ground floor of your skyscraper.

Before you get started, you need to get your Workplane and ViewCube working so that you can make sure that your walls are in the right place.

You want your Workplane to sit on the top face of the floor slab. That way, when you place your shapes to form your walls, they will sit on the top face of the floor slab. Simply follow these steps:

1. **With your skyscraper design open, select the Workplane icon at the top right of the Tinkercad design screen.**

2. **Click on the top face of the floor slab.**

   If you haven't created a floor slab, see Chapter 10.

   Just before you click on the top face of the floor slab, you will see that Tinkercad highlights the face with a transparent square shape on your cursor so that you know which face you're clicking on.

   The Workplane then turns a yellow color and becomes the top face of the slab, as shown in Figure 11-1.

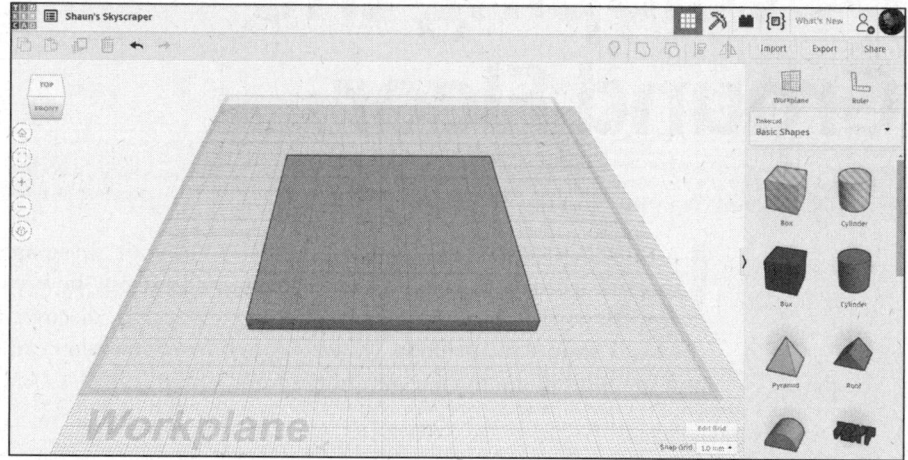

FIGURE 11-1: The Tinkercad design screen, with the Workplane now set to the top face of the floor slab.

You also need to make sure that you're in the preset Top view from the ViewCube, top left of the Tinkercad design screen. Click on that view on the ViewCube, and the view changes accordingly.

TIP

To make life easier later, make sure that you switch to orthographic view using the icon menu on the left (bottom icon). Changing to the view, which is shown in Figure 11-2, turns off any perspective so that you can see exactly where shapes and objects align with the Workplane grid.

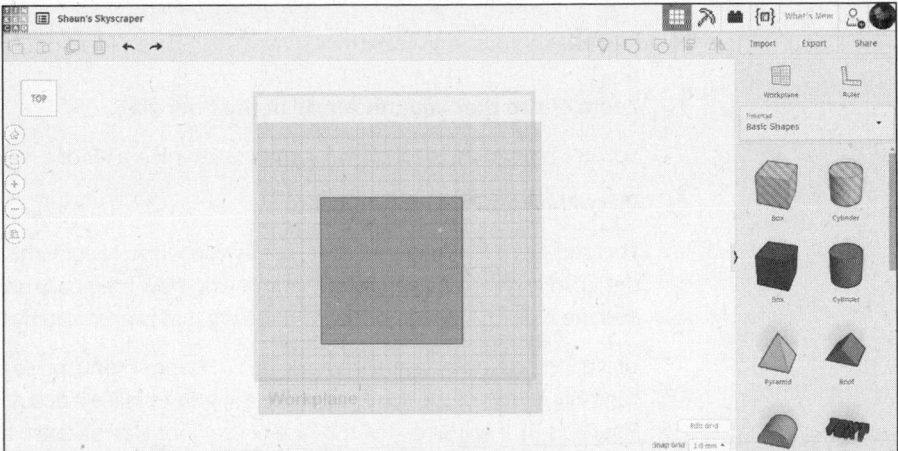

FIGURE 11-2:
The preset Top view, switched to orthographic view, with the Workplane set to the top face of the floor slab.

You also need to make sure that the floor slab aligns with the grid squares on the Workplane. Simply select the floor slab and drag it so that it aligns with the grid in the preset Top view, as shown in Figure 11-3. Zooming in a bit may make this easier.

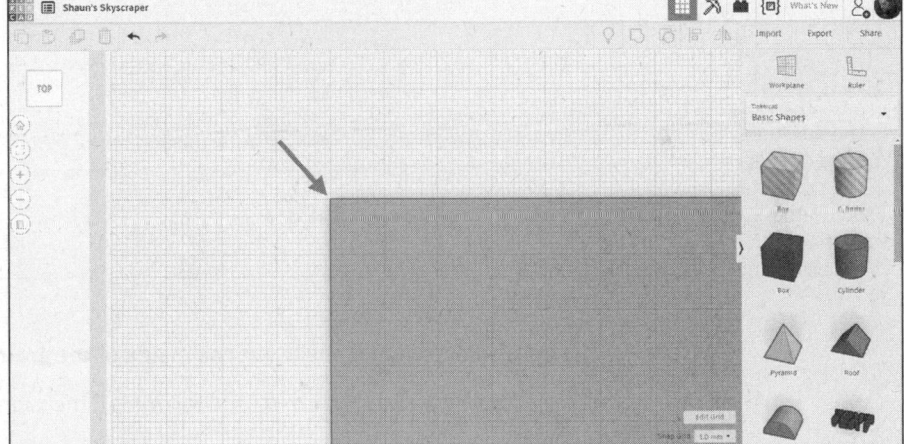

FIGURE 11-3:
The floor slab aligned with the grid squares on the Workplane. Note the view is magnified after being zoomed in for clarity.

Adding Walls

After you have the floor slab aligned with the grid (see preceding section), you can use the grid to place other shapes that will allow you to create the walls of your skyscraper's ground floor.

To add walls to your skyscraper:

1. **Zoom out so that you can see all of the floor slab.**

You are now going to follow what you may think is a bit of a weird workflow.

2. **Place the hole on the floor slab.**

This sequence may seem strange, but as you work through this part of the design, it will become apparent that this workflow is actually easier when you add the hole first to cut out the open space that is enclosed by the walls.

Using the Box (hole) shape from the Basic Shapes menu, place the box (hole) centrally on top of the floor slab using the grid to place it accurately (see Figure 11-4). It will sit on the top face of the floor slab because the Workplane is already placed on that face.

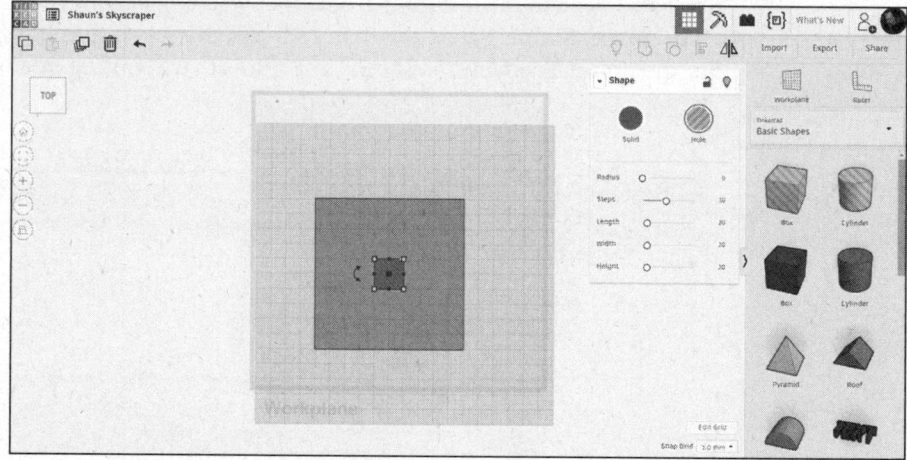

FIGURE 11-4: The box (hole) placed centrally on top of the floor slab using the grid for alignment.

3. **Size the box (hole) so that it shells out the inside of the ground floor.**

You can use the Shape dialog box to set the following dimensions (see Figure 11-5):

    Length: 85 (mm)

    Width: 85 (mm)

    Height: 80 (mm)

If you're using imperial dimensions, you can use these dimensions as a guide:

Length: 3.4 (in)

Width: 3.4 (in)

Height: 3.2 (in)

So you now have a hole sitting on the ground floor slab, and while that may seem a bit weird, go with the flow. It all comes out right in the end!

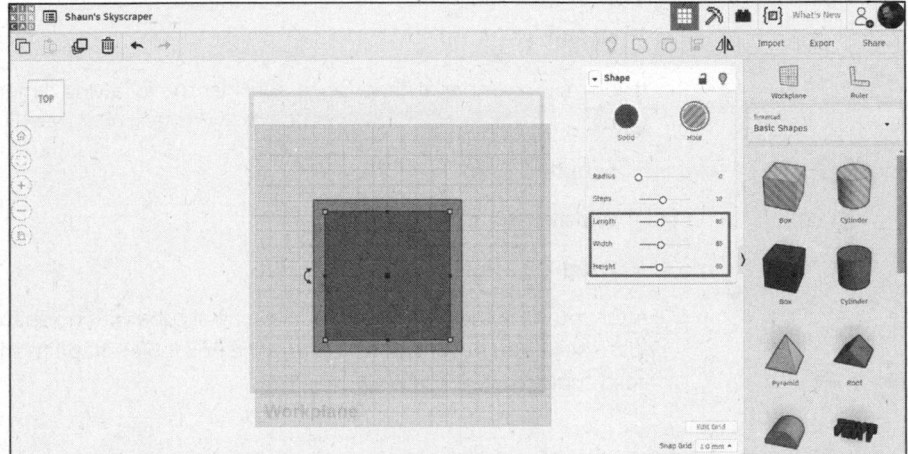

FIGURE 11-5:
The Box (hole) shape in place with the metric dimensions applied.

Using Hide to Your Advantage

After you have a hole sitting on top of your ground floor slab, you need to complete the steps in the preceding section, but with a full Box shape this time around. You then end up with a Box shape and a Box (hole) shape occupying the same space, but the Box shape will be slightly larger. When you shell out the Box shape, with the Box (hole) shape, you will end up with your walls.

Before you do that, though, to make placing the full Box shape easier, you can hide the Box (hole) shape.

To hide the Box (hole) shape:

1. **Select the Box (hole) shape and then click on the little lightbulb icon in the Shape dialog box.**

Alternatively, you can also use the keyboard shortcut CTRL+H (or if using a Mac, use the keyboard CMD+H).

2. From the Basic Shapes menu, select the Box shape, which is normally red, and place it centrally like you did the Box (hole) shape in the preceding section.

You may need to zoom in to ensure it is aligned to the grid.

3. Apply the following dimensions to the Box shape, which are shown in Figure 11-6:

Length: 90 (mm)

Width: 90 (mm)

Height: 80 (mm)

If you're using imperial dimensions, consider the following dimensions as a guide:

Length: 3.6 (in)

Width: 3.6 (in)

Height: 3.2 (in)

After you place the Box shape, you have a full cube with no space inside. It is just a solid. You now need to re-utilize the Box (hole) shape to shell out that solid cube to create the walls.

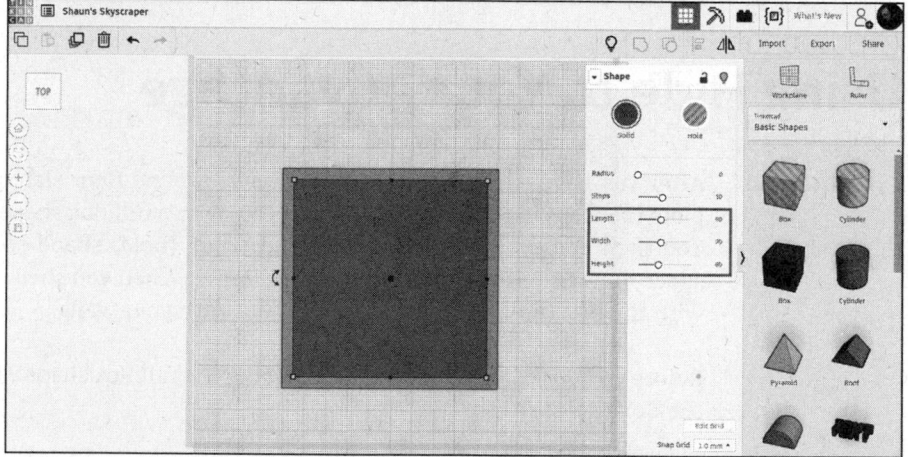

Before you placed the box shape, you used the Hide command to hide the Box (hole) shape. You now need to bring it back onto the screen by unhiding it so that it occupies that same space as the full Box shape.

4. **Deselect the box shape you placed in Step 2.**

   To do this, click in the white area around your workspace.

5. **Click on the lightbulb icon on the top-right toolbar.**

   This step executes the Show All command. You can also use the keyboard shortcut CTRL+SHIFT+H (CMD+SHIFT+H on a Mac).

   You now see the box (hole) shape appear inside the box shape, sharing the same space, ready to shell out the interior of your ground floor to give you walls.

6. **Go to the ViewCube and select the bottom-right corner.**

   The Top/Front/Right preset isometric view appears. You can now see the box shape and the box (hole) shape more clearly, as shown in Figure 11-7.

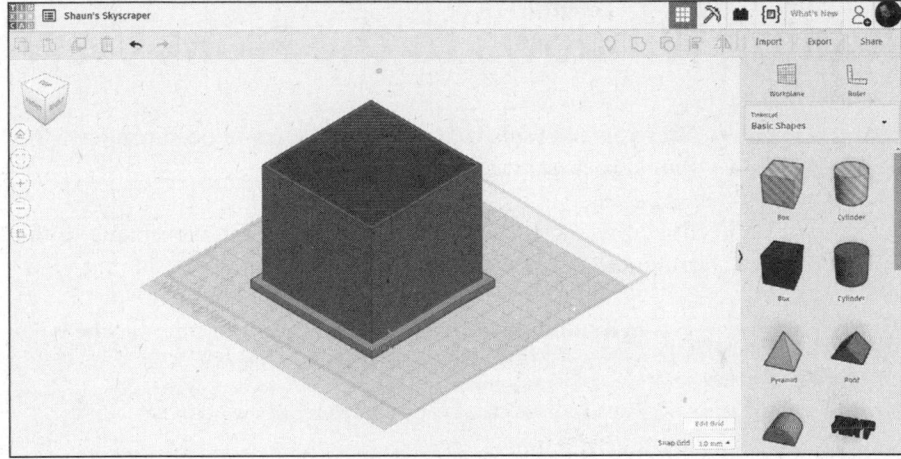

FIGURE 11-7:
The box shape and box (hole) shape sitting on the Workplane on the top face of the floor slab in a preset isometric view.

In the isometric view, you can select both the box shape and the box (hole) shape.

7. **Click on the Group command icon on the top-right toolbar.**

   You can also use the keyboard shortcut CTRL+G (CMD+G on a Mac).

   The box (hole) shape has shelled out the box shape, giving you walls for your ground floor (see Figure 11-8).

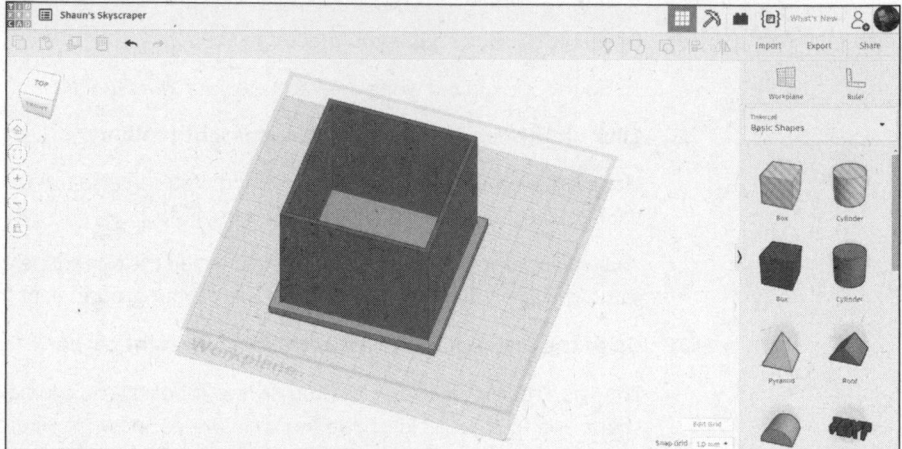

FIGURE 11-8:
The shelled out ground floor with walls after using the Group command (view has been orbited slightly for clarity).

Adding Windows to the Front View

After you add walls to the ground floor, you need windows. It will be very dark in your skyscraper without them, right?

To add windows, you first need to align the Workplane to the Front face of your ground floor, to use the wall that is in the selected Front view.

1. **In a suitable isometric view on the ViewCube, set the Workplane to the appropriate wall face (in this case, Front).**

   The Front wall is already complete with windows.

   The Workplane is now aligned with the Front wall of the ground floor, as shown in Figure 11-9.

2. **Align the Workplane with the Front wall in the isometric view.**

3. **Set the view to the required view on the ViewCube.**

   The Workplane should be set to the Front wall, so you need to be in the preset Front view on the ViewCube.

4. **Place the appropriate number of Box (hole) shapes from the Basic Shapes menu on the Front wall to represent windows.**

   Figure 11-10 shows you a typical position for the two window shapes.

TIP

   You may need to zoom in to see the grid for accuracy, and you can place more than two box (hole) shapes, if you want. In this example, though, I use two, purely for clarity. You can also pan by holding down the middle mouse wheel as a button and dragging the mouse in the direction you want to pan.

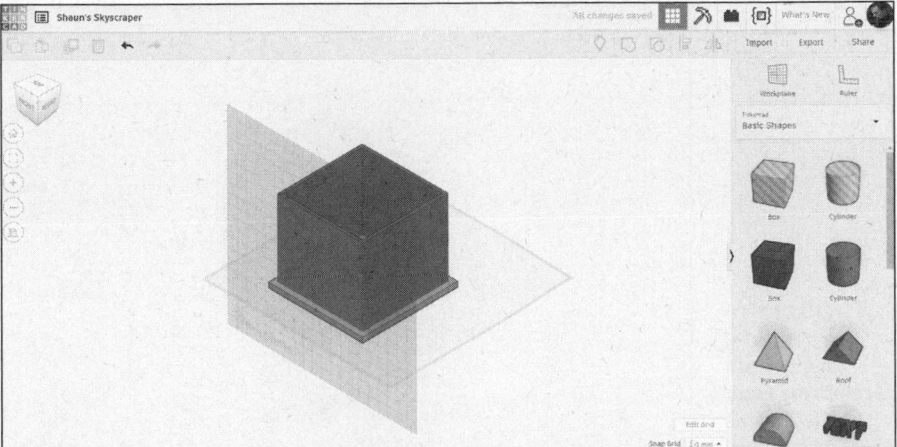

FIGURE 11-9:
The Workplane aligned with the Front view on the ViewCube and the Front wall of the ground floor design.

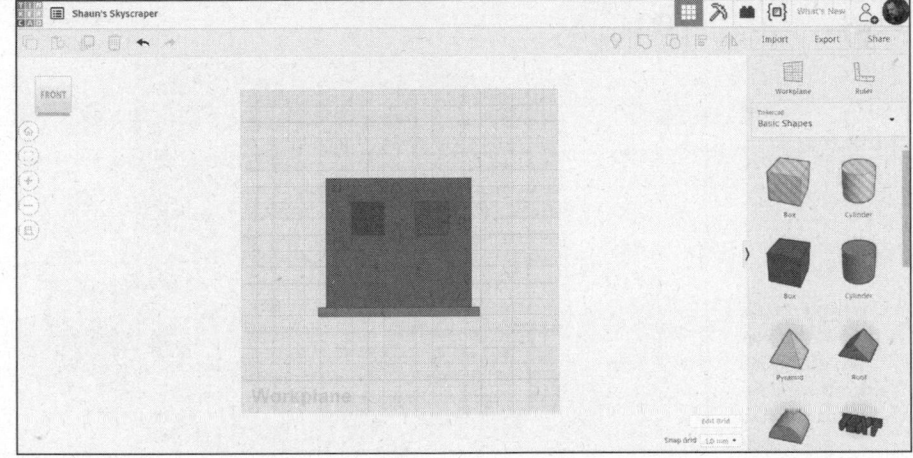

FIGURE 11-10:
The two box (hole) shapes being used for windows on the Front view of the ground floor design.

5. **Go back to the previous isometric view on the ViewCube.**

You see that the box (hole) shapes are sitting flush with the wall right now, as shown in Figure 11-11. If you group them like this with the wall, they will not make holes to represent windows because they need to go through the wall to make that happen.

6. **Select one of the Box (hole) shapes and use the axis arrow to move the Box (hole) shape so that it goes through the corresponding wall face.**

Zooming in closer here may help. Make sure you can see the shape that represents the window in the view. Figure 11-12 shows one of the Box (hole) shapes selected with the axis arrow highlighted.

7. **Repeat this process for the second Box (hole) shape so that both hole shapes are going through the Front wall.**

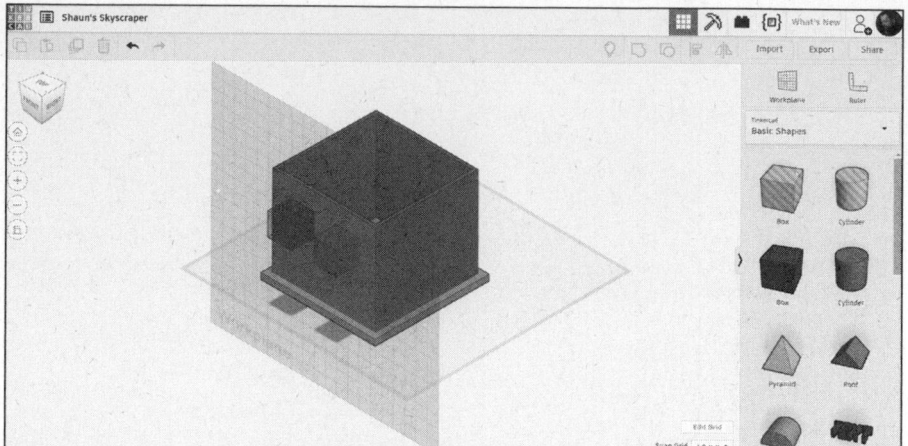

FIGURE 11-11:
The box (hole)
shapes flush
against the Front
wall in the
isometric view.

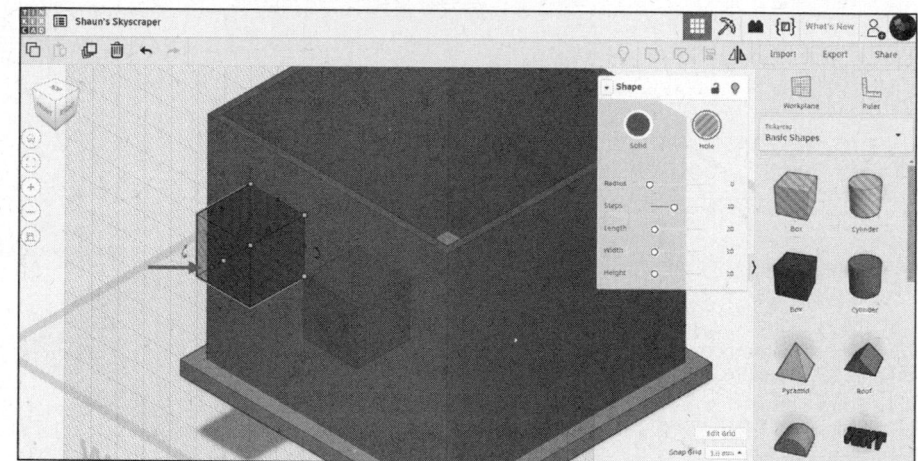

FIGURE 11-12:
One of the Box
(hole) shapes
selected with the
axis arrow
highlighted.

8. **Go to the Top view on the ViewCube to check that the box (hole) shapes are going through the wall in plan.**

   In my example, I have two Box (hole) shapes to represent the windows, but you may have more.

   If you go to the Top view on the ViewCube, you can check to make sure all of the Box (hole) shapes are going through the Front wall. Figure 11-13 demonstrates this.

9. **In isometric view, hold down the SHIFT key and select the Box (hole) shapes and the walls in the design.**

   Three objects are now selected in total, and it should read Shapes (3) on the Shape dialog box (top right), as shown in Figure 11-14.

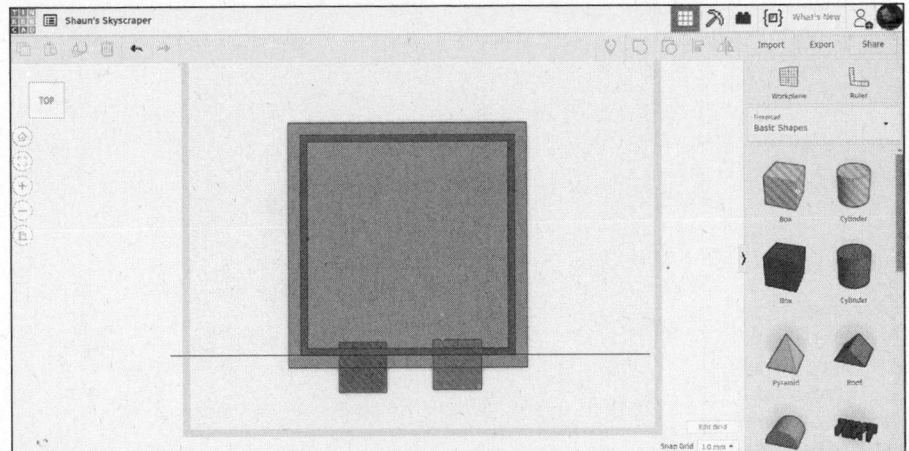

FIGURE 11-13:
The Top preset view on the ViewCube with the box (hole) shapes going through the Front wall in plan.

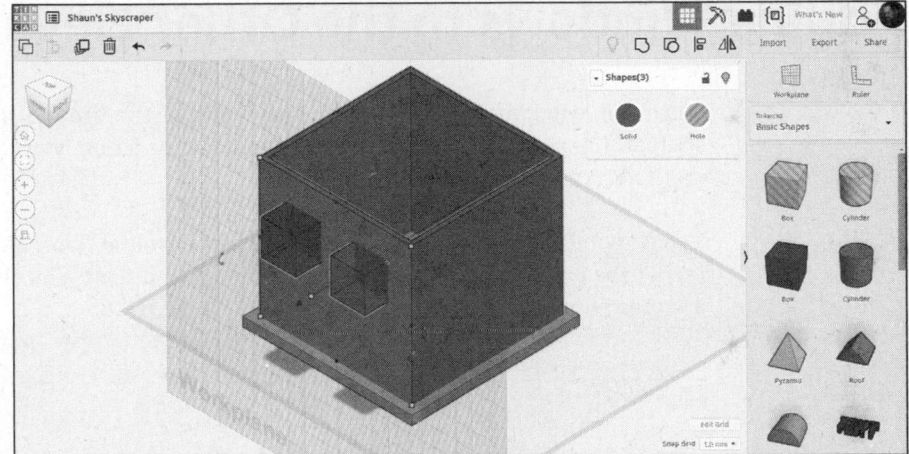

FIGURE 11-14:
The two box (hole) shapes and the walls selected in the isometric view.

10. **Group the Box (hole) shapes and the walls.**

The Front view of the ground floor now has a set of windows.

You can see that the Box (hole) shapes form openings in the Front wall. These shapes represent windows. Figure 11-15 shows you how they should look.

Your windows are in your Front view, which is known as the Front elevation. You can now see your skyscraper (in miniature) taking shape.

TIP

Once you are at a point where you have completed a workflow in Tinkercad, it is often a good idea to go to an isometric view where you can sanity check the new details. Also, make sure that you set the Workplane back to its default position by using the Workplane command and clicking in a space away from your design.

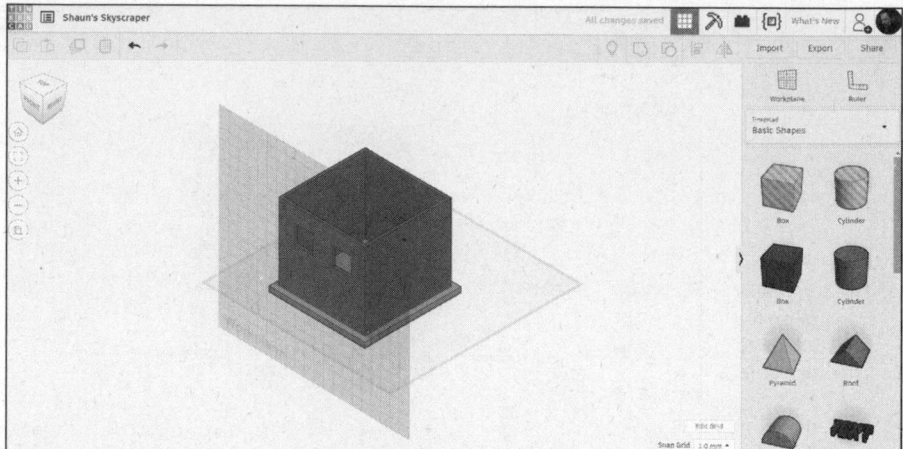

FIGURE 11-15:
When grouped,
the box (hole)
shapes form
window openings
in the Front wall.

Adding Windows to the Other Elevations

You want windows on each of the four walls of the ground floor of your skyscraper. If you followed the steps in the preceding section, you have windows only on the Front elevation.

To add windows to the other elevations on your ground floor, all you have to do is repeat the process for each other side of the ground floor. You should end up with a ground floor similar to the one shown in Figure 11-16.

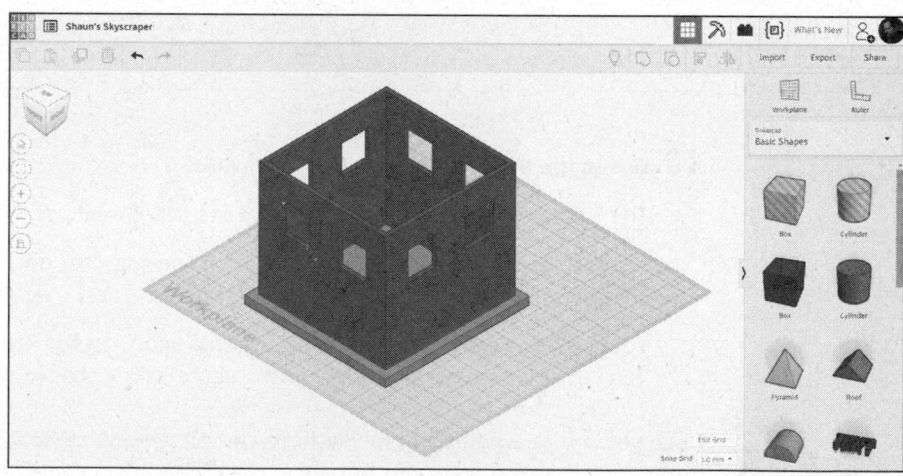

FIGURE 11-16:
The finished walls
with windows
provided on each
side (elevation) by
the box (hole)
shapes. Note that
the Workplane is
back in its default
position on the
bottom face of
the floor slab.

Adding the Ceiling

As you now have a ground floor, with a floor slab, and some windows, you need a ceiling to sit on top of the ground floor walls.

This part of the design is quite easy compared to the windows, as there is only one ceiling with no repetitive tasks to perform this time.

To add a ceiling:

1. **Get into a suitable isometric view on the ViewCube.**

2. **Set the Workplane to the top face/edge of the ground floor walls.**

If you refer to Figure 11-17, you can see the Workplane aligned with the top face/edge of the walls.

FIGURE 11-17:
The ground floor design in an isometric view, with the Workplane aligned to the top face/edge of the ground floor walls. The view has been orbited slightly for clarity to show the Workplane alignment.

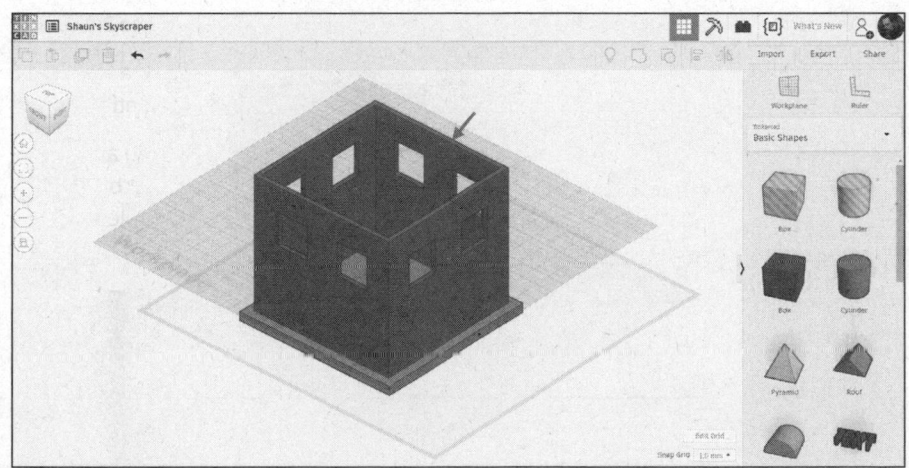

3. **Set the ViewCube to the preset Top view and switch to Orthographic view as well.**

4. **Align the walls and the floor slab to the grid on the Workplane.**

You may need to zoom in to make sure this alignment to the grid is accurate here. You can see the correct alignment in Figure 11-18.

TIP

5. **Position a box shape centrally.**

You may want to also give it a different color to distinguish it from other objects in the design. Check Figure 11-19 to see the color change.

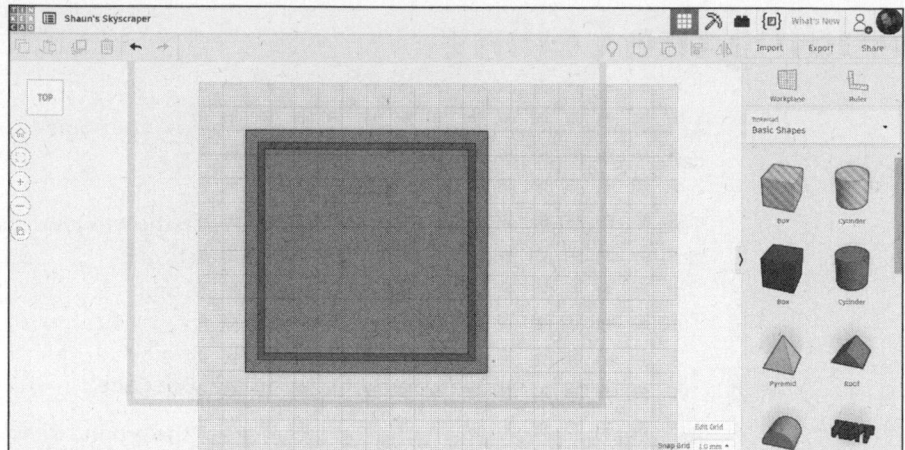

FIGURE 11-18:
The Top view of the walls and the floor slab, aligned accurately to the grid on the Workplane.

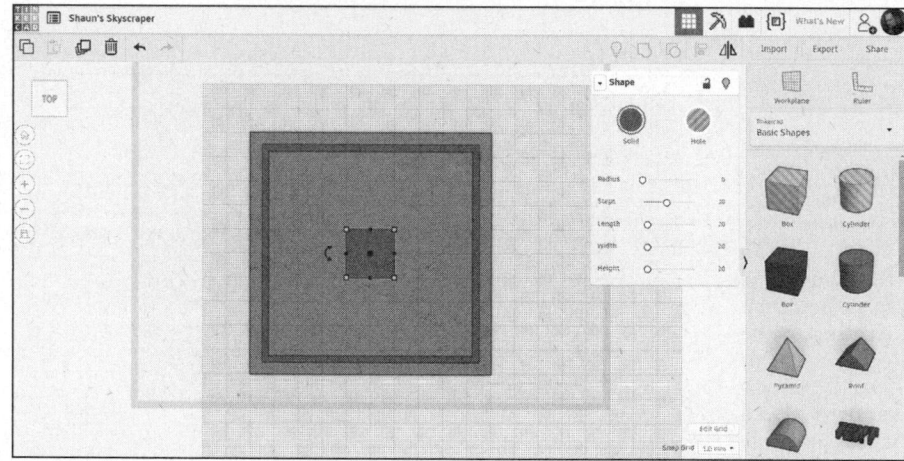

FIGURE 11-19:
The new box shape, placed centrally on the grid in the Top view. Note the color of the box shape is different to other objects in the design.

6. **With the box shape being used for the ceiling selected, size the ceiling to exactly fit the walls below it.**

In my example, I use the following dimensions (which you can see in Figure 11-20):

Length: 90 (mm)

Width: 90 (mm)

Height: 5 (mm)

If you're using imperial dimensions, here is a guide to the dimensions you can use:

Length: 3.6 (in)

Width: 3.6 (in)

Height: 0.2 (in)

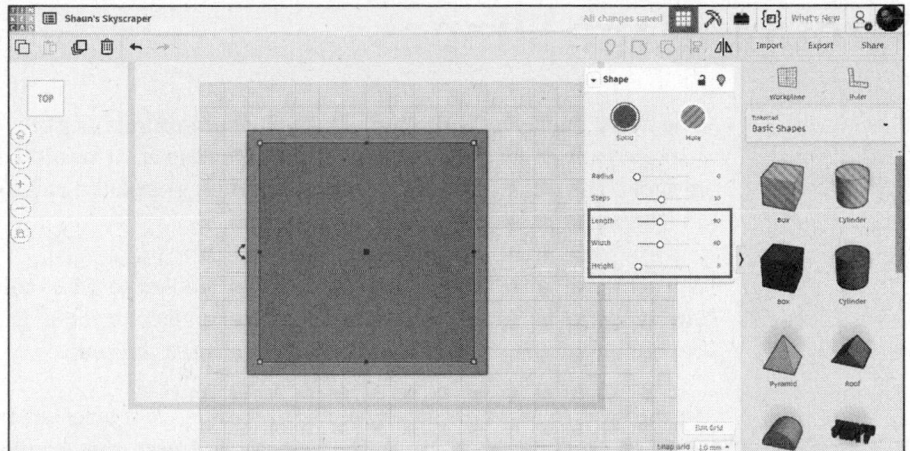

FIGURE 11-20:
The new ceiling formed from the box shape with the metric dimensions displayed in the Shape dialog box to the right.

7. **Change to an isometric view.**

You can now see the ceiling sitting flush on top of the walls of the ground floor. As it is a different color, it is easy to spot.

Always check your corners by zooming in and panning. If they are not as exactly flush as you may expect, tidy them up accordingly to make the ceiling flush on each corner.

8. **Reset the Workplane back to its default position.**

Figure 11-21 shows you the ceiling in place with the Workplane set back to its default position.

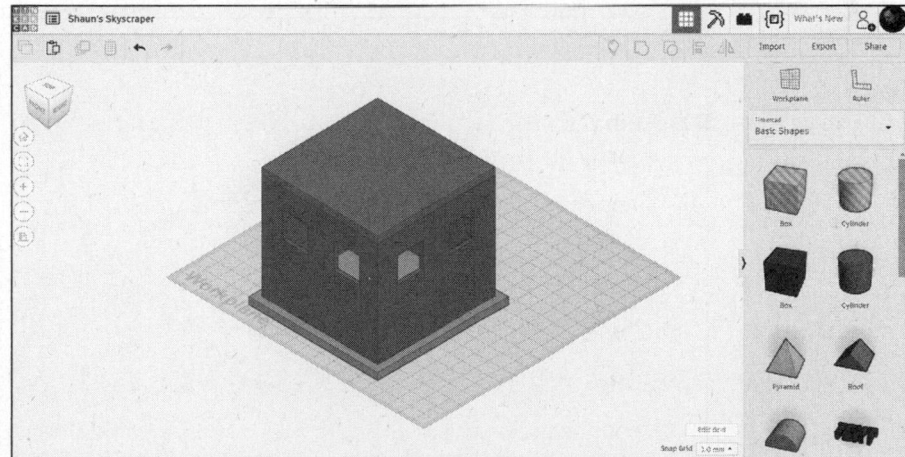

FIGURE 11-21:
The ceiling in place on top of the ground floor walls. The Workplane is back in its default position.

Grouping the Shapes

The walls, windows, and ceiling make up your ground floor of your skyscraper. To make creating more floors of the skyscraper easier, it would be beneficial if you grouped the walls (with their window openings) and the ceiling as one object in the skyscraper design.

TIP

At this point, you have to make a final decision as to what color you want your skyscraper to be. Grouping will assume an overall color for all the shapes grouped, depending on the color of the first shape selected to group.

In the case of Shaun's Skyscraper, if the walls were selected first, the grouping would go red. If the ceiling were to be selected first, the group would be a brown color.

Color selection is totally subjective and in the eye of the beholder, so to speak, so decide on your color before you group the shapes together or change it after the grouping operation.

Use the Group command to group the walls and ceiling together. With the grouped object seleceted, change the object color to a color of your choosing.

The ceiling and the walls (and windows) become one shape and one color.

Figure 11-22 shows the finished ground floor after grouping as one shape, with one color, in an isometric view.

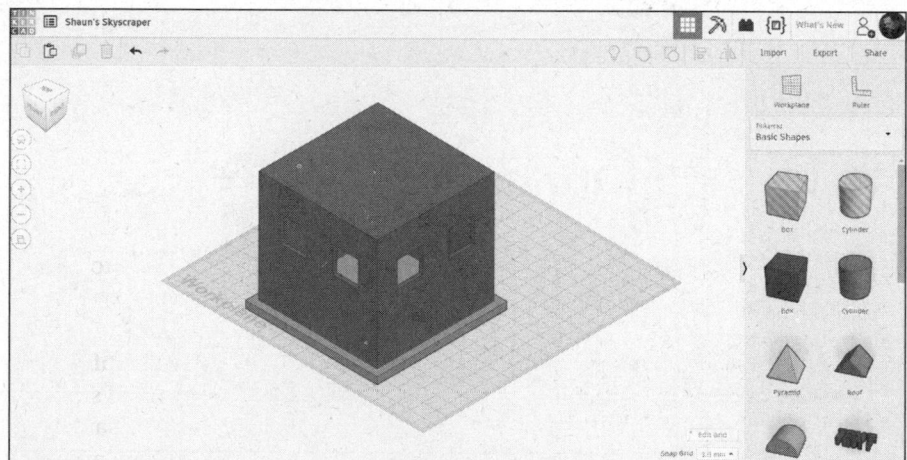

FIGURE 11-22:
The finished ground floor after grouping as one shape, in an isometric view.

Chapter **12**

Copying the Floors as You Build

I n Chapter 11, you create your ground floor and group it into a shape that you can easily copy, move, and manipulate to help you build up extra floors in your skyscraper design in Tinkercad.

In this chapter, you utilize the Copy and Paste functions of Tinkercad and use the user interface and your mouse to your advantage to place extra floor shapes as you increase the height of your Tinkercad skyscraper.

Copying Floor Elements

After you have a floor shape/object, you can use it to create other floors in your skyscraper design.

The Copy and Paste commands in Tinkercad are helpful when you want to re-use design content quickly and effectively. The keyboard shortcuts for Copy and Paste are CTRL+C and CTRL+V, respectively. They are the same keyboard shortcuts used in most Microsoft Windows-based applications. On a Mac, you use the keyboard combinations CMD+C and CMD+V, respectively.

To copy and paste Tinkercad shapes and objects, make sure you are in your sky-scraper design in Tinkercad.

1. **Set your skyscraper design to the Front view of the ViewCube.**

   It is much easier to use an elevation to copy and paste Tinkercad shapes and objects. Figure 12-1 shows you how your view should be looking.

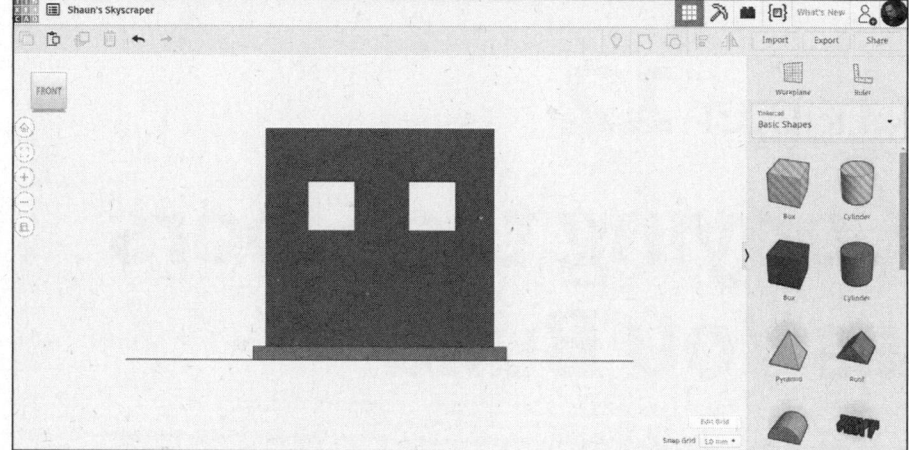

FIGURE 12-1: The ground floor and floor slab of the skyscraper design in the Front view of the ViewCube.

2. **Zoom out slightly so that you have a little bit of space around the Front view of the ground floor.**

3. **Select the ground floor shape and then click on Copy on the top-left toolbar.**

   You can also use the keyboard commands, if you want. The ground floor shape is now copied to the clipboard.

4. **Click on Paste on the top-left toolbar.**

   Another ground floor shape appears sort of next to and on top of the original shape. You can see this shown in Figure 12-2.

TIP

The Duplicate command in the top-left toolbar can also be operated by pressing CTRL+D on the keyboard (CMD+D on a Mac). Duplicate allows you to duplicate a shape as many times as you like, but they will all be in the same space (on top of the original shape). This command is great for duplicating a number of shapes really quickly, but be careful: It can get confusing when you don't know how many duplicated shapes are on top of the original shape!

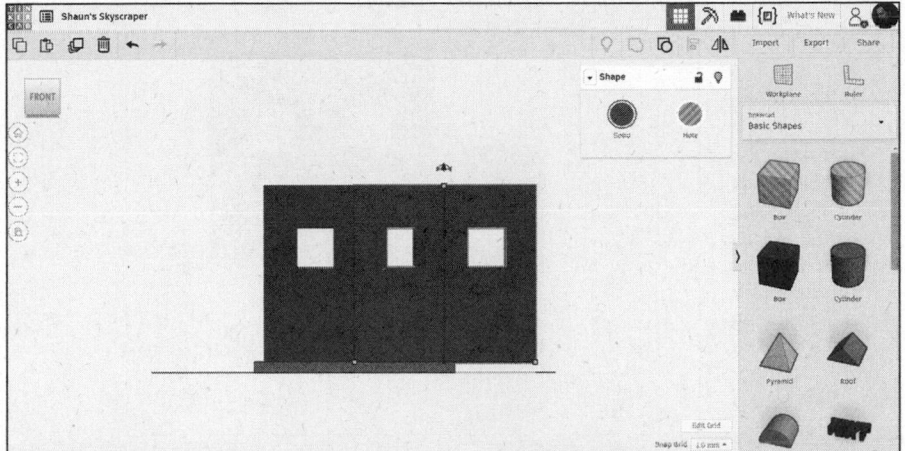

FIGURE 12-2:
The copied and
pasted ground
floor shape next
to the original
ground floor
shape in the
Front view.

Getting the Placement of the Floors Right

After you copy the ground floor, you can place it on top of the existing ground floor to create the first floor:

1. **Select the copied ground floor shape, if it's not selected already.**

   The axis arrow appears either above or below the shape.

   Although you can drag the shape horizontally along the screen using the mouse, you can't move it upwards or downwards in the vertical plane. This is because it is constrained in the plane it was created in.

   You can, however, use the axis arrows to move the copied shape vertically.

2. **Place the new floor shape on top of the existing floor shape by clicking and dragging upwards on the axis arrow.**

   You see the temporary dimensions appear. These dimensions will be useful. Figure 12-3 shows the temporary dimensions being displayed.

3. **Change the vertical temporary dimension to 90 mm (or the corresponding imperial dimension to 3.4 inches) and press Enter.**

   This dimension includes the height of the floor shape (80 mm), plus the depth of the floor slab (10 mm).

   As the vertical temporary dimension is measured from the Workplane in its default position, the 90 mm will place the copied floor shape exactly on top of the ground floor shape, as shown in Figure 12-4.

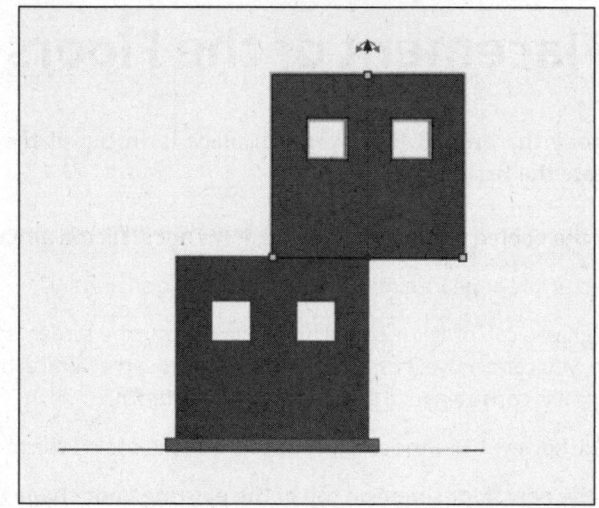

FIGURE 12-3:
The copied floor shape being dragged upwards with the temporary dimensions being displayed. The vertical temporary dimension is arrowed.

FIGURE 12-4:
The copied floor shape sitting exactly on top of the ground floor shape.

4. **With the copied floor shape still selected, start to drag it to the left.**

The horizontal temporary dimension appears on the bottom right.

5. **Make that temporary dimension 45 mm (1.7 inches) and press Enter.**

The copied floor moves exactly to the centralized position above the ground floor shape below it.

When you created the floor shape originally from the original box shape, it was positioned centrally on the grid. You then made it 90 x 90 mm (3.4 inches), so if you move it from its central point by 45 mm, it then moves to where it needs to be. That's why you made sure you placed the box shapes centrally when you created the walls for the ground floor.

Figure 12-5 shows you the copied floor shape with the temporary dimension highlighted.

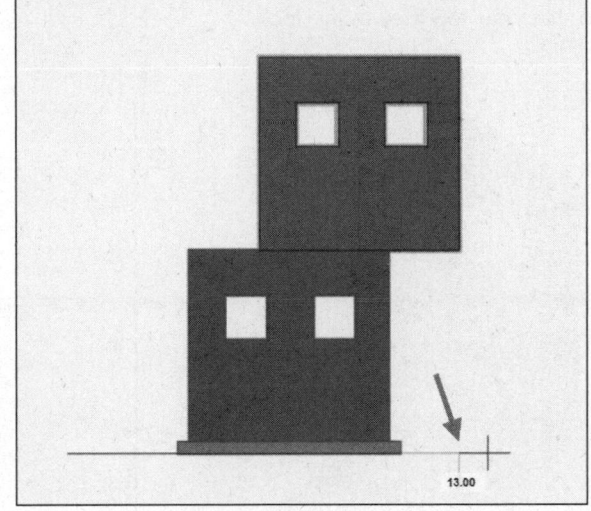

FIGURE 12-5: The copied floor shape with the horizontal temporary dimension arrowed.

6. **After you have your first floor placed exactly above the ground floor, verify that it's in the correct position.**

   You can do this by zooming in or by picking a corner of the ViewCube to go in to an isometric view.

   Figure 12-6 shows the copied (first) floor shape placed exactly above the ground floor shape.

FIGURE 12-6: The copied (first) floor shape placed exactly above the ground floor shape.

7. Go to a suitable isometric view on the ViewCube to check that the two floors are positioned correctly.

Figure 12-7 shows the two floor shapes in correct alignment in an isometric view to show you how they should look.

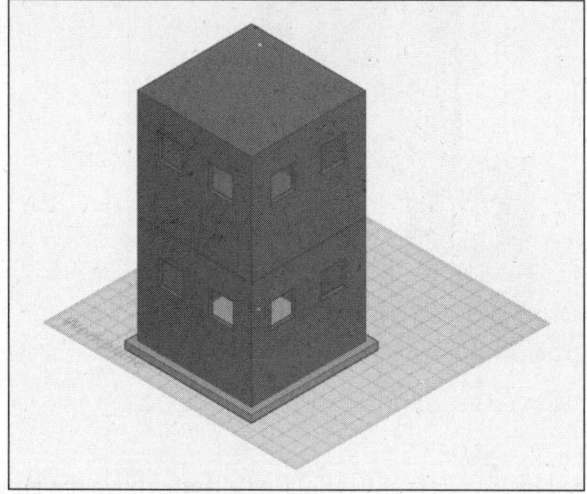

FIGURE 12-7:
The two floors positioned correctly in an isometric view set by the ViewCube.

Adding More Floors

You may need to add more floors. In my example, I have a total of five floors in my skyscraper.

To add each floor, follow the steps listed in the two preceding sections.

Figure 12-8 shows the skyscraper with its five floors in an isometric view.

TIP

When you start to add extra floors to your skyscraper, use all of the Tinkercad tools available to you. When in an isometric view, align the Workplane with the top face of the floor shape you have just placed. That way, you know that it is all zeroed on the top of the last floor, and you can then make sure that your vertical temporary dimension is always zero to get the floors to align at each level. The horizontal temporary dimension will always be 45 mm (1.7 inches) as you're working from the center each time. If you use Duplicate instead of Copy and Paste, always stay aware of how many duplicates you create.

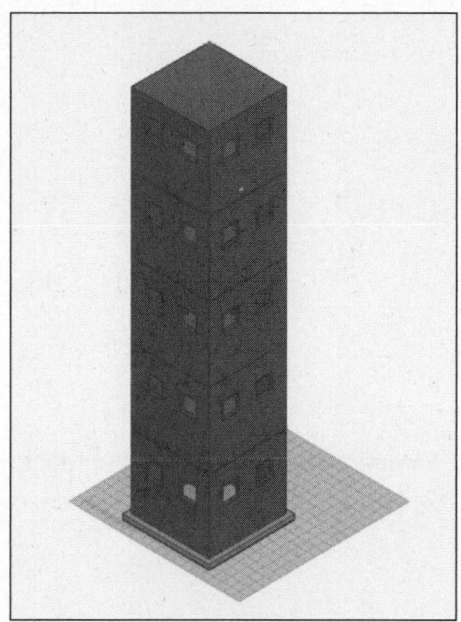

FIGURE 12-8:
The skyscraper
with five floors in
an isometric view.

TIP

Another quick workflow you could use is to put the Workplane at the top of the story you are on, choose the top story, and click CTRL+D (CMD+D on a Mac) to duplicate. You can then just change the vertical to the number 0 to get it directly above. This method is super useful when you want to add a story quickly and correctly.

The steps to take are as follows:

1. **Look at the top of the skyscraper.**
2. **Set the Workplane to the top face.**
3. **Click the top story.**
4. **Duplicate using CTRL+D (or CMD+D on a Mac).**
5. **Start moving it up and change the temporary location to zero (0).**
6. **Repeat for each story.**

REMEMBER

Keep an eye on the number of duplicates you create.

Chapter **13**

Adding the Roof to Stop the Rain

I n Chapter 12, you develop your skyscraper and add more floors to it. There is no such thing as a one-story skyscraper.

In this chapter, you develop the roof of your skyscraper and add a curved edge to allow for rain runoff.

Picking the Right Shape for Your Roof

If you watch movies, a lot (and I mean a lot) of tall buildings have a roof on them that doubles as a helipad. The roof for your skyscraper will double as a helipad, but it will be even cooler: It will have a curved edge that allows the rain to run off of it, too!

The following steps guide you through adding a helipad to your skyscraper. You find out how to add a shape that represents the helipad and also see how to add a curved edge to a shape in Tinkercad.

1. **Open your skyscraper design in Tinkercad.**

2. **Using an isometric view, align the Workplane to the top face of the top floor of the skyscraper.**

   Figure 13-1 shows the Workplane aligned to the top face of the top floor of the skyscraper.

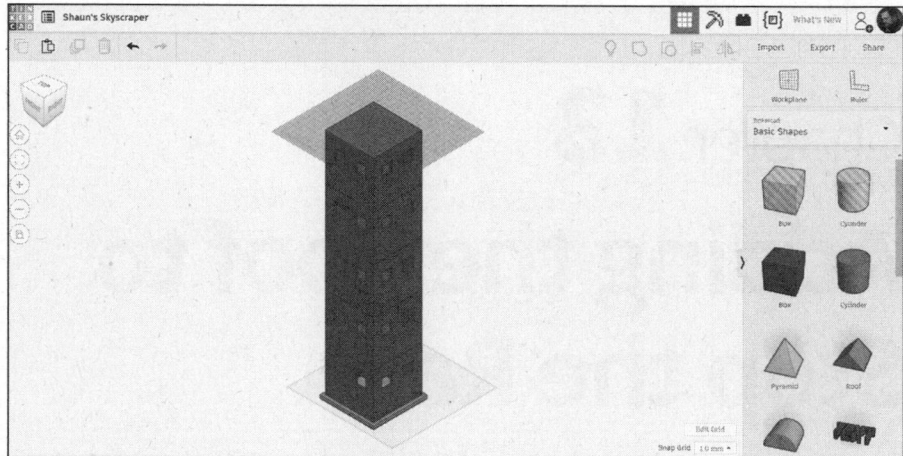

FIGURE 13-1:
The Workplane aligned to the top face of the top floor in an isometric view.

3. **Go to the Top view on the ViewCube and place the shape that will form the roof of your skyscraper.**

   Zoom in if you need to for clarity and to be able to see the grid for accurate shape placement.

4. **In Orthographic view, align your skyscraper to the grid appropriately.**

   Figure 13-2 shows the Top view of the skyscraper aligned to the Workplane grid.

   Your roof is going to be a polygon with ten sides, also known as a decagon. On the Tinkercad Basic Shapes menu is a Polygon.

5. **Using the grid on the Workplane, place the default polygon centrally on the top face of the top floor of your skyscraper.**

   This placement should happen automatically because your Workplane is the top face.

6. **In the Shape dialog box, change the number of sides to 10 and press Enter.**

   The polygon changes shape accordingly, as shown in Figure 13-3.

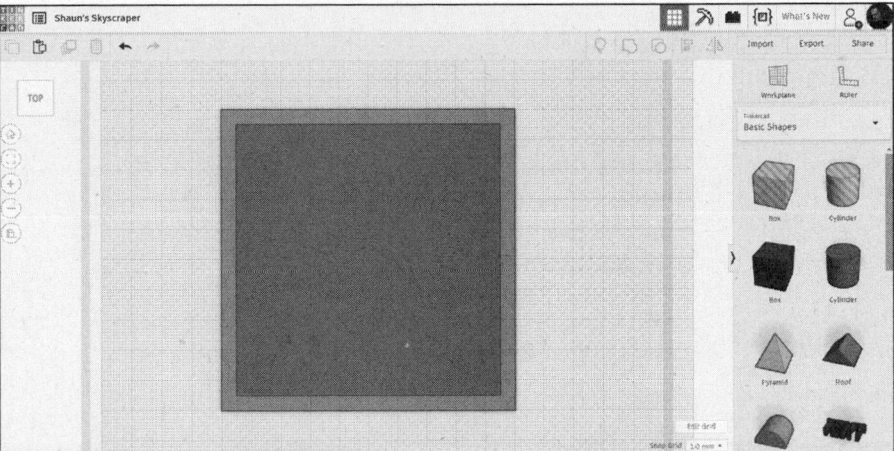

FIGURE 13-2:
The Top view of the skyscraper, aligned to the Workplane grid, ready for placement of the shape that will form the skyscraper roof.

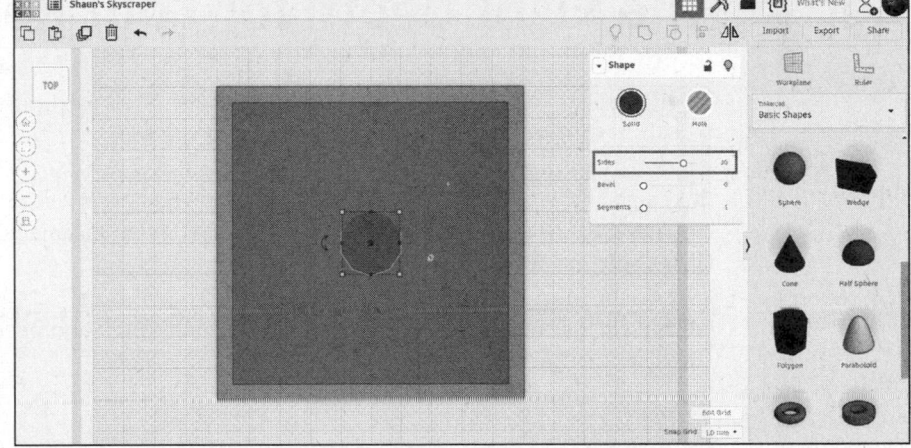

FIGURE 13-3:
The decagon in place on top of the skyscraper, with the number of sides highlighted in the Shape dialog box.

7. **Use the small black squares on the decagon edges to click and drag the edges of the decagon to the corresponding outer edges of the floor slab in plan.**

   Do not drag them to the floor shape.

The roof does not cover the floor shape exactly because of its nature as a polygon (decagon), but you can develop this later, if you want, by adding more refined detail to your skyscraper.

Figure 13-4 shows the revised decagon in place.

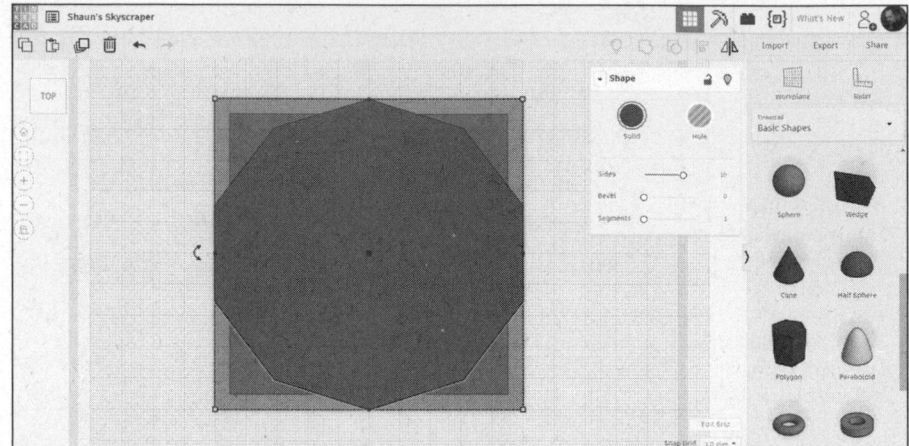

FIGURE 13-4:
The decagon
(roof) with its new
shape on top of
the skyscraper.

Getting the Right Depth for Your Roof

In the earlier sections of this chapter, you have been working in plan (the Top view). In this section, you adjust the height of the roof.

If you go to isometric view, you will notice that the height of the roof is quite high and needs to be changed. However, there is no Height variable in the Shape dialog box when you select the decagon (polygon).

As you can see in Figure 13-5, the new roof is quite high and needs to be adjusted.

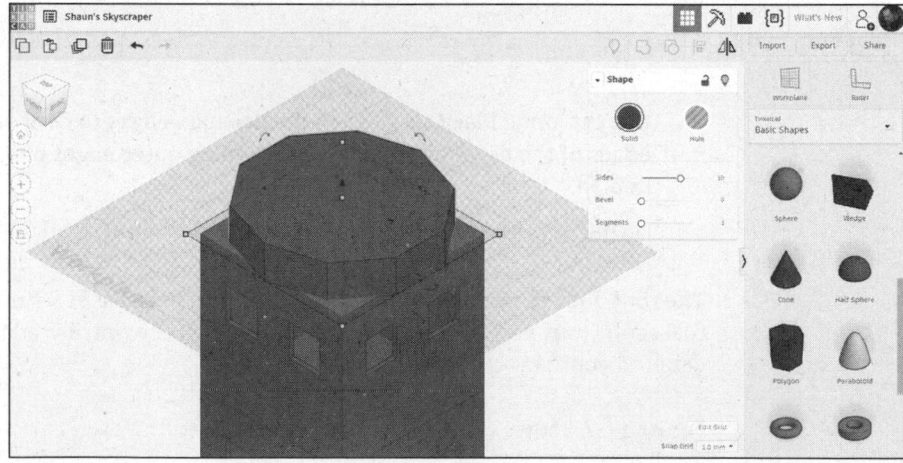

FIGURE 13-5:
The top of the
skyscraper in an
isometric view,
giving an
indication of the
height of the
new roof.

To change the height of your skyscraper roof, you need to go to the Front view on the ViewCube and zoom and pan with your mouse so that you can see the roof and the top of your skyscraper.

After you're in the Front view, you can change the height of your new skyscraper roof:

1. **Select the roof and then hover over the top middle grip on the roof.**

   You see the temporary dimension showing the height of the roof. In metric millimeters, the default height of the roof is 20 mm (8 in), which you can see in Figure 13-6.

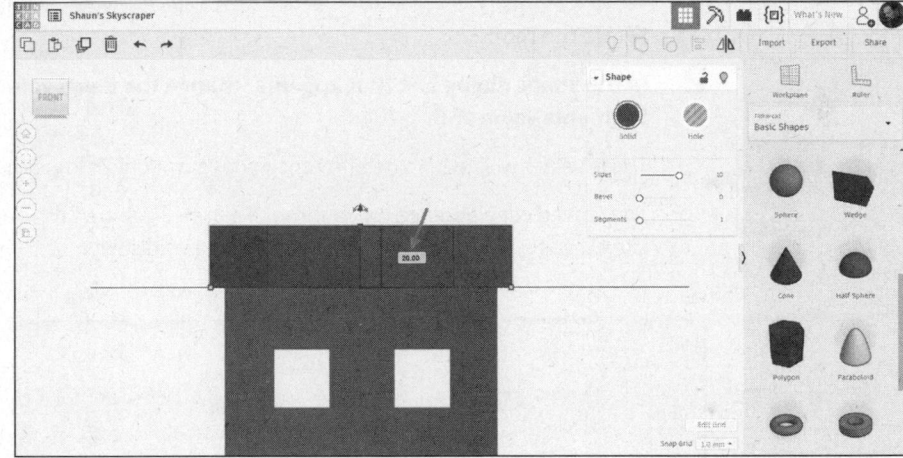

FIGURE 13-6:
The roof on the skyscraper in the Front view, with the roof height temporary dimension arrowed.

2. **Change the roof height to 10 mm (4 in).**

   To do so, just hover over the top middle grip on the roof and then click and drag downwards until the temporary dimension reads 10 (or 4). The roof height changes accordingly. Refer to Figure 13-7.

You now have a roof height that is more sensible and ready for its curved edge for rain runoff.

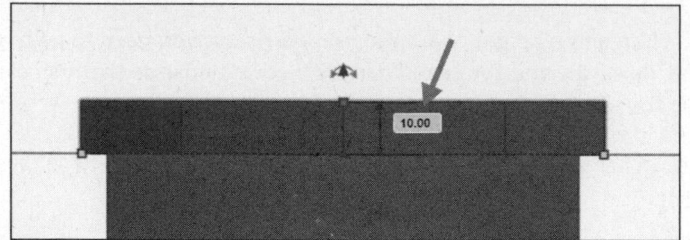

FIGURE 13-7:
The Front view of
the roof with the
grip highlighted
in red with the
temporary
dimension
displayed.

Adding the Curved Roof Edge

In Front view, you can set the curve on your decagon roof edge:

1. **Select the roof.**

2. **In the Shape dialog box that appears, change the Bevel value to 2 and the Segments value to 5.**

REMEMBER

These values will need to be different if you're working in imperial measurements.

The curved edge appears on your roof. Figure 13-8 shows the new roof with its curved edge and the Bevel and Segments values displayed.

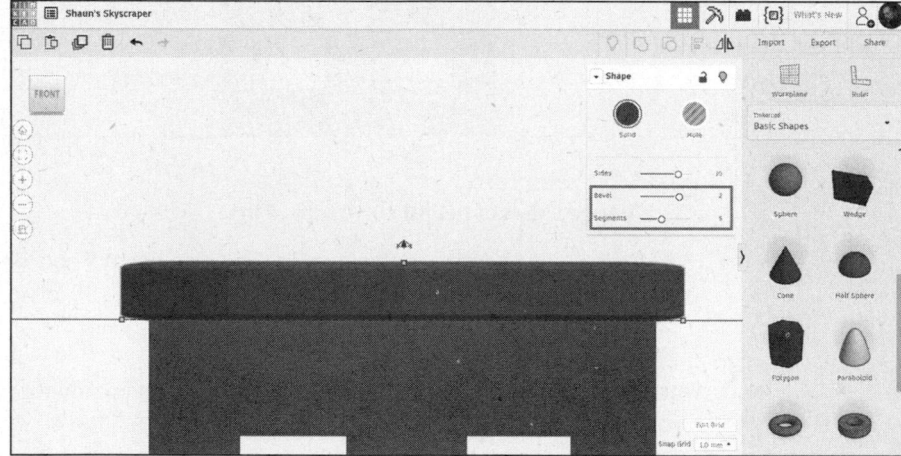

FIGURE 13-8:
The new roof with
its curved edge
and the Bevel and
Segments values
displayed in the
Shape dialog box.

3. **In a suitable isometric view, zoom accordingly so that you can admire your new skyscraper!**

4. **Set the Workplane back to its default position.**

   You can do so by selecting the Workplane command and clicking in the pale blue area at the bottom of the skyscraper, in this case.

   Figure 13-9 gives you an idea of how your new skyscraper should look with its shiny new curved roof!

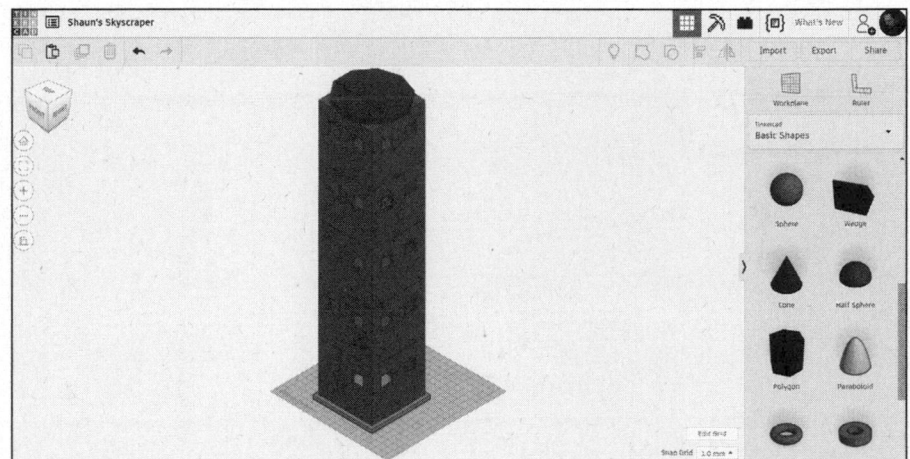

FIGURE 13-9: The new skyscraper in all its glory with its new curved roof.

Chapter **14**

The Sky's the Limit: Adding a Helipad

I n Chapter 13, you add your decagon roof to your skyscraper in preparation for it to also become a helipad — you know, a cool helipad for the rich and famous to land on when they are visiting your skyscraper, right?

In this chapter, you develop a big H using Tinkercad text. You make sure that it's flush with the skyscraper roof so that it looks as though it has been painted onto the roof's surface.

Getting to the Right View

With your skyscraper design open in Tinkercad, you want to be in an isometric view, zoomed in to the top of the skyscraper, with a clear view of the skyscraper roof. Figure 14-1 gives you an idea of the view you need.

In the isometric view, you need to set the Workplane to the top face of the top floor of the skyscraper, not the top face of the roof.

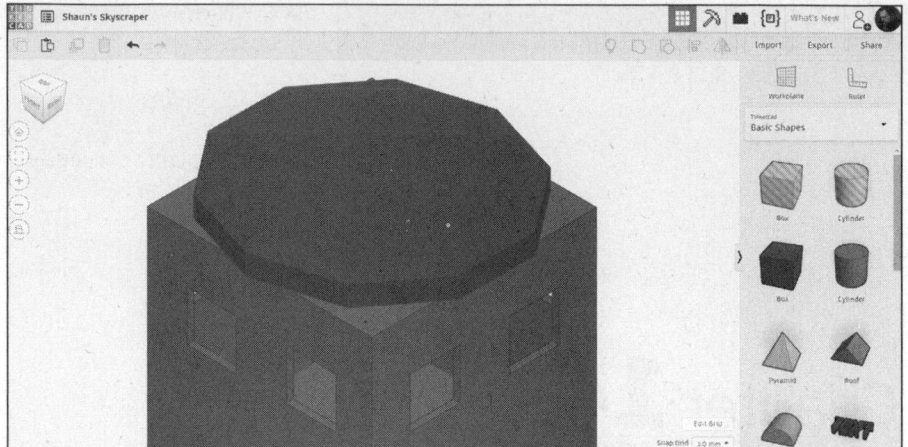

FIGURE 14-1:
The top of the skyscraper in an isometric view so that the roof can be seen clearly.

Select the Workplane command and click on a part of the exposed top face of the top floor, where the decagon roof does not cover it. That way, you can embed the helipad H in the decagon shape that forms the roof.

Then, select the Top view on the ViewCube so that you're working in plan, looking down on the roof. You may need to zoom in for clarity. Figure 14-2 shows you how your view should look for this.

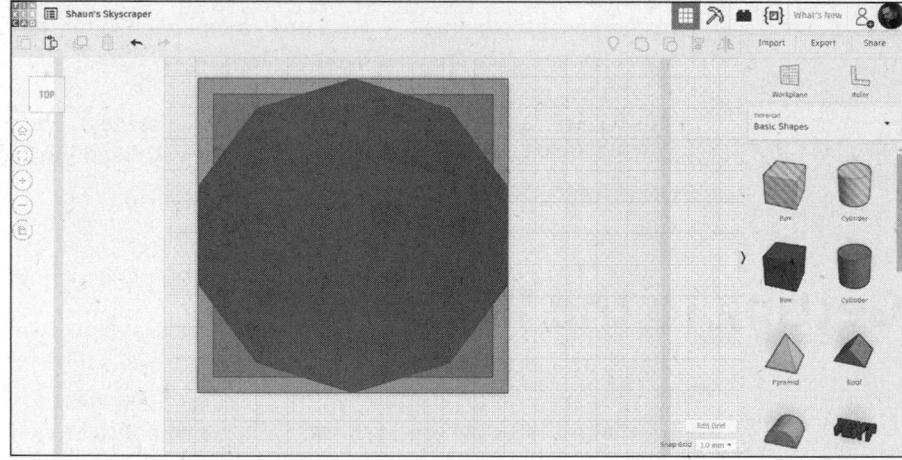

FIGURE 14-2:
The skyscraper roof in plan in the Top view on the ViewCube, ready for the helipad H to be added.

Choosing Your H

You need to decide where your big letter H for Helipad is going to go on the roof.

The reason you have set the Workplane to the top face of the top floor (see the preceding section) is so that you can embed the H into the roof and give the Tinkercad text the same height as the skyscraper roof. This will be a height of 10 mm (4 in).

From the Tinkercad Basic Shapes menu, select the Text shape. Then drag and drop the Text shape to the center of the roof as the text will snap to the center of the roof as you drag it into place.

The Text shape reads TEXT by default and is shown in position in Figure 14-3.

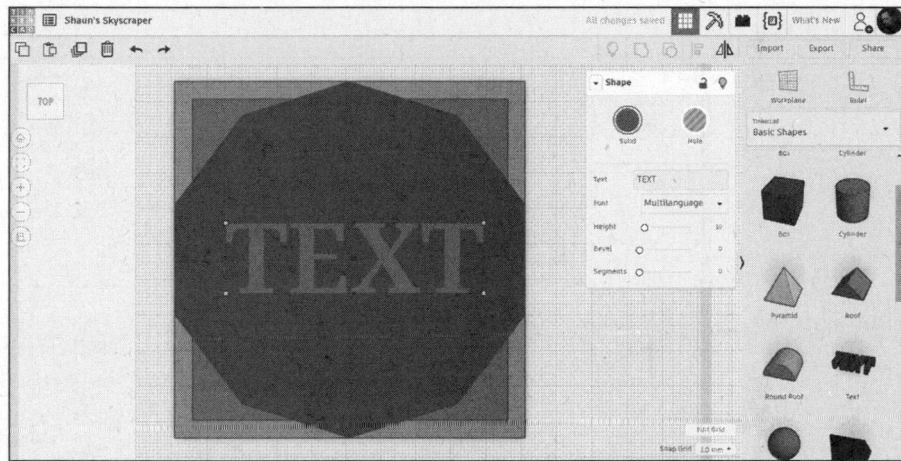

FIGURE 14-3: The default Tinkercad text in place, centered on the roof of the skyscraper.

Changing the Text Settings

The text on your helipad is set to the default settings. You can alter the text, check its height, and make sure that it's using a cool font.

To change the text, font, and height:

1. **Select the Text shape.**

2. **In the Shape dialog box that appears, change the text in the Text field to H and select the Sans font.**

   The text for the helipad changes accordingly. Adjust the positioning of the H, if necessary, to make sure that it is centered.

   Also, note that the height of the text is 10 mm (4 in), so it will be flush with the top face of the roof. This can sometimes affect visibility of the text in Tinkercad.

3. **Make the height of the text 10.5 mm (4.1 in) so that it shows through the top surface of the roof.**

   Figure 14-4 shows the new text settings for the H for the helipad.

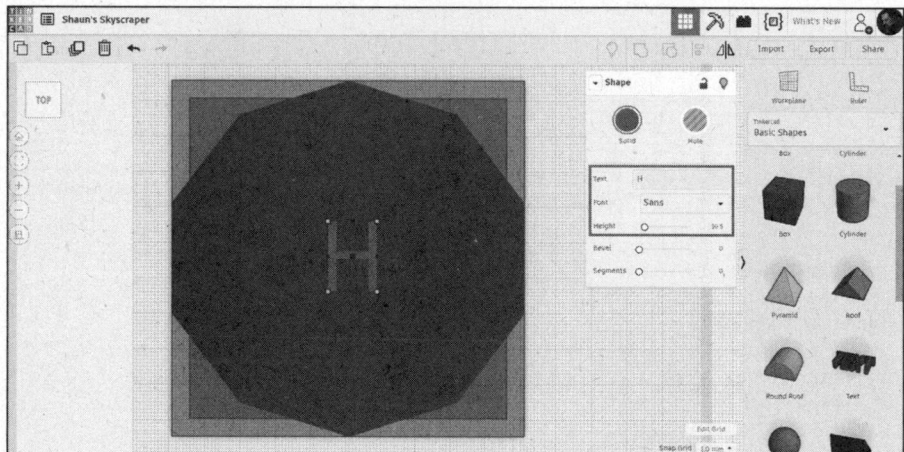

FIGURE 14-4:
The new text settings for the helipad H.

Getting the H to Fit the Roof

With the new helipad H text selected, you see that the text has just as many adjustment grips as a regular Tinkercad shape. These grips allow you to adjust the size of the H to suit the size of the roof.

Click on a grip and drag the grip in the direction you need to go. You need to do this in both horizontal directions and both vertical directions as the H is a bit small at the moment!

Work through each grip methodically until you have an H you are happy with.

Figure 14-5 shows you how your H should look after adjustment.

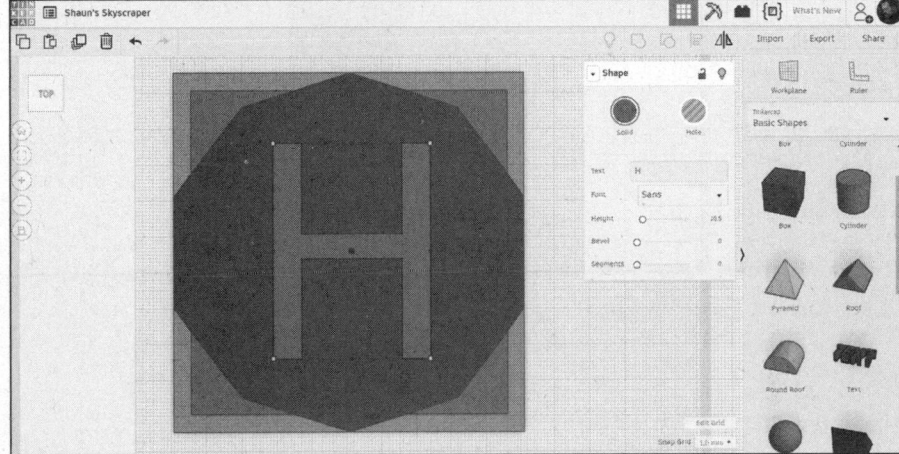

FIGURE 14-5:
The H on the helipad resized with the adjustment grips and now looking much more in context on the skyscraper helipad.

Adding the Finishing Touches

As a finishing touch, you may want to change the color of the H (they are normally white in color).

Change to an isometric view and reset the Workplane back to the pale blue area down toward the bottom of the skyscraper (ground level, as it is known).

Then, just get a good zoom and pan to fit in the isometric view, and you have a helipad on top of your skyscraper!

Figure 14-6 shows you the finished skyscraper (in miniature).

Your skyscraper is now complete.

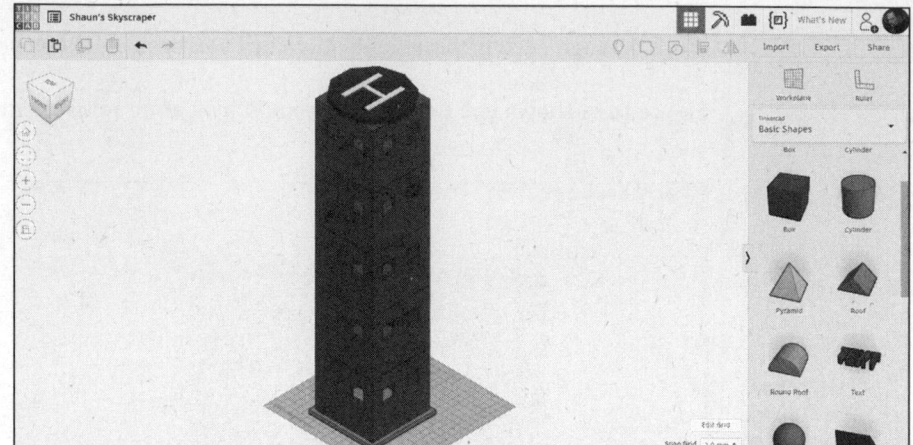

FIGURE 14-6:
The finished skyscraper, complete with roof and helipad, in an isometric view, with the Workplane back in the default position.

4

Making It Happen: 3D Printing Your Designs

IN THIS PART . . .

Tidy up your design for 3D printing and then choose the type of file to export to 3D print.

Select specific 3D shapes from your design to 3D print and then 3D print piece by piece to build up your 3D design components.

Download your Tinkercad design as an STL file.

Download your Tinkercad design as an OBJ file.

Download your Tinkercad design as an SVG file.

Chapter **15**

Getting Started with 3D Printing

After you design your nameplate and your skyscraper, you're ready to take the plunge and dive into the pool of 3D printing. Your Tinkercad design is about to become a real physical thing.

In this chapter, you perform all the checks and balances to make sure that your design can be 3D printed. You also decide what method of 3D printing is the best for your Tinkercad design.

Verifying That You Included Everything

Before you even consider 3D printing, you need to ensure that you have included everything. If you have solid shapes and shapes used as holes and objects that are used for other reasons, you must make sure they're included in your design.

The easiest way to do this is to make sure that all necessary objects that you want to 3D print are grouped as one object. If you are unfamiliar with grouping, it is covered in a number of the previous chapters.

Using the nameplate design as an example, you may want to 3D print the nameplate baseplate as one object and the nameplate text as another object. Therefore, your nameplate body should be one object, while your nameplate text should be another separate object.

TIP

The main reason you keep the text separate is purely for editing reasons. Plus, if you do group it with the nameplate body, it will all be the same color, too, which won't make the text legible.

Figure 15-1 shows the nameplate selected as one object.

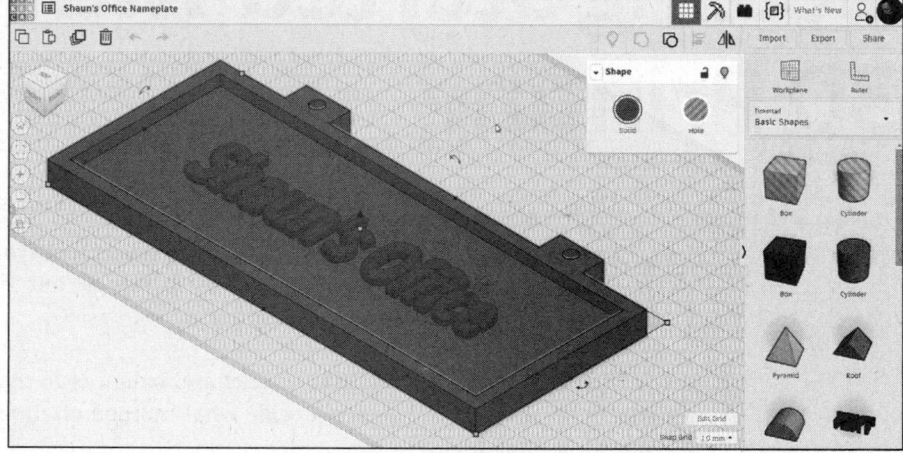

FIGURE 15-1: The nameplate selected as one object. The Shape dialog box indicates only one shape is selected also.

REMEMBER

Don't forget to check your text settings before committing to the 3D printing. Check the color, text, font, height, bevel, and segments to make sure that they're all what you want to them to be. You can't change them once you start the 3D print process!

Figure 15-2 shows the nameplate text selected with the settings in the Shape dialog box.

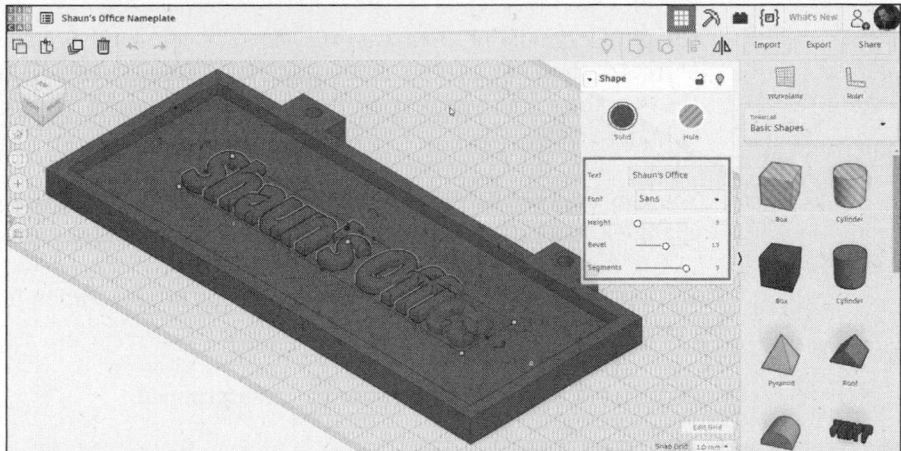

FIGURE 15-2:
The nameplate
text selected with
the settings in the
Shape dialog box
highlighted.

Tidying Up Your Design

You may think that your design is complete, with not a single issue. More often than not, that is not the case.

All designs have their flaws. It is only when you start to revisit and revise your designs that you see areas you can tweak. For example, you can fillet sharp edges to a smooth curved edge with a radius, and so on.

Elements of the nameplate design can even be tidied up a little. Take the holes for hanging the nameplate, for example. The hole surrounds are squared off, and you can make them softer with a curve by adding a nice bevel with segments set correctly.

For example, if you select the nameplate body and look at the shape in the Shape dialog box, you'll notice there is no option to adjust any curve, fillet radius, or anything else for that matter.

If you want curved soft edges, you need to ungroup all the shapes that make up the nameplate, edit each individual shape, and then group them again to join them all together as one shape again.

Sometimes, you may have used the Group command more than once during a workflow to get to your finished 3D design. This means that to get back to your starting point to perform a redesign, you may need to use the Ungroup command more than once to reverse the workflow.

A typical example of a redesign may be that you need to change the outer edge objects of the hanging holes on the nameplate. These were originally created using the Box shape, but you now want curved edges instead, and you want to use the Cylinder shape.

You can ungroup to the point where the original Box shape was used and then change it to a suitable Cylinder shape, adjusting the sizes accordingly.

You can then group the objects again, perhaps in preparation for a 3D print of the design.

Figure 15-3 shows the nameplate object ungrouped.

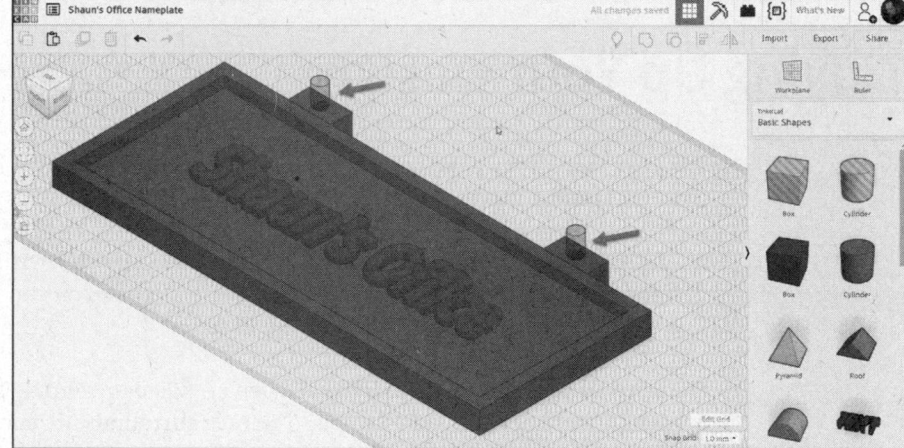

FIGURE 15-3:
The nameplate object ungrouped. Note that you can see the hole shapes and the joins between the solid shapes used.

Knowing What Type of File to Export

You need to consider what type of file you want from the outset. You need to be aware of what types of 3D print files are available and what will give you the best results.

You can export three types of files:

» **STL:** The best file format to download to if you want to use external 3D printing services or your own 3D printer. The majority of 3D CAD modelers support this format (just in case your design needs refining in a more complex modeler).

>> **OBJ:** Another great file format to use for external 3D printing services or your own 3D printer. However, OBJ is more complex than the STL file format, with the ability to represent textures and colors, too.

>> **SVG:** The perfect file format for laser cutting. If your 3D design requires many layers to be built up (a bit like the contour lines of a mountain on a map), with each layer requiring laser cutting, this file format is the one you need.

Choosing a Printing Option

You can also choose other options when printing your design, such as adding descriptions, tags, or even a URL link to share your design. The most important one, though, is that you can decide which 3D printing option you are going to use: Download for 3D Printing or Order 3D Print.

Figure 15-4 shows the dialog box where these two options are available.

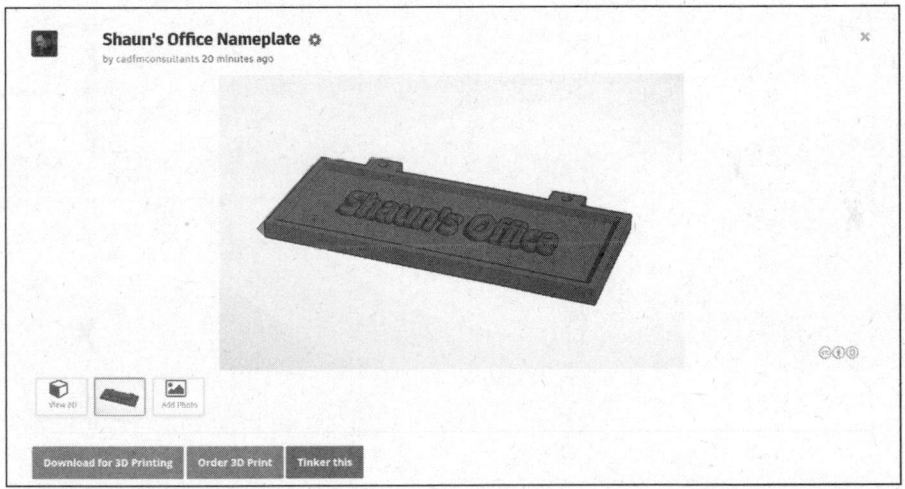

FIGURE 15-4:
The dialog box that gives you the options for 3D printing your Tinkercad design.

If you Download for 3D Printing, you can select which file type you want to download to so that you can print your design: STL, OBJ, or SVG. You can then send that filetype to a 3D printer and 3D print.

If you choose to Order 3D Print, you can choose from several 3D print providers through Tinkercad.

Figure 15-5 shows you the options you have for 3D print providers.

FIGURE 15-5:
The 3D print
providers
available through
Tinkercad should
you choose Order
3D Print in the
dialog box.

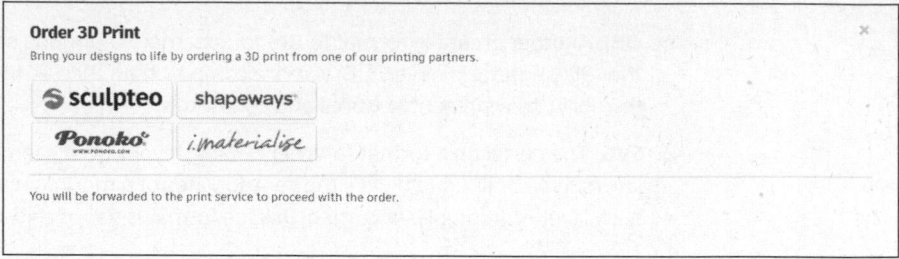

Order 3D Print
Bring your designs to life by ordering a 3D print from one of our printing partners.

sculpteo   shapeways

Ponoko   i.materialise

You will be forwarded to the print service to proceed with the order.

Exit your design screen by clicking on the Tinkercad logo (top left) so that you can see all of your designs.

To access 3D printing, simply click once on the design you want to print. In the dialog box that appears, simply select which Tinkercad 3D printing partner you want to use and click on the icon. Onscreen instructions guide you on what to do and how to pay for your 3D printing service.

Chapter **16**

3D Printing Selected Shapes

I n this chapter, you consider 3D printing selected parts of your 3D design and look into the possibilities of printing your design in parts, which makes the design interchangeable with different design and usage options.

In the case of your nameplate, you may consider 3D printing the nameplate base as one part, and the nameplate text as a separate part. Think about this. You could have designs for all different types of text to go on your nameplate and use magnets of Velcro to attach them.

The possibilities are endless with Tinkercad, right?

Selecting Specific Shapes from Your Design

Ideally, you want different designs for specific shapes that you want to 3D print. In the case of the nameplate, you want two designs: nameplate body and nameplate text.

TIP

Here's a little trick you can use: Use the Duplicate command to duplicate your nameplate design twice so that you have two copies. You can then use one copy for the nameplate body and one for the nameplate text and retain the original design as well. Figure 16-1 shows you where to find the Duplicate command so that you can duplicate your Tinkercad design.

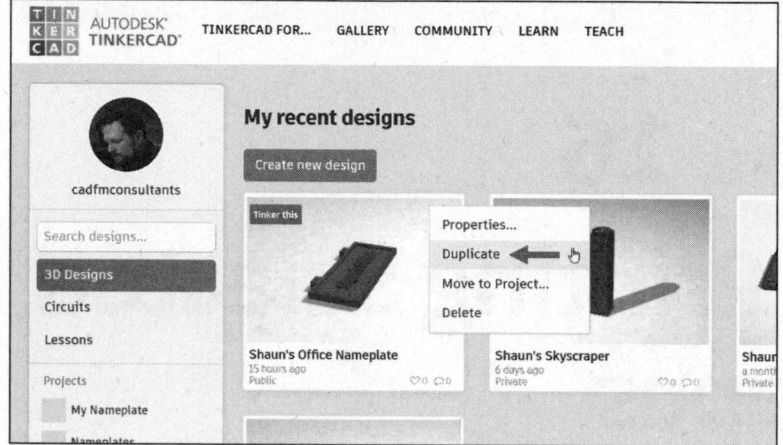

FIGURE 16-1:
Duplicating the
nameplate.

WARNING

Be aware that you have a Duplicate command both in your Tinkercad homepage and in your Tinkercad design screen, too. Don't get them confused! At this point, you are looking at duplicating designs on the Tinkercad homepage, not shapes within a Tinkercad design.

TIP

When you're duplicating designs in your Tinkercad homepage, it is always good practice to retain any original designs. Firstly, it means you always have a point of reference to refer back to from a design audit/archive perspective, and secondly, you just never know when you might need that design again!

You should now have two copies of your original nameplate design, as shown in Figure 16-2.

Rename the new copies of your nameplate design. Make sure you do this in the Properties dialog box for each new copy of your nameplate design.

I suggest using the following names:

>> NAMEPLATE – Nameplate Body

>> NAMEPLATE – Nameplate Text

FIGURE 16-2:
An excerpt of
the Tinkercad
homepage,
showing the
original nameplate
design (on the
right) and the
two dupliates
of the design.

This naming philosophy ties each design to the main nameplate design, but also allows for identification of each particular nameplate part: body and text.

TIP

You may also want to rename your original nameplate design as something like NAMEPLATE – Original Design, too.

Figure 16-3 shows all three Tinkercad design files named appropriately.

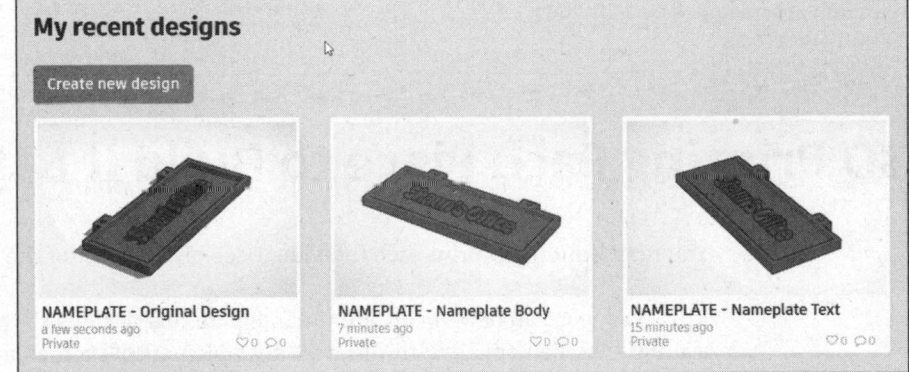

FIGURE 16-3:
All three
Tinkercad design
files renamed
appropriately.

Open up the NAMEPLATE – Nameplate Body design by hovering over it in the Tinkercad homepage and clicking on Tinker This.

Once you are in the Tinkercad design screen, simply delete the text object from the design. Yep, delete it!

Once you're done, click on the Tinkercad logo (top left) to return to the homepage.

Then, repeat the process for the NAMEPLATE – Nameplate Text design, but in this case, delete the nameplate body object.

Again, once you're done, click on the Tinkercad logo to return to the homepage.

You now have three Tinkercad designs: original, nameplate body, and nameplate text.

Figure 16-4 shows all three revised designs on the Tinkercad homepage, all named appropriately. Notice that the thumbnail views now show the appropriate design content, too.

My recent designs

Create new design

NAMEPLATE – Nameplate Body
a few seconds ago
Private

NAMEPLATE – Nameplate Text
a few seconds ago
Private

NAMEPLATE – Original Design
20 minutes ago
Private

FIGURE 16-4:
The three designs on the Tinkercad homepage, all named appropriately with the thumbnails showing the design content.

3D Printing Each Piece to Build It Later

You may want to 3D print each individual design as a part of the total design.

That way, you can develop different nameplate text designs so that you can make a multi-use nameplate with different text elements, such as a name, an office name, or a quote. The list is endless, and with Tinkercad, you could design any of these.

The nameplate design aligns itself to either the STL or OBJ file format for 3D printing:

>> **STL file format:** Use the STL file format if you want to consider importing your designs into another 3D modeler to refine your design and then 3D print. Typical modelers you might consider are Autodesk Inventor and Autodesk's Fusion 360.

>> **OBJ file format:** Use the OBJ file format to develop a more sophisticated 3D model that includes textures and colors. You might want your 3D print to have a metallic texture and color perhaps. Again, though, you can import the OBJ file format into other 3D modelers to refine the design further before 3D printing, if you want.

Printing Your Design

All you have to do now is select each separate design to 3D print so that you have component parts of the same original nameplate design.

From your Tinkercad homepage, click on each of the separate designs and then select the appropriate 3D printing option:

>> **Download for 3D Printing:** This option allows you to download your design into a particular file format. The nameplate design aligns itself to the STL and OBJ file formats, as it is a 3D design, not 2D. The SVG file format is primarily a 2D cutting file format.

>> **Order 3D Print:** This option allows you to order a 3D print from a suggested 3D printing partner. When you select this option, you see four 3D printing partner icons. Click on one and follow the onscreen instructions to order and pay for your 3D print.

Figure 16-5 shows one of the selected designs with the two 3D printing options at the bottom left of the Tinkercad screen.

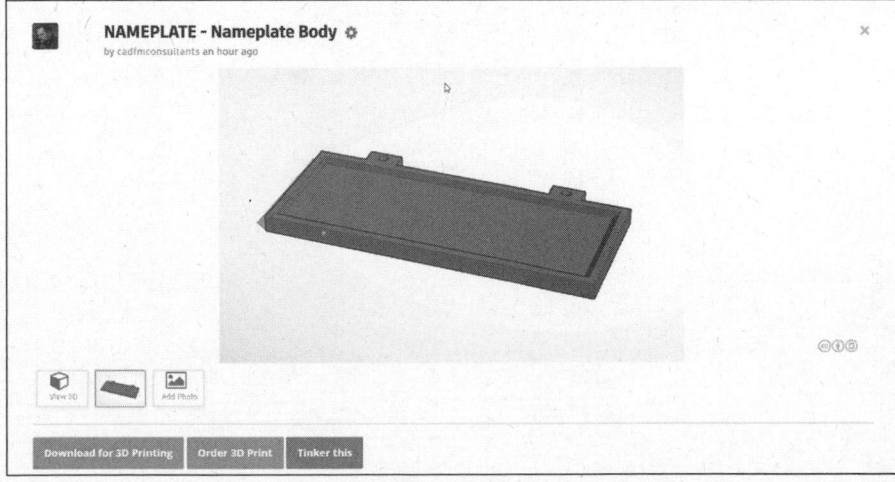

FIGURE 16-5: The dialog box that appears when you click on a design in the Tinkercad homepage. The two 3D printing options are bottom left.

Chapter **17**

STL Files

You are now at that final stage where 3D printing is going to go ahead and you want to export your design to the appropriate file format to get it 3D printed.

In this chapter, you find out exactly what an STL file is and how to export one out of Tinkercad based on one of your designs.

What Is an STL file?

STL is an abbreviation of STereoLithography and is a file format native to the stereolithography CAD software created by a company called 3D Systems. STL has several nicknames, including Standard Triangle Language and Standard Tessellation Language.

Many other 3D modelers use the STL file format as one of their native formats or as a file format for easy design interchange. Typical examples from Autodesk include Inventor and Fusion 360.

Figure 17-1 shows both a CAD representation and an STL representation of a 3D shape known as a *torus*. In a 3D view, a torus looks like a donut or a rubber ring a child might wear at the beach or at a swimming pool.

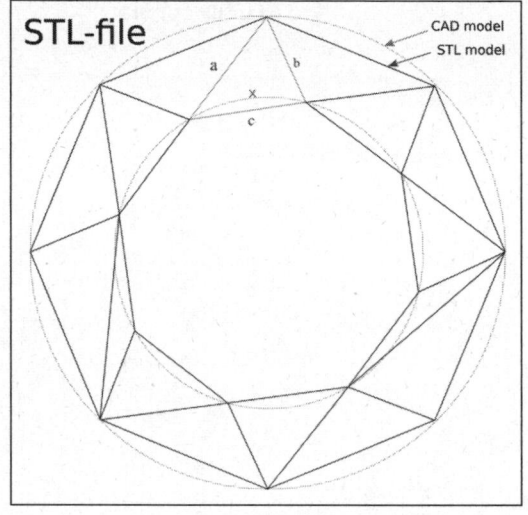

FIGURE 17-1:
A CAD representation of a torus and an STL approximation of the same shape.

The red circles in Figure 17-1 represent the CAD interpretation of the torus in a plan view (from the top), and the blue lines represent how an STL file would interpret those circles/curved faces. The angled lines of the STL file break down the circles/curves into triangles to allow for easier calculation/approximation of the STL file. The higher the definition of the STL file, the more triangles there would be.

Downloading as an STL File

In order to get your Tinkercad design to the STL file format, you need to select the appropriate Tinkercad design that you want to 3D print from your Tinkercad homepage. Note that you do not have to open your design using the *Tinker This* icon.

To get your design ready for 3D printing as a downloaded STL file, follow these steps:

1. **Hover over the chosen design on the Tinkercad homepage and click.**

2. **In the dialog box that appears, select the Download for 3D Printing option.**

   In the dialog box that appears, you can see the .STL button, as indicated in Figure 17-2.

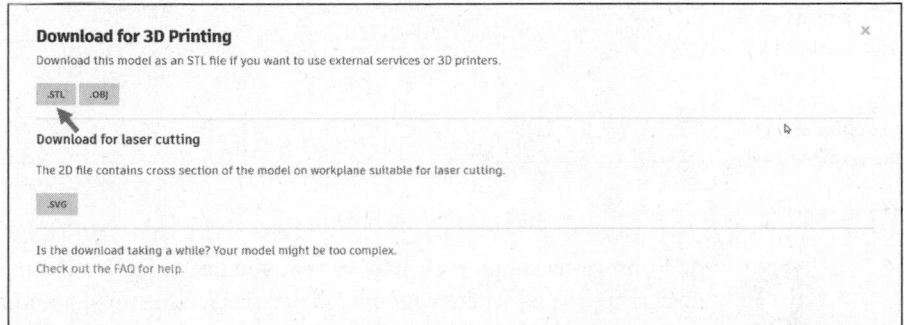

Download for 3D Printing

Download this model as an STL file if you want to use external services or 3D printers.

.STL .OBJ

Download for laser cutting

The 2D file contains cross section of the model on workplane suitable for laser cutting.

.SVG

Is the download taking a while? Your model might be too complex.
Check out the FAQ for help.

FIGURE 17-2:
The Download for 3D Printing dialog box with the .STL button indicated.

3. **In the Download for 3D Printing dialog box, select the .STL button to download your design as an STL file.**

   The file downloads in whichever browser you are using.

   In the case of the original nameplate design file, NAMEPLATE – Original Design, the STL file will be called NAMEPLATE – Original Design.stl. You can find the file in your folder used for downloads from your chosen browser.

   You can check out the STL file in the proprietary 3D Builder app that is part of the Windows 10 operating system. Just double-click on your exported STL file to get an idea of what it looks like.

   Figure 17-3 shows the downloaded STL file in the Microsoft app, 3D Builder.

   If you're using a Mac to work with Tinkercad, you can consider using STL Viewer 3D, which can be downloaded at minimal cost. There is also a free download-able viewer, simply called STL Viewer.

   You now have an exported STL file, ready for use in another 3D modeler or to be sent to the 3D printer to be 3D printed.

FIGURE 17-3:
The exported STL
file in the
Microsoft
proprietary app,
3D Builder.

TIP

As in previous chapters, it may be that you are going for the modular component design approach, where your overall design is made up of a number of subdesigns, such as the nameplate body and nameplate text being two separate designs within one design. In this case, you need to export an STL file for *each* design.

Chapter **18**

OBJ Files

W hen you're ready to print, it's important that you export your design to the appropriate file format to get it 3D printed.

In this chapter, you find out what an OBJ file is and how to export one out of Tinkercad based on one of your designs.

What Is an OBJ File?

The original OBJ file was first developed by a company called Wavefront Technologies. It is a geometry definition file format that was created for use with the Advanced Visualizer animation package created by Wavefront Technologies. It is an open file format, which has been adopted by several 3D modeling software vendors.

An OBJ file represents 3D geometry only in a simple data format in the file. In the file itself, you will find the geometry and coordinates of each point (known as a *vertex*), along with texture coordinate vertex UV position (for material surface mapping), vertex normal, and the faces of each polygon. Each polygon face is defined in the OBJ file as a list of *vertices* (plural of vertex), as well as a list of vertices for textures. The coordinates in an OBJ file have no defined units, but an OBJ file can contain scaling information.

Many 3D modelers, such as Blender, use the OBJ file format as one of their native formats or as a file format for easy design interchange.

Blender is another free 3D modeler available online from The Blender Foundation. It is much more sophisticated than Tinkercad and provides a 3D modeling application that can be used for professional purposes. Tinkercad is your entry-level 3D modeler, and you might consider graduating up to Blender after you are fully proficient with 3D modeling with Tinkercad, for example. Bear in mind that Blender is a downloaded application that you install and is not cloud-based like Tinkercad.

Blender is used for animation, visual effects, and (like Tinkercad) creating 3D models. It is also used in the development of video games, due to its integrated games engine.

Blender has other extensive features that include texturing, raster graphics editing, rigging, skinning, and fluid and smoke simulation. It can also sculpt and animate, too.

For more information on Blender, see Chapter 22.

Figure 18-1 shows a typical OBJ file after it has been imported into Blender.

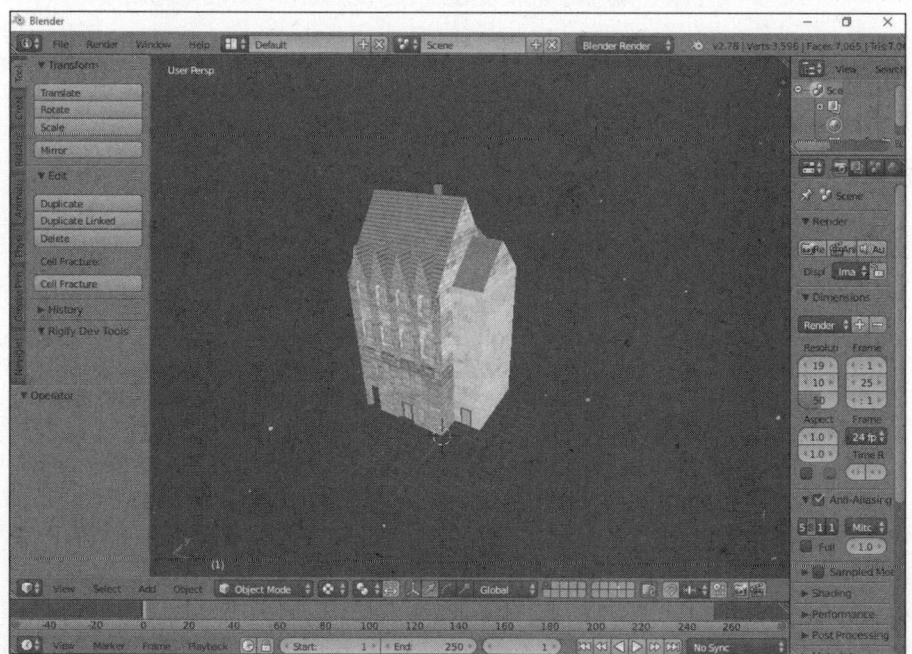

FIGURE 18-1:
A typical OBJ file after it has been imported into the 3D modeler Blender.

Credit: *http://blender.stackexchange.com.*

Downloading as an OBJ file

In order to get your Tinkercad design to the OBJ file format, you need to select the appropriate Tinkercad design that you want to 3D print from your Tinkercad homepage. Note that you do not have to open your design using the Tinker this icon.

To get your design ready for 3D printing as a downloaded OBJ file, follow these steps:

1. **Hover over the chosen design on the Tinkercad homepage and click.**

2. **In the dialog box that appears, select the Download for 3D Printing option.**

   Figure 18-2 shows the Download for 3D Printing dialog box with the .OBJ button highlighted.

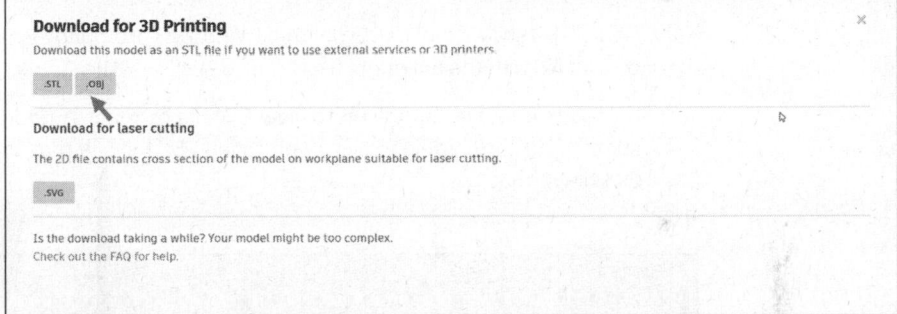

FIGURE 18-2:
The Download for 3D Printing dialog box with the .OBJ button indicated.

3. **In the Download for 3D Printing dialog box, select the .OBJ button to download your design as an OBJ file.**

   The file downloads as a ZIP file in your browser. In the case of the original nameplate design file, NAMEPLATE – Original Design, the OBJ file will be in a ZIP file called NAMEPLATE – Original Design.zip. You can find the file in your folder used for downloads from your chosen browser.

4. **Open the ZIP file.**

   You can use a program such as WinRAR to open a ZIP file. You can also open ZIP files natively in Windows 10 and on a Mac in Mac OS.

Opening a ZIP file natively on either operating system is pretty simple.

- **Windows:** Right-click on the appropriate ZIP file and choose Open with ⇨ Windows Explorer. You are then able to open the compressed file (or folder).

- **Mac OS:** Double-click on the appropriate ZIP file and the file (or folder) will be decompressed into the same folder the compressed file or folder is in.

In the zipped OBJ Tinkercad file are two files:

- **tinker.obj:** The Tinkercad geometry in the OBJ file format

- **obj.mtl:** The material geometry for the associated OBJ file. If any material geometry is associated with the OBJ file, keep it in the same folder as its associated OBJ file.

You can check out the OBJ file in the proprietary 3D Builder app that is part of the Windows 10 operating system.

5. **If the obj.mtl file is not in the same folder as the tinker.obj file, upload it at the 3D Builder prompt when you double-click on the tinker.obj file.**

Figure 18-3 shows the 3D Builder app (Windows) prompting you to load the obj.mtl file with the tinker.obj file.

If you are on a Mac and want to view OBJ file formats, Autodesk provides a superb OBJ compatible viewing app called FBX Review that supports the OBJ file format.

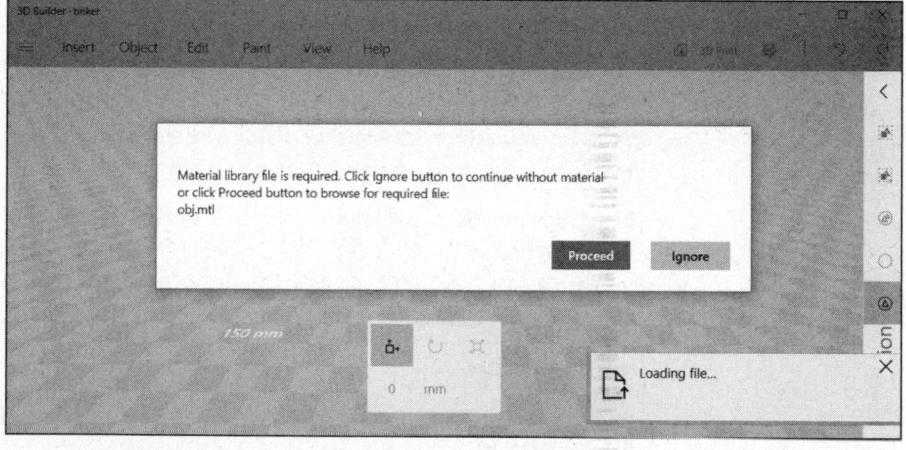

FIGURE 18-3: The Microsoft 3D Builder app, with the prompt asking for the obj.mtl to be loaded with the tinker.obj file.

Credit: Microsoft, Inc.

If you have made sure that both the tinker.obj file and the obj.mat file are in the same folder, 3D Builder will go ahead and load the tinker.obj file, using the textures mapped in the obj.mtl file.

Figure 18-4 shows the 3D Builder app (Windows) displaying the tinker.obj file with the textures (colors) map from the obj.mtl file.

FIGURE 18-4:
The exported OBJ file (tinker.obj) in the Microsoft proprietary app, 3D Builder, with the textures (colors) mapped from the obj.mtl file.

You now have an exported OBJ file, with its associated MTL file, all ready for use in another 3D modeler or to be sent to the 3D printer to be 3D printed.

Chapter **19**

SVG Files

I n this chapter, you find out exactly what an SVG file is and how to export one out of Tinkercad based on one of your designs.

What Is an SVG File?

An SVG file or Scalable Vector Graphics file is an eXtensible Markup Language (XML)–based vector image format, developed by the World Wide Web Consortium (W3C) in 1999.

SVG files are used primarily for 2D graphics with support for interactivity and animation and are an open source file standard, like the OBJ file format.

An SVG file comes out of Tinkercad as a 2D slice based on the location of the Workplane and allows you to take slices through a 3D Tinkercad design.

Extensible Markup Language (XML) allows the user to create a set of rules to code documents (XML files) that can be human-readable, but also (more importantly) machine-readable.

Due to this, all SVG files and their behavior are defined in XML text files. As XML files, SVG files can be created and edited with any text editor, as well as with drawing and modeling software.

An SVG file can be opened in most simple text editors to be read (human-readable). You can open an SVG file in Windows NotePad or NotePad++. You can even (although it is not really recommended) open an SVG file in Microsoft Word. In Windows, all you need to do is right-click on an SVG file, choose Open with from the menu, and then choose the text editor of your choice (as long as it is installed on your PC). If you are using a Mac, you can use the default Apple TextEdit or a proprietary text editor, as long as it is installed on your Mac. Alternatively, you can open SVG files by choosing a web browser instead of a text editor.

All modern browsers support the SVG file format and there are numerous software applications that support the SVG file format also. A typical example of this is Autodesk's Fusion 360.

Fusion 360 is another cloud-based 3D modeler from Autodesk, but is a more professional, industry-specific modeler. Tinkercad is entry-level. You may upgrade to using Fusion 360, after you become fully proficient on Tinkercad and understand 3D in more depth (if you will pardon the pun).

You may bring your SVG file into Fusion 360 to take your Tinkercad slice, refine it further, and then consider 3D printing it via Fusion 360. There are numerous workflows and methodologies where the SVG file can be used. That would be just one of them.

Figure 19-1 shows a typical imported SVG file in Autodesk's Fusion 360.

FIGURE 19-1:
A typical imported SVG file in the Autodesk application, Fusion 360.

Credit: Autodesk, Inc.

Downloading as an SVG file

In order to get your Tinkercad design to the SVG file format, you need to select the appropriate Tinkercad design that you want to slice. Imagine going to the butcher and asking for some slices of ham. The butcher will pick up the ham joint (the Tinkercad design) and then cut off some slices using a big slicing machine. Those ham slices represent the SVG file's 2D slices.

To get your design ready for 3D printing as a downloaded SVG file, follow these steps:

1. **Hover over the chosen design on the Tinkercad homepage and click.**

2. **In the dialog box that appears, select the Download for 3D Printing option.**

    Figure 19-2 shows the Download for 3D Printing dialog box with the .SVG button highlighted.

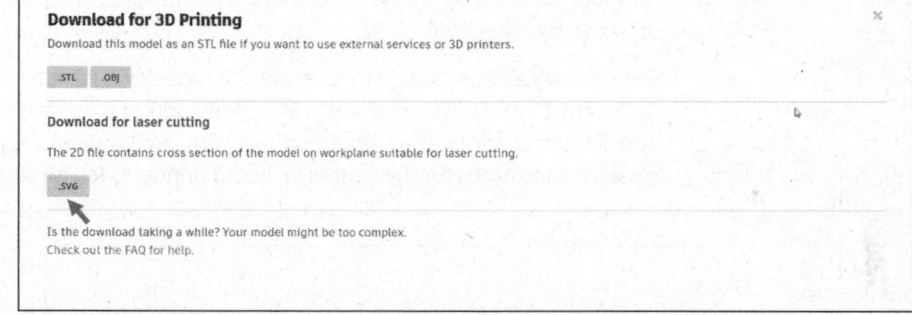

FIGURE 19-2:
The Download for
3D Printing dialog
box with the .SVG
button indicated.

3. **In the Download for 3D Printing dialog box, select the .SVG button to download your design as an SVG file.**

    Next to the .SVG button is text telling you that the SVG file will be a cross-section of the Tinkercad Workplane for laser cutting.

    Do you remember those cardboard dinosaurs you used to get as a kid? You know the ones that were made out of cardboard slices and you had to build up the dinosaur, slice by slice? Those slices are your SVG files. Each slice of the dinosaur is an individual SVG file, the location of the slice being where the Workplane is located in the 3D model.

The file downloads as an SVG file in your browser. In the case of the original nameplate design file, NAMEPLATE – Original Design, the SVG file will be called NAMEPLATE – Original Design.svg. You can find the file in your folder used for downloads from your chosen browser.

4. **Double-click on your exported SVG file to get an idea of what the slice looks like.**

TIP

Note that to get different shaped SVG file slices, you will need to adjust the Workplane in Tinkercad to go through the 3D design at the position you want your SVG slice. Figure 19-3 shows your Tinkercad slice in Google Chrome. Note that this is only one slice of many in your 3D design.

Now you may think to yourself, "Do I have to export every single slice from Tinkercad?" The simple answer is no. There are numerous apps available (free or at cost) that can look at your 3D model in Tinkercad and then create many SVG files based on the thickness of each layer (slice) in your model. These can then be fed into a 3D cutting machine in order to create the 3D print you need, but in slices of wood, cardboard, plastic, or any material.

A typical slicing app is called Slic3r, and it can be downloaded from the Internet for most operating systems. You can find Slic3r at http://manual.slic3r.org/intro/overview.

Basically, what Slic3r does is to take your 3D model and translate it into the SVG format, which, in turn, allows a 3D cutting printer to understand the files. The 3D cutting printer then slices up the model into horizontal layers and generates the paths for the cutters in the 3D printer to follow.

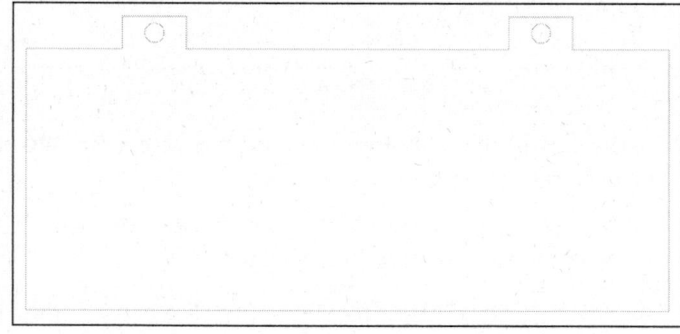

FIGURE 19-3:
An SVG slice loaded in Google Chrome. Note that it is a single-line, flat, 2D image.

You now understand how to generate an exported SVG file (slice), all ready for use in another 3D modeler or to be sent to the 3D printer to be cut. Apps, such as Slic3r, will create all of those slices of your 3D design for you.

And just for those of you who loved those dinosaurs made from slices, there is a hippo constructed in a similar fashion in Figure 19-4.

FIGURE 19-4:
A typical cardboard model of a hippo made from slices that have been laser cut using an SVG file per slice.

5

The Part of Tens

Discover 3D printing materials and how they work with 3D printers to create your 3D designs.

Find out how 3D printers work.

Discover alternative 3D modeling applications and the software companies that provide them.

Chapter **20**

Ten Great 3D Printing Materials

I n this chapter, you find out about the ten greatest 3D printing materials, as suggested by the Tinkercad team at Autodesk.

A lot of this information, including a number of figures, actually comes from the Tinkercad blog page over at https://blog.tinkercad.com/materialsguide. It is a useful guide when you consider 3D printing your Tinkercad designs.

Here are the ten great materials that the guys at Tinkercad recommend.

Choosing a Material

It is often really tough to decide on what materials to use when 3D printing. You should consider numerous factors, including the

» Type of material

» Minimum thickness of the printed material

>> Texture of the printed material

>> Cost of the material (probably the most important)

The cost also depends on whether the 3D print will be a prototype for a design, a gift, or even a product to sell. You need to consider all of the preceding factors, regardless of whether you are a business expecting to create multiple 3D prints as products, or a hobbyist just 3D printing because you can.

Choosing a material all comes down to the bottom line, and that is cost. In manufacturing, the cost of raw materials has always been the make-or-break factor as to whether a particular product could be designed, manufactured, and then sold to cover those material costs and overhead. As you progress into 3D printing, you will see this factor's impact.

TIP

Create a simple spreadsheet that lists materials, volumes of those materials, costs of the materials purchased, and the amount of material used per 3D design. You can then calculate how much each 3D print costs. Then factor in your time to design the 3D printed object, and 3D print the object and then add a nominal hourly rate for your time. Sure, you may be a hobbyist, but this experience will stand you in good stead if you ever decide to start selling your 3D prints. You never know. The Internet is an amazing place where starting small often ends up big, so never stop designing!

Nylon (Polyamide)

Nylon (polyamide) comes in a raw powder format that is normally white, but it can be dyed, sprayed, or smoothed to pretty much any 3D print of any 3D design. It is also known as white plastic, durable plastic, or strong plastic.

When 3D printing, the laser in the 3D printer melts the nylon powder in layers that are microns thick at exactly 170°C (338°F), thus giving you incredible flexibility in your 3D printing of your design due to this incredible accuracy. This is known as *laser sintering.*

Laser sintering can sometimes take up to one and a half days on a complex 3D print, and the cooldown period can take up to two days. After that time, you can touch the print, which will often be a large block of the white nylon powder that you have to dig into, to find your 3D print.

According to the Tinkercad materials guide, nylon polyamide has a 1 mm minimum wall thickness and is naturally white, but can be colored, if required. It normally 3D prints about 10 layers per 1mm in a 3D printer. As it is made from a powder, it can be used to 3D print alumide, which is polyamide plus aluminum, thus creating a metallic polymer that is strong but flexible. It can be used for interlocking, movable parts, such as a chain, and regular nylon polyamide can be used for simple plastic components, such as phone cases. The guys at Tinkercad created Tinkercad-branded phone cases for promotional purposes, and you can see them in the Tinkercad materials guide, shown in Figure 20-1.

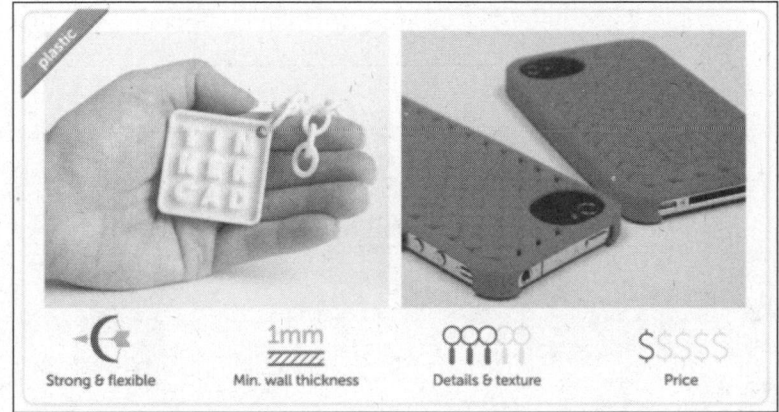

FIGURE 20-1: The Tinkercad materials guide for nylon (polyamide).

ABS (Home Printers)

ABS stands for Acrylonitrile Butadiene Styrene and is often used in home-based 3D printing.

ABS is classified as a *thermoplastic*, which means the ABS softens to be molded when heated and hardens when cooled. ABS has been widely used in many industries because of its ability to take on many forms and maintain high quality in those forms.

ABS can endure extreme weather and is also chemical resistant. Due to those qualities, ABS forms many of the products you use or encounter on a daily basis.

ABS plastics are a core ingredient to 3D printing. Companies, hobbyists, and 3D printing enthusiasts will always continue their search for the holy grail of 3D printing materials, but ABS will come pretty close. The overall quality of ABS prints are hardness, toughness, electrical insulation properties, and gloss, which give it incredible durability in the real world. ABS can also be printed to have a certain level of resistance and toughness to meet specific standards needed for a specific product or design to be considered usable.

Many other 3D printing materials can be used to create the aesthetics wanted by 3D designers, but ABS is still preferred by engineers and makers who want to accomplish the mechanical use of the 3D print they create.

The Tinkercad materials guide states that ABS is a very strong, durable plastic, similar to the plastic that Lego bricks are made from. It is formed of a spaghetti-like filament with many color options, and it normally 3D prints to about 3 layers per 1mm and has a 1mm minimum wall thickness. Figure 20-2 shows 3D prints made from ABS, as shown in the Tinkercad materials guide.

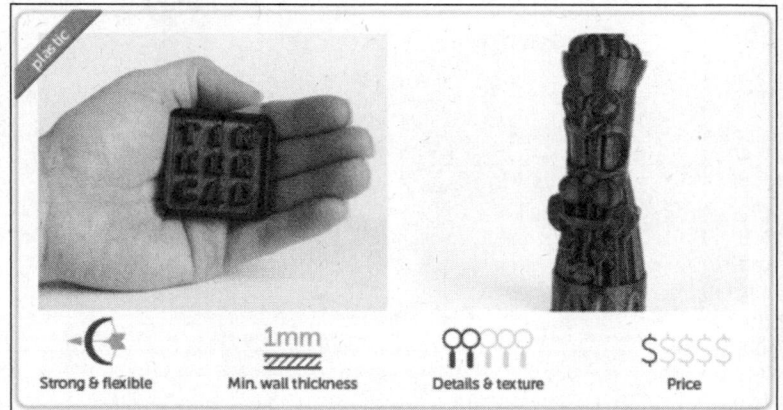

FIGURE 20-2: The Tinkercad materials guide for ABS.

Resin (Multiple Options)

Instead of using powder or filament, STL files use a liquid resin to produce 3D prints. It is a liquid material, so more often than not, you will need to provide a support structure for overhanging parts and cavities.

A resin 3D print is created in a tank filled with liquid resin. The 3D printing process starts with a layer of UV-sensitive liquid polymer being spread over a platform. A UV laser is then used to harden selected parts of the liquid, hardening where the laser beam strikes. The remaining material remains a liquid. Then, the platform is lowered, making room for the next layer of polymer to be drawn (hardened) on top of the previous one. This process is repeated until the 3D model is complete. The supports, for overhanging parts and cavities, are automatically generated, and once the process is finished, the 3D model can be raised out of the tank and the supports removed.

Resin comes in five forms:

>> Standard resin

>> Gray resin

>> Mammoth resin

>> Transparent resin

>> High detail resin

The names of each type of resin are self-explanatory: Standard resin is translucent, gray resin gives a gray metallic finish, mammoth resin allows for larger 3D prints, transparent resin has a glass-like quality, and high detail resin allows for a high level of detail in the 3D model.

The Tinkercad materials guide states that resin comes in many options. You can have white, black, or transparent resin. There is white detail resin, high detail resin, and transparent, paintable resin. It can be rigid and sometimes delicate. It is a liquid photopolymer cured with ultraviolet (UV) light. It comes in white and black and most typical colors. It 3D prints to about 10 layers per 1mm and has a 1mm minimum wall thickness. Figure 20-3 shows some resin prints from the Tinkercad materials guide.

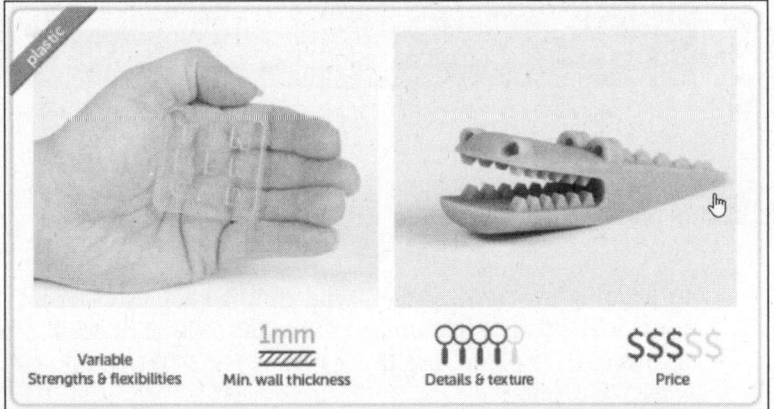

FIGURE 20-3:
The Tinkercad materials guide for resin.

Resin (Paintable)

Paintable resin provides all of the qualities of resin (see preceding section), but it has a rougher surface that provides a key for paint and color. To paint on a 3D model effectively, you need a *key*, which is a slightly rougher surface that allows the paint to adhere to that surface.

The maker and hobbyist communities love paintable resin because they can 3D print a design and then apply colored paints to give the 3d print realism and make it look real world. Numerous fantasy modeling communities around the world have jumped into the world of 3D printing so that they can model, 3D print, and paint fantasy characters from the likes of Marvel Comics and DC Comics and use them for ornaments, board gaming figures, and mascots for their desks.

Refer to the preceding section to see what the Tinkercad guys have to say about resin as a 3D printing material. Figure 20-4 shows an action figure made from paintable resin to give you an idea of what it would look like before and after painting.

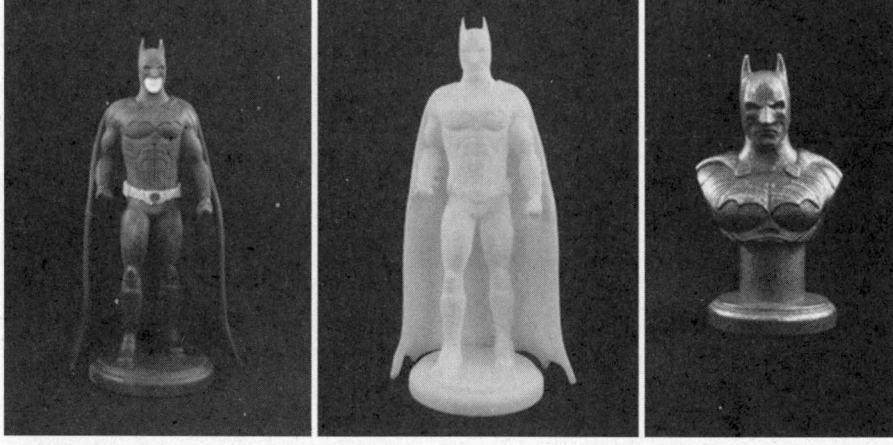

FIGURE 20-4:
An action figure made from paintable resin, both painted and unpainted.

Credit: https://i.materialise.com.

Stainless Steel

3D printing in stainless steel (type 316L) combines excellent surface quality 3D prints with great resolution and a significant level of detail. Stainless steel is not as strong as titanium, but it does allow for better detail and thinner walls at a much lower price.

As with nylon (polyamide), the 3D printing technology prints a stainless steel model by binding together layers of ultra-fine grains of stainless steel powder in an inkjet-like printer. A layer of stainless steel powder is spread across the base of what is called a build box, and then a special print head moves back and forth over that layer, depositing a binding agent at specific points, as directed by a computer and your design file, such as a Tinkercad design. Once that layer is finished and has been dried with heaters, a new layer of powder is spread, and the process begins again. Layer by layer, your part is created.

Once the 3D printing is complete, the 3D model is carefully taken out, and any extra powder that was not bound is removed. The printed part is still fragile, and this *green state* is then followed by being sintered in an oven at 1300°C, in either sand or on a ceramic plate. Sand is used for designs that are irregular and don't have a flat base, and the ceramic plate is used more often for technical pieces with a flat base.

After cooling, the 3D model is put into a mechanical polishing machine for finishing.

The Tinkercad materials guide states that stainless steel is a very strong 3D printing material. It is normally 3D printed in multiple steps or directly from a powder medium. It has various coloring options, including gold and bronze plating, and normally 3D prints to about six layers per 1mm and has a 3mm minimum wall thickness. Figure 20-5 shows you some 3D stainless steels prints from the Tinkercad materials guide.

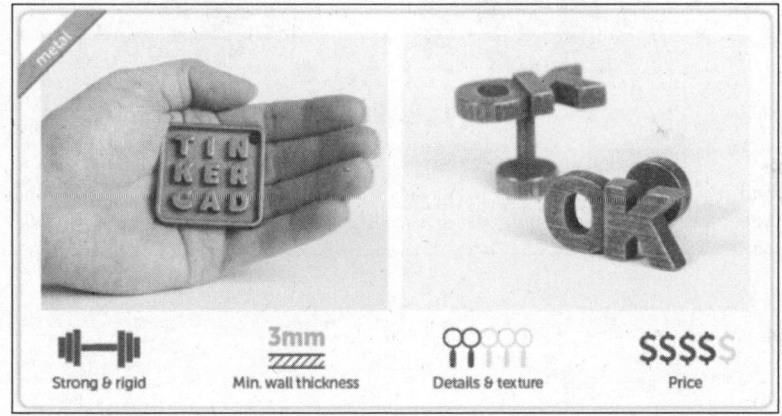

FIGURE 20-5: The Tinkercad materials guide for stainless steel.

Gold

Gold is rarely 3D printed directly. Most often, gold is printed using a wax 3D print with lost wax casting process. This process uses STL files with a wax-like resin. Support structures are printed along with the model (which is often quite delicate) to ensure that the model does not fall apart during the process. These support structures are normally automatically generated and manually removed once the printing process is complete.

The 3D wax cast (which is normally the original 3D design) is covered in a fine plaster, which, once solidified, is put in an oven until the wax has completely burned away (the lost wax casting). Gold is poured into the empty plaster cast, creating a 3D printed gold model. The model is then normally polished and finished manually.

Gold is often used to create 3D printed jewelry and is of high cost as a raw material, hence it is rarely, if ever, 3D printed for that reason.

The Tinkercad materials guide classes gold as an incredibly strong 3D printed material, using a highly expensive 3D printing process, due to the amount of material that is wasted to form the end result. The wax used for the lost wax casting normally prints at about 10 layers per 1mm and has a 0.5mm minimum wall thickness. Figure 20-6 shows you some 3D gold prints from the Tinkercad materials guide.

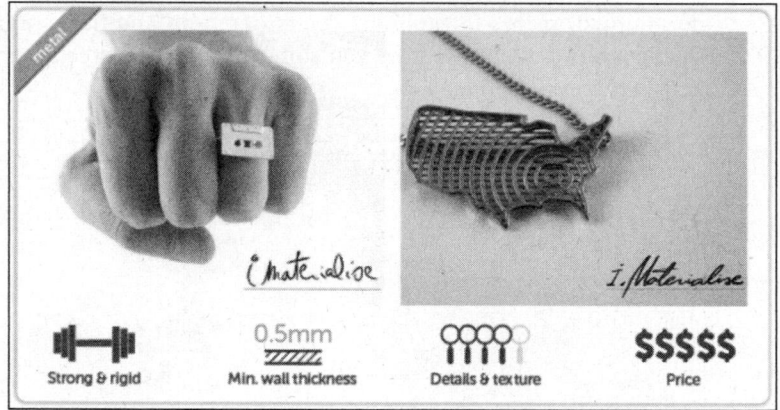

FIGURE 20-6:
The Tinkercad materials guide for gold.

Silver

As with gold (see preceding section), wax 3D printing and lost-wax casting are used to build your design when using silver. The wax printing process uses STL files with the same wax-like resin with support structures that are printed along with the model to make sure the 3D model doesn't fall apart. These support structures are automatically generated and manually removed after the printing process. After the support structures are removed and the model is cleaned, the model can be prepared for casting.

One or more wax sprues will be attached to your model. Then, the sprue(s) and model will be attached to a wax tree, together with a bunch of other models. The tree is then placed in a flask and covered in fine plaster. The solidified plaster forms the mold for silver casting. It is then put in an oven where the wax is completely burned out.

Molten silver is poured to fill the cavities left behind by the wax. Once the silver has cooled and solidified, the plaster mold is broken (carefully!) to get at the silver models, which are removed manually. The model is then filed and sanded to lose the sprues and then sanded, polished, or sandblasted to achieve the appropriate finish. Silver, 3D printed in this way, is often used for jewelry, such as rings, cufflinks, bracelets, pendants, and earrings.

Here are some interesting things you may not know about silver:

» Pure silver is too soft for durable jewelry, so an alloy is added to harden it for longer wear.

» Due to lost-wax casting and printing being used in the production of silver, interlocking or enclosed parts are not possible.

» Sterling silver is a standard alloy used for jewelry purposes and, for this reason, is safe to wear on your skin.

» The fine quality of a 3D printed silver model is comparable to the kind of jewelry you can find in jewelry stores.

» Silver is made up of 93 percent silver, 4 percent copper, and 3 percent zinc.

The Tinkercad materials guide classes silver, like gold, as another incredibly strong 3D printed material. The process used to create 3D prints made from silver is the same as gold.

It is actually possible to 3D print directly with silver and gold, but it costs tens of thousands of dollars, which is why the processes described are more cost-effective. It also allows for wax prototypes to be made before the casting is done in order to ensure that the design has full integrity before any silver or gold is used.

The company ZMorph has a superb article on *Medium* about a jeweler who 3D prints her designs to create a unique jewelry range. You can find ZMorph on Medium at `https://medium.com/@ZMorph`. Simply search for the article on 3D printed jewelry. Figure 20-7 shows you some of the ZMorph 3D printed jewelry designs that can be made.

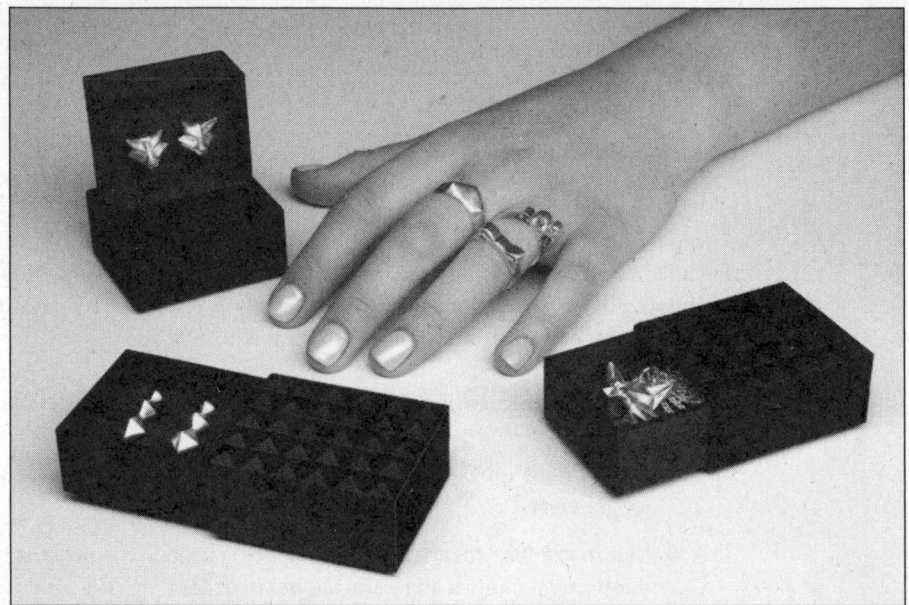

FIGURE 20-7:
The 3D printed jewelry range mentioned in the ZMorph article on `Medium.com`.

Credit: `https://medium.com/@ZMorph`.

Titanium

Titanium is a metal used for 3D printing because it has numerous advantages over many other 3D printed metals. It is lightweight and, mechanically, very strong. More importantly, though, it is biocompatible and resists corrosion very well, hence its extensive use in high-tech fields, such as aeronautics and space exploration, and in the medical field.

3D printing with titanium has many advantages over traditional manufacturing methods. When it comes to complexity of titanium 3D printed parts, titanium can produce complex shapes that otherwise may not be possible. This creates many design possibilities and parts optimization.

Titanium parts that are 3D printed always retain their mechanical properties when batch produced, reducing the need for welding, which can sometimes create impurities and areas of weakness in a design. It also reduces production time and gives increased flexibility because 3D printing takes away several of the traditional manufacturing steps, allowing parts to be produced (sometimes) in hours, not days.

Titanium is an expensive metal, and traditional methods can produce titanium waste, which can quickly increase raw material costs. 3D printing keeps waste to a minimum, which keeps raw material costs down. However, titanium 3D printing is still expensive. The 3D printing industry needs more innovation and invention to overcome these challenges and improve the 3D printing technology — for example, reducing the cost of titanium powder, which is used for 3D printing.

The Tinkercad materials guide classes titanium as the strongest material used for 3D printing. It is 3D printed using a process called Direct Metal Laser Sintering (DMLS), where an STL file is used by the DMLS operator to orientate the model geometry and add support structures where needed. Once this build file is complete, it is then sliced into the appropriate layer thicknesses for the 3D printing process to begin. DMLS uses titanium powder that is fused in to the 3D print by the laser. It can print up to 30 layers per 1mm and has an incredible 0.2mm minimum wall thickness. Figure 20-8 shows you some 3D printed titanium designs from the Tinkercad materials guide.

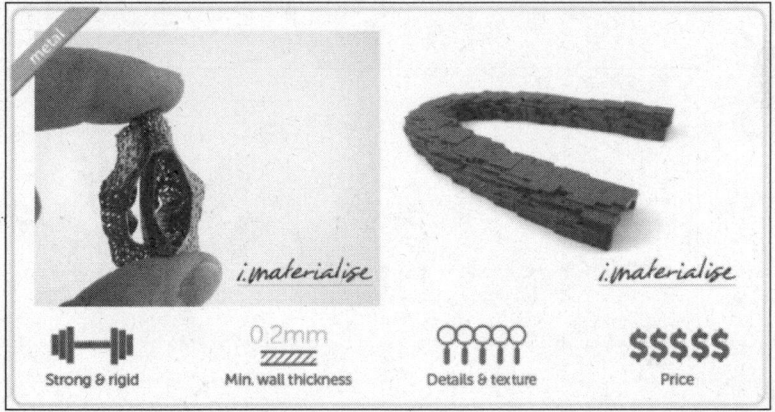

FIGURE 20-8: The Tinkercad materials guide for titanium.

Ceramic

Ceramic 3D printing is done using specially designed 3D printers. The printers use ceramic powder, placed on a powder bed to build a model, layer by layer, from bottom to top. The ceramic powder is made up of miniscule, ultra-fine particles of alumina silica ceramic. Once finished, the 3D print is removed and placed in a drying oven. This drying process strengthens the 3D print, but it is still fragile. Once drying is completed, the model is fired as it would be traditionally in an oven, followed by a preglazing coating. It is then fired again, glazed, and put through the final firing, to set the glaze, just like traditional ceramics.

Ceramic 3D prints have good thermal properties, but the high melting point can be a challenge when 3D printing is involved. Ceramics, unlike metals and thermoplastics, do not easily fuse together when heat is applied to them. They can resist high temperatures of up to 600°C (1112°F) which means they are suitable for 3D printing different objects but can undergo various finishing processes like other materials.

Ceramic 3D printing creates objects that are expected to have superior qualities compared to their traditional counterparts. In addition to printing ceramic household objects, such as tableware and cooking utensils, scientific lab equipment with the ability to withstand high temperatures can also be 3D printed.

The Tinkercad materials guide states that ceramics, as a 3D printed material, are rigid and delicate and are often used to 3D print decorative items, such as homewares. When a ceramic 3D print is first printed, it is often a ceramic white, which is then glazed to give it color. Ceramics normally 3D print to about six layers per 1mm, with a 3mm minimum wall thickness. Figure 20-9 shows some ceramic 3D prints from the Tinkercad materials guide.

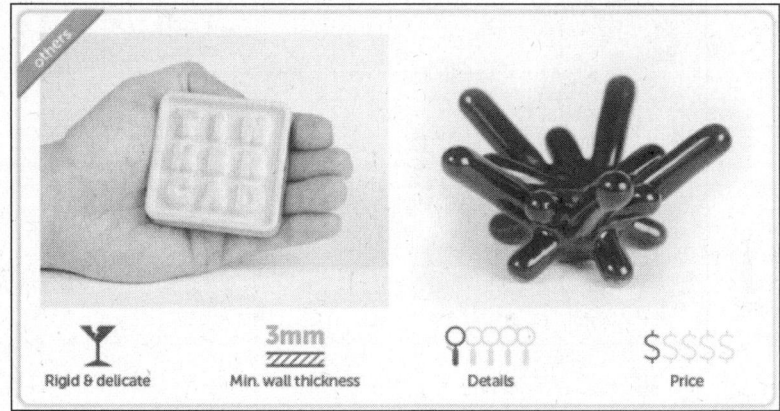

FIGURE 20-9: The Tinkercad materials guide for ceramic.

Gypsum

Gypsum is used in powder form when 3D printing. A technology called powder binding is often used with gypsum to create 3D prints. The powder binding technique was invented at MIT in 1993. It is an additive manufacturing (AM) method that works by solidifying a powder with a binder. In 1995, the American company Z Corporation obtained the exclusive rights to this technology, and in 2012, it was acquired by 3D systems, which renamed the company to ColorJet Printing.

Like with all 3D printing techniques, the 3D object must be pre-modeled using a CAD software, such as Tinkercad. The model is then exported to the printing software, which instructs the 3D printer on what to do with the 3D model.

In order to use powder binding with gypsum, a 3D powder binding printer is needed. These printers are made up of two tanks and a platform (bed) where the printer prints the object. When the 3D printing process starts, one of the tanks is empty, while the second tank holds the powdered printing material (in this case, the gypsum). The 3D printing then begins by lowering the platform upon which the first layer of gypsum powder is spread by a leveling roller. The gypsum is then solidified with a binder and colored according to the instructions that have been transmitted to the computer. The platform gets lower and lower, creating a new layer of powder each time, which will then be spread and bound in turn by the binder. Layer by layer, the 3D print takes shape in this way.

The Tinkercad materials guide states that gypsum is also called sandstone, rainbow ceramics, or multicolor ceramics. It is a rigid and delicate 3D printed material, made from powder. Normally, it is naturally white, but it can be obtained in colors for 3D printing as well. It normally 3D prints to about 10 layers per 1mm, and has a 2mm minimum wall thickness. Figure 20-10 shows you some typical 3D gypsum prints in the Tinkercad materials guide.

FIGURE 20-10: The Tinkercad materials guide for gypsum.

You can download the Tinkercad materials guide, in PDF format, at the following link:

```
https://blogdottinkercaddotcom.files.wordpress.com/2012/06/material_guide.pdf
```

Chapter **21**

Ten Great 3D Printers

This chapter gives you ten of the more commonly available 3D printers. The list is not exhaustive, and many other models are out there.

Factors to Consider When Choosing a 3D Printer

You need to consider many aspects of 3D printing when purchasing a 3D printer, including

» **Materials:** What materials are supported, and are they cheaper and accessible?

» **Time to print:** How long does a simple 3D model take to print?

» **Colors:** Does the 3D printer support colored materials?

» **Size:** What size of model can be printed?

» **Software:** Does the printer need specific software to print?

» **Connectivity:** Does the printer support WiFi/Internet/Bluetooth?

» **Power:** What sort of power requirements does the printer have or require?

All these factors are important. I provide this information, when available, for each printer in this chapter so that you can make an informed decision.

If you are going to consider getting your own 3D printer, be sure to examine all the marketplace has to offer and make sure you invest in one that fulfills all of your needs and requirements, as they are quite an investment financially.

Quite simply, do your research.

Ultimaker: Ultimaker 2+

```
https://ultimaker.com/en/products/ultimaker-2-plus
```

The Ultimaker 2+ is a highly engineered, robust 3D printer. It is quoted as being reliable, efficient, and user-friendly. It supports a wide range of materials, including nylon and ABS, and is suitable for most 3D printing applications, such as prototypes, all the way up to customized tools. It is seen as one of the best all-around 3D printers on the market and provides consistent 3D prints.

Factors to consider:

>> **File support:** STL, OBJ, X3D, 3MF, G, GCODE, BMP, GIF, JPG, and PNG.

>> **Materials:** PLA, ABS, CPE, CPE+, PC, Nylon, TPU 95A, and PP.

>> **Time to print:** Data not available.

>> **Colors:** Most colors available based on material support.

>> **Size of model:** 223 x 223 x 205 mm (8.8 x 8.8 x 8.1 inches).

>> **Software:** Ultimaker Cura (Windows, Mac OS, and Linux).

>> **Connectivity:** Standalone 3D printing from SD card (included).

>> **Power:** 100 to 240V, 4A, 50 to 60Hz, 221 W max.

Figure 21-1 shows a typical image of the Ultimaker 2+.

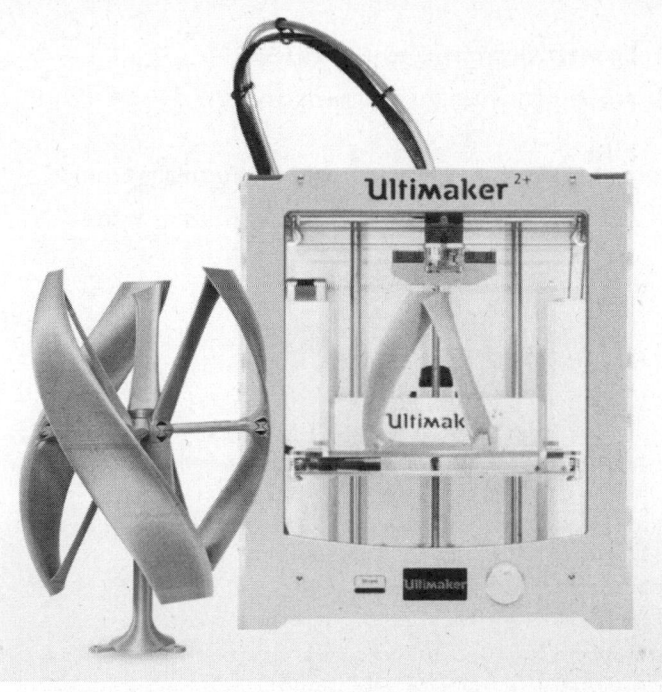

Credit: *https://ultimaker.com/en.*

Formlabs: Form 2

https://formlabs.com/3d-printers/form-2/

The Formlabs Form 2 is another popular 3D printer out there in the maker/hobbyist community. It provides industrial standard 3D printing at a fraction of the cost and offers high resolution 3D prints that support the STL file format. It also has a unique automated resin tank fill system that automatically ensures that you have resin all the time when 3D printing.

Factors to consider:

>> **File support:** STL and OBJ file support.

>> **Materials:** Formlabs provide an entire range of resins.

>> **Time to print:** Data not available.

>> **Colors:** Most colors available based on material support.

>> **Size of model:** 145 x 145 x 175mm (5.7 x 5.7 x 6.9 inches).

>> **Software:** PreForm software (Windows and Mac OS).

» **Connectivity:** WiFi, Ethernet, and USB.

» **Power:** 100 to 240 V, 1.5A, 50to 60 Hz, 65 W.

Figure 21-2 shows a typical image of the Formlabs Form 2.

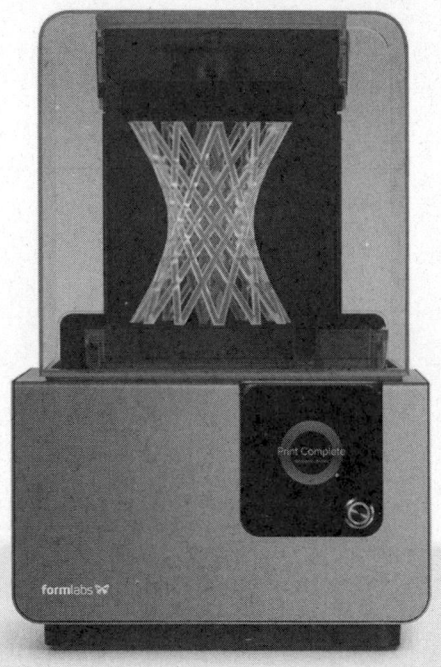

FIGURE 21-2:
The Formlabs
Form 2.

Zortrax: Zortrax M200

https://zortrax.com/printers/zortrax-m200/

The Zortrax M200 was a crowd-funded 3D printer, funded by a Kickstarter campaign. It won the hearts of thousands of users very quickly with its reliability and efficiency. It is very competitively priced in the maker space, putting itself up against other 3D printers that are more expensive but giving the same incredible depth of precision. It works in an integrated system and can be used with a wide selection of professional materials with a variety of qualities and colors.

Factors to consider:

» **File support:** STL, OBJ, DXF, and 3MF.

» **Materials:** Own brand materials: Z-ULTRAT, Z-HIPS, Z-ABS, and Z-GLASS.

» **Time to print:** Data not available.

» **Colors:** Most colors available based on material support.

» **Size of model:** 200 x 200 x 180mm (7.9 x 7.9 x 7.1 inches).

» **Software:** Z-SUITE software (Windows and Mac OS).

» **Connectivity:** SD card (included).

» **Power:** 110 V ~ 4 A, 50 to 60 Hz, 240 V ~ 1.7 A 50/60 Hz.

Figure 21-3 shows a typical image of the Zortrax M200.

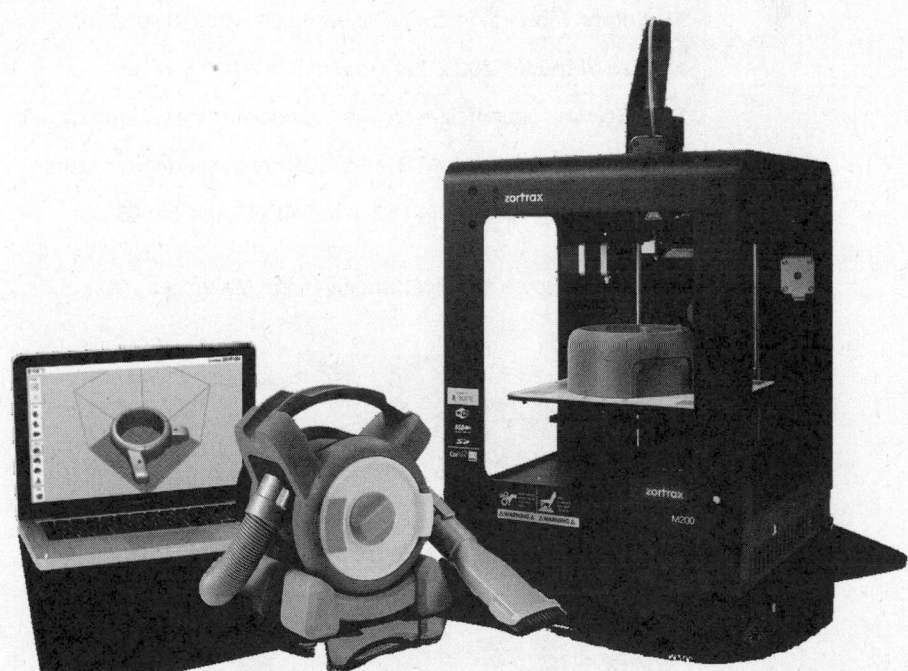

FIGURE 21-3:
The Zortrax M200.

Credit: www.zortrax.com.

Makergear: Makergear M2

https://www.makergear.com/products/m2

The Makergear M2 is a modular 3D printer made up of high-quality components, all manufactured in the United States, and built to a high standard. The Makergear M2 is often regarded as the best 3D printer for industrial-level precision but for an affordable price. One of the main reasons is that it is modular. This means that if any part needs to be replaced, it can be done so quickly and easily, which reduces any downtime.

Factors to consider:

>> **File support:** Numerous recognized file formats.

>> **Materials:** PLA, ABS, PET, HIPS, HDPE, TPU, polycarbonate, and composite.

>> **Time to print:** Data not available.

>> **Colors:** Most colors available based on material support.

>> **Size of model:** 200 x 250 x 200 mm (8 x 10 x 8 inches).

>> **Software:** Simplify3D software (Windows, Mac OS, and Linux).

>> **Connectivity:** SD Card Reader, USB connection to computer.

>> **Power:** 100 to 120 V (4 A)/220 to 240 V (2 A), 47 to 63 Hz.

Figure 21-4 shows a typical image of the Makergear M2.

FIGURE 21-4:
The Makergear M2.

Credit: www.makergear.com.

Aleph Objects: LulzBot TAZ 6

`www.lulzbot.com/store/printers/lulzbot-taz-6`

The LulzBot TAZ 6 is seen as one of the most reliable and easy-to-use 3D printers in the maker space at the moment. It is self-leveling and self-cleaning and has a modular tool head for flexible and multi-material upgrades. It has one of the largest print volumes in its class and has easy-to-use printing technology suited to intermediate users of 3D printing.

Factors to consider:

>> **File support:** STL, OBJ, and GCODE.

>> **Materials:** PLA, ABS, nylon (polyamide), and many more.

>> **Time to print:** Data not available.

>> **Colors:** Most colors available based on material support.

>> **Size of model:** 280 x 280 x 250 mm (11.02 x 11.02 x 9.8 inches).

>> **Software:** Cura LulzBot software (Windows, Mac OS, and Linux).

>> **Connectivity:** SD Card Reader, 4GB SD card (included).

>> **Power:** 100 to 240 V AC. 5.3 A (US), 2.65 A (EU).

Figure 21-5 shows a typical image of the LulzBot TAZ 6.

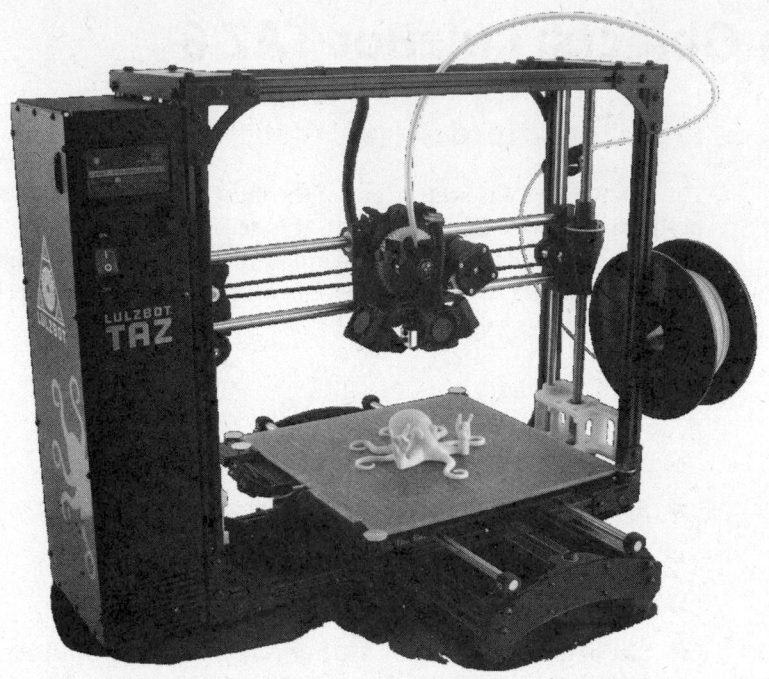

BCN3D Technologies: BCN3D Sigma

www.bcn3dtechnologies.com/en/3d-printer/bcn3d-sigma/

The BCN3D Sigma is another intermediate user 3D printer that is out there at the moment. It provides full support for Tinkercad (cool) and offers a dual extrusion service, called Meshmixer, whereby you can get multi-colored 3D prints using more than one color of material in the print from a standard STL file.

Factors to consider:

>> **File support:** STL, OBJ, AMF, and GCODE.

>> **Materials:** PLA, ABS, PVA, TPU, Nylon, HIPS, and Specials.

>> **Time to print:** Data not available.

>> **Colors:** Most colors available based on material support.

>> **Size of model:** 210 x 297 x 210mm (8.3 x 11.7 x 8.3 inches).

>> **Software:** Cura-BCN3D, Simplify3D, and Slic3r (Windows, Mac, and Linux).

>> **Connectivity:** SD card (autonomous) and USB.

>> **Power:** AC 84 to 240V, AC 3, 6-1, 3A, 50 to 60Hz.

Figure 21-6 shows a typical image of the BCN3D Sigma.

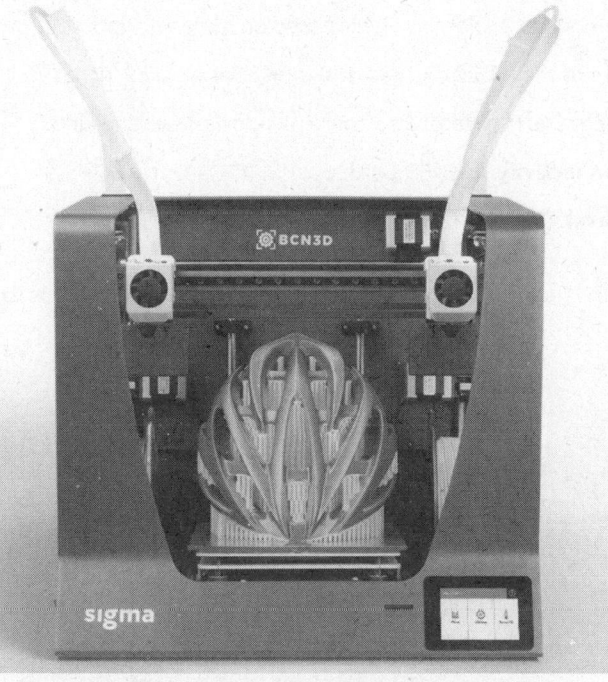

FIGURE 21-6:
The BCN3D
Sigma.

Credit: www.bcn3dtechnologies.com.

FlashForge: FlashForge Creator Pro

http://www.flashforge.com/creator-pro-3d-printer/

The FlashForge Creator Pro is a very reliable 3D printer with excellent precision and professional quality. It has a sturdy metal frame for stability, which allows for enhanced stability of the moving parts of the printer. It has 10 mm Z-axis guide rods for precise movement of the z-axis, and it has a build plate made from 6.3mm aluminum alloy, the same grade used in the aerospace industry. It has excellent heat distribution to prevent deformation, and its print chamber provides different printing environments for different materials.

Factors to consider:

>> **File support:** STL and OBJ.

>> **Materials:** PLA and ABS.

>> **Time to print:** Data not available.

>> **Colors:** Most colors available based on material support.

>> **Size of model:** 227 x 148 x 150 mm (8.9 x 5.8 x 5.9 inches).

>> **Software:** ReplicatorG software (Windows, Mac, and Linux).

>> **Connectivity:** USB, SD Card.

>> **Power:** 100 to 240 V, ~2amps, 50 to 60 Hz, and 350 W.

Figure 21-7 shows a typical image of the FlashForge Creator Pro.

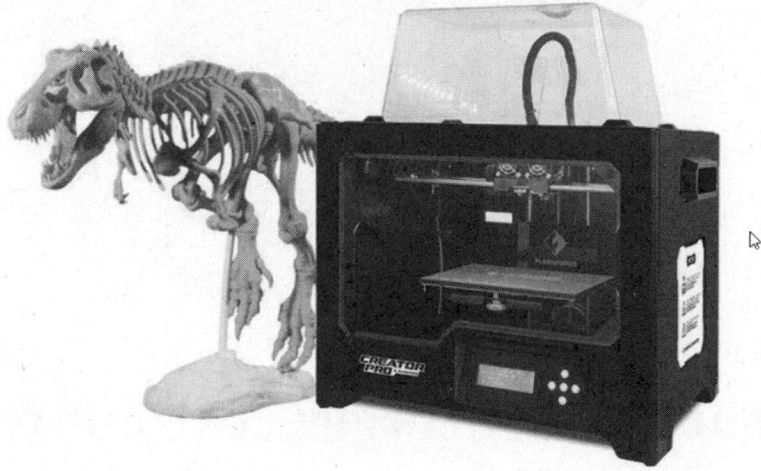

FIGURE 21-7:
The FlashForge
Creator Pro.

Credit: www.flashforge.com.

Prusa Research: Original Prusa i3 MK2S

https://shop.prusa3d.com/en/3d-printers/59-original-prusa-i3-mk2-kit

The Original Prusa i3 MK2S is one of the most popular 3D printers worldwide. One of its benefits to makers/hobbyists is that it can be purchased as a kit to build. This gives great insight into how the printer works and also allows for greater knowledge of maintenance, when parts need to be replaced. It has a heatbed with cold corners compensation, and a maintenance-free PEI surface and supports a wide range of printing materials. The MK2S is also the 3D printer of the year 2017 and 2018 in *MAKE: Magazine*.

Factors to consider:

>> **File support:** STL and OBJ.

>> **Materials:** PLA, ABS, PET, HIPS, Flex PP, and many more.

>> **Time to print:** Data not available.

>> **Colors:** Most colors available based on material support.

>> **Size of model:** 250 x 210 x 200 mm (9.84 x 8.3 x 8 inches).

>> **Software:** Slic3r Prusa Edition (Windows, Mac, and Linux).

>> **Connectivity:** Integrated LCD and SD card (8GB card included).

>> **Power:** Data not available.

Figure 21-8 shows a typical image of the Original Prusa i3 MK2.

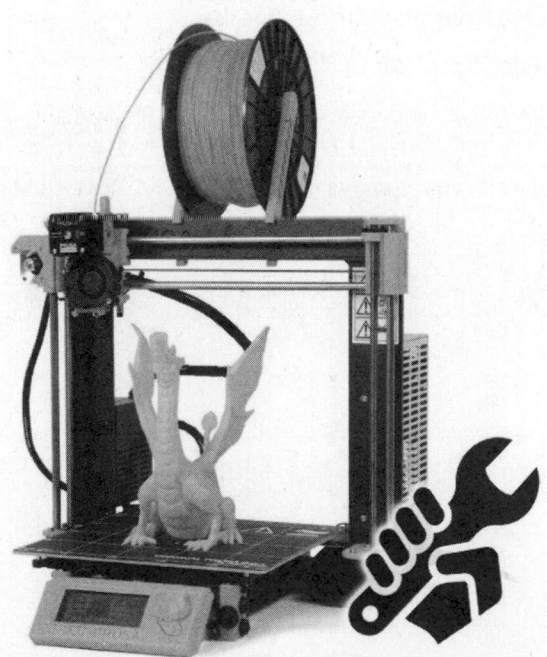

FIGURE 21-8:
The Original
Prusa i3 MK2.

Credit: www.prusa3d.com.

SeeMeCNC: Rostock Max

`www.seemecnc.com/products/rostock-max-v3-desktop-3d-printer-diy-kit`

The Rostock Max is another 3D printer that can be ordered in kit form to be built by the end user. It has an all-metal design with a PTFE liner as a heat break, allowing nylon (polyamide) up to 250 degrees Celsius and other materials up to 280 degrees Celsius. It can be calibrated to automate your 3D printing and has an onyx heatbed to prevent warping and heat distortion. It comes with an EZT Struder print head and has a three-part fan for excellent cooling of your 3D prints.

Factors to consider:

>> **File support:** STL and OBJ.

>> **Materials:** PLA and ABS.

>> **Time to print:** Data not available.

>> **Colors:** Most colors available based on material support.

>> **Size of model:** 250 x 210 x 200 mm (9.84 x 8.3 x 8 inches).

>> **Software:** MatterControl (Windows and Mac).

>> **Connectivity:** SD card (card included) and USB.

>> **Power:** 110v or 220v (input power selectable) at 350 watts.

Figure 21-9 shows a typical image of the SeeMeCNC Rostock Max.

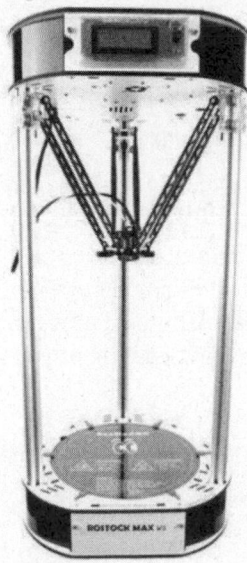

FIGURE 21-9:
The SeeMeCNC
Rostock Max.

Credit: www.seemecnc.com.

PrintrBot: PrintrBot Simple Pro

`https://printrbot.com/shop/simple-pro-base-model/`

The original model of the Simple Pro, it is a 3D printer base model manufactured from premium hardware components. This printer has a 32-bit brain known as the Printrboard G2. This is the basic model of the printer and does not come provided with a heatbed, but there is a model with the heatbed available. It also has a touchscreen and has wifi and cloud support too. It is another 3D printer manufactured in the United States.

Factors to consider:

» **File support:** STL (possibly others, but data not available).

» **Materials:** PLA and ABS (and other exotics, according to website).

» **Time to print:** Data not available.

» **Colors:** Most colors available based on material support.

» **Size of model:** 200 x 150 x 200mm (8 x 6 x 8 inches).

>> **Software:** Cura 2 (Windows and Mac).

>> **Connectivity:** Direct wifi and USB. Also uses printrbot in the cloud.

>> **Power:** 12V (6 A) laptop power supply (included).

Figure 21-10 shows a typical image of the PrintrBot Simple Pro.

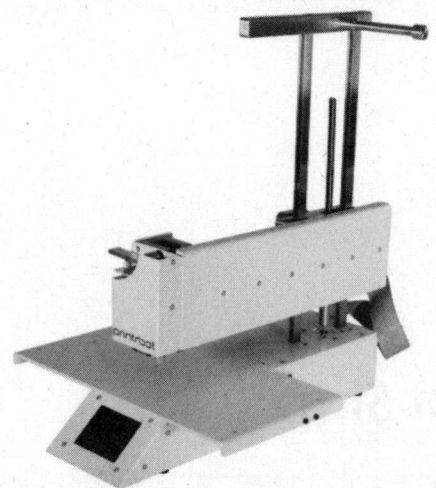

Chapter **22**

Ten 3D Applications

M any other 3D applications besides Tinkercad are available. In this chapter, you find out about ten 3D applications that you may have heard of.

You can find a lot of this information on the Internet. I provide the web address for each application so that you can find out additional details, if you want.

Like with any software applications, you may find a particular application that you like or prefer in this list of ten 3D applications, or the one you really like isn't there. Bear in mind that many 3D applications are out there, and it can come down to personal preference, file format, or even just company standards that define which one you use.

If you are going to consider using 3D applications and modelers other than Tinkercad, make sure you examine what you need first. Find the application that suits your needs and, more importantly, your pocket! One of the big benefits nowadays is that many 3D modeling applications can be free and open source, such as Blender, but also numerous applications are now subscription based, so you can pay a monthly fee, instead of being stung with a huge financial investment before you have even started.

Also, be aware that some of the 3D applications listed are not compatible with Tinkercad. They have been listed because there will come a point where you move away from Tinkercad and go to the next level of 3D. Tinkercad is an entry-level 3D modeler and has its limitations, but the benefits of Tinkercad to get you into the 3D world and into 3D modeling are priceless.

Autodesk: 3D Studio Max

www.autodesk.com/products/3ds-max/overview

Known as 3ds Max, this 3D application by Autodesk is used to develop the 3D scenery, characters, and props used in most of the console-based games out there. It is also used by designers worldwide who want to animate their 3D models. It includes easy-to-use, powerful modeling tools, high-end rendering for materials and textures, and realistic 3D animation.

>> **File support:** 3DS and MAX (native) and OBJ.

>> **Operating system:** Microsoft Windows only.

>> **Price:** $1,470 per year (subscription).

>> **Compatible with Tinkercad:** Yes, with OBJ file export.

>> **Output to 3D printing:** Yes, with OBJ file export.

>> **Community:** https://area.autodesk.com/

>> **User level (above or below Tinkercad):** Above.

Figure 22-1 shows you a typical image of 3ds Max.

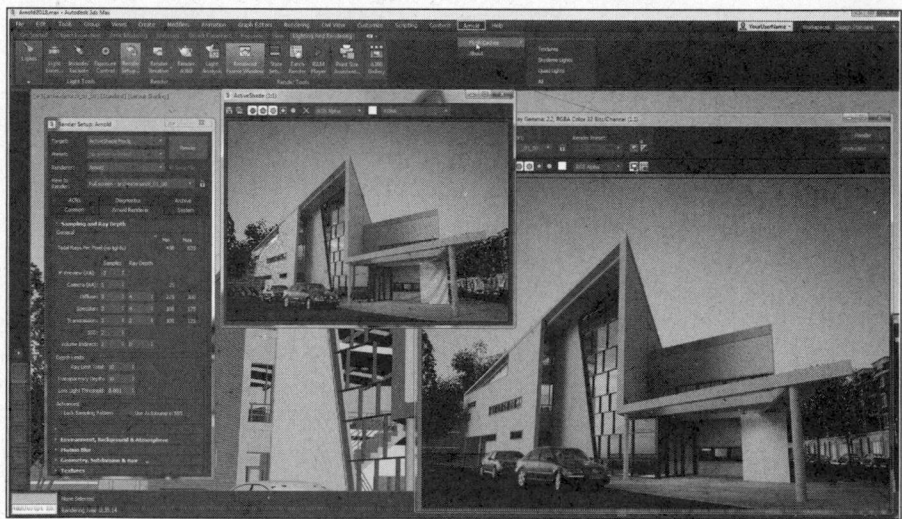

FIGURE 22-1: A typical 3ds Max screenshot.

Credit: Autodesk,Inc.

Autodesk: Maya

www.autodesk.com/products/maya/overview

Maya provides incredible 3D animation, modeling, simulation, and rendering in a software environment that incorporates an integrated, powerful toolset. It is often used for animation, environments, motion graphics, virtual reality, and character creation. Many action movies and TV shows use Autodesk Maya CGI (Computer Generated Images) in their scenes nowadays.

» **File support:** Maya IFF (native) and OBJ, STL, SVG.

» **Operating system:** Windows, Mac OSX, and Linux.

» **Price:** $1,470 per year (subscription).

» **Compatible with Tinkercad:** Yes, with OBJ, STL, and SVG file export.

» **Output to 3D printing:** Yes, with OBJ, STL, and SVG file export.

» **Community:** https://area.autodesk.com/

» **User level (above or below Tinkercad):** Above.

Figure 22-2 shows a typical still from a Maya showreel.

FIGURE 22-2:
A typical still from a Maya showreel.

Autodesk: Inventor

www.autodesk.com/products/inventor/overview

Autodesk's Inventor 3D CAD software is used for 3D mechanical design, documentation, and product simulation, providing industry-standard 3D models for product design and manufacturing. It is used in many commercial environments, such as aerospace, automotive, and factory-based manufacturing.

>> **File support:** IPT (native) and IAM (native) and STL.

>> **Operating system:** Microsoft Windows only.

>> **Price:** $1,890 per year (subscription).

>> **Compatible with Tinkercad:** Yes, with STL file export.

>> **Output to 3D printing:** Yes, with STL file export.

>> **Community:** https://forums.autodesk.com/t5/inventor/ct-p/70

>> **User level (above or below Tinkercad):** Above.

Figure 22-3 shows a typical screenshot from Autodesk Inventor.

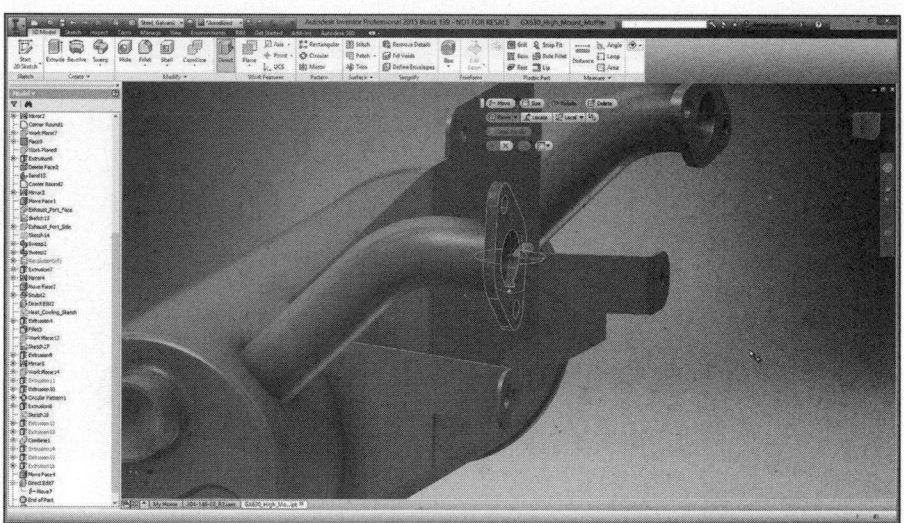

FIGURE 22-3: A typical Inventor screenshot.

Credit: Autodesk,Inc.

Autodesk: Fusion 360

www.autodesk.com/products/fusion-360/overview

Autodesk's Fusion 360 is a cloud-based 3D modeler, just like Tinkercad, but is more biased to the commercial marketplace. It allows for quick iterations on design ideas with sculpting tools to explore form and modeling tools to create finishing features. It also provides tools to test fit and motion, perform simulations, create assemblies, and make photorealistic renderings and animations, with links to CAM software to generate nondestructive prototypes.

>> **File support:** F3D (native), CAM360 (native), OBJ, and STL.

>> **Operating system:** Windows and Mac OSX.

>> **Price:** Free to students and educators; $300 per year otherwise.

>> **Compatible with Tinkercad:** Yes, with OBJ or STL file export.

>> **Output to 3D printing:** Yes, with OBJ or STL file export.

>> **Community:** https://fusion360.autodesk.com/community

>> **User level (above or below Tinkercad):** Slightly above (commercial).

Figure 22-4 shows a typical Fusion 360 screenshot.

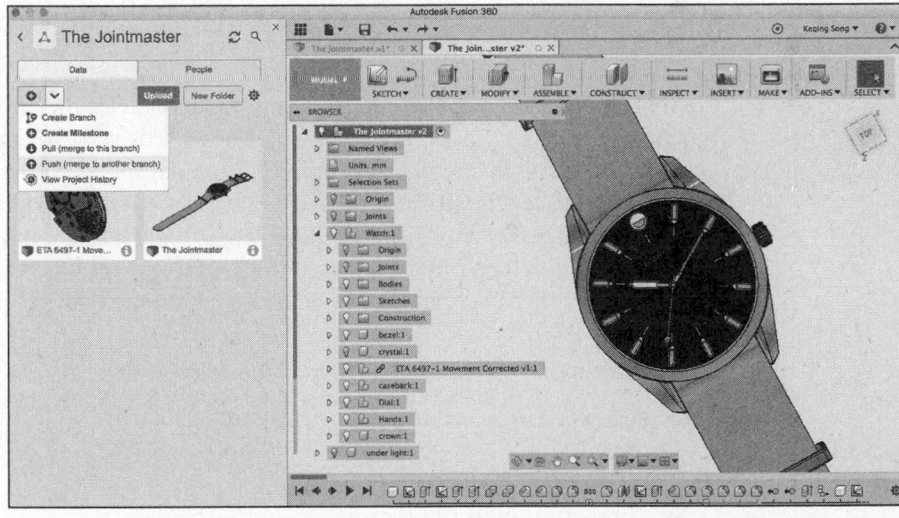

FIGURE 22-4:
A typical Fusion 360 screenshot.

Credit: Autodesk, Inc.

Smith Micro Software: Poser

http://my.smithmicro.com/poser-pro-11 (latest version)

Poser provides human and animal models that are prepared for you to start designing and posing immediately. The Poser figures are pre-rigged so 3D artists can click and drag to pose body parts, sculpt faces, or create ethnic varieties. Poser can provide the 3D artist with thousands of poses, morphs, clothing, hair, and materials.

>> **File support:** CR2, PPZ, PP2, MC5, MC6 plus others (native), and OBJ.

>> **Operating system:** Windows and Mac OSX.

>> **Price:** Digital copy $129.99; pro version $349.99.

>> **Compatible with Tinkercad:** Yes, with OBJ file export.

>> **Output to 3D printing:** Yes, with OBJ file export.

>> **Community:** https://forum.smithmicro.com/category/9/poser

>> **User level (above or below Tinkercad):** Above (commercial).

CLO Virtual Fashion: Marvelous Designer

www.marvelousdesigner.com/product/overview

Marvelous Designer allows you to create 3D virtual clothing from basic shirts to intricately pleated dresses and rugged uniforms. The software can virtually replicate fabric textures and physical properties. It allows you to edit and drape garments onto 3D forms with high-fidelity simulation. This innovative pattern-based approach has been adopted by top game studios, such as EA and Konami, and can be seen in big-screen films, including *The Hobbit* and *The Adventures of Tin Tin*, created by Weta Digital. Figure 22-5 shows a typical Marvelous Designer screenshot.

>> **File support:** ZPAC, APT, POS plus others (native), and OBJ.

>> **Operating system:** Windows and Mac OSX.

>> **Price:** $50 per month; $300 per year; or $499 perpetual.

>> **Compatible with Tinkercad:** Yes, with OBJ file export.

>> **Output to 3D printing:** Yes, with OBJ file export.

CLO Virtual Fashion: CLO3D

www.clo3d.com/

CLO3D has some of the most advanced 3D modeling algorithms in the 3D industry, allowing the fashion industry to reduce design lead times from weeks to minutes. The software allows the 3D artist and fashion designer to confirm and fine-tune the 3D clothing design before the material is cut, made, and trimmed. This eliminates the excess fabric sample rounds and over-development, reducing excessive costs.

>> **File support:** ZPAC, ZPRJ and others (native), and OBJ.

>> **Operating system:** Windows and Mac OSX.

>> **Price:** POA (Price On Application).

>> **Compatible with Tinkercad:** Yes, with OBJ file export.

>> **Output to 3D printing:** Yes, with OBJ file export.

>> **Community:** https://support.clo3d.com/hc/en-us/community/topics

>> **User level (above or below Tinkercad):** Above (commercial).

Figure 22-6 shows you a typical CLO3D screenshot.

EFI: Optitex

https://optitex.com/

Optitex provides a smooth, efficient workflow for clothing and fashion design for clothing companies, such as Under Armour. The 3D software allows for designing from the first stitch to the final finished product, highlighting any changes made in 2D or 3D automatically. The 3D design can then be leveraged across all business processes, from product development and merchandising, all the way through to sales and marketing.

>> **File support:** DSN, PDS, 3DS and others (native), STL, and OBJ.

>> **Operating system:** 3D Product Creation Suite – Microsoft Windows only.

>> **Price:** POA (Price On Application).

>> **Compatible with Tinkercad:** Yes, with STL and OBJ file export.

>> **Output to 3D printing:** Yes, with STL and OBJ file export.

>> **Community:** Customer page https://optitex.com/our-customers/

>> **User level (above or below Tinkercad):** Above (commercial).

Figure 22-7 shows a typical Optitex screenshot.

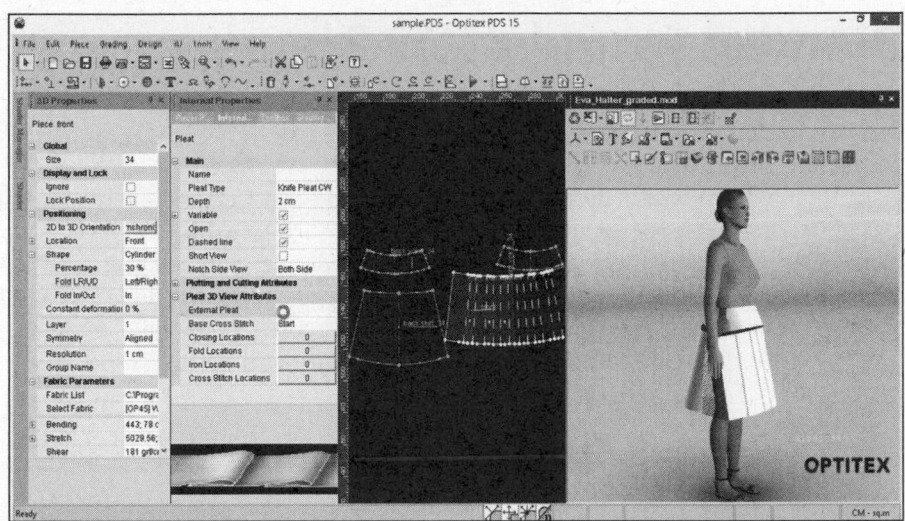

FIGURE 22-7:
A typical Optitex
screenshot.

Trimble: SketchUp

www.sketchup.com/

SketchUp by Trimble was originally Google SketchUp. SketchUp is a user-friendly, forgiving, 3D modeling software application that allows you to develop functional designs by drawing lines and shapes, which can then be pushed and pulled into 3D surfaces and then into 3D forms.

>> **File support:** SKP (native) and STL.

>> **Operating system:** SketchUp Pro – Windows and Mac OSX.

>> **Price:** SketchUp Pro $695.

>> **Compatible with Tinkercad:** Yes, with STL file export.

>> **Output to 3D printing:** Yes, with STL file export.

>> **Community:** https://forums.sketchup.com/

>> **User level (above or below Tinkercad):** Above (commercial).

Blender Foundation: Blender

```
www.blender.org/
```

Blender by the Blender Foundation is a free and open source 3D creation suite. Blender allows you to follow the entire 3D workflow pipeline from modeling, rigging, animation, simulation, rendering, compositing, and motion tracking. It even allows for video editing and game creation. Blender is a public project, made by people from around the world, studios and individual artists, professionals and hobbyists, scientists, students, VFX experts, animators, game artists, modders, and the list goes on.

>> **File support:** BLEND (native) and STL.

>> **Operating system:** Windows, Mac OSX, and Linux.

>> **Price:** Free – open source software.

>> **Compatible with Tinkercad:** Yes, with STL file export.

>> **Output to 3D printing:** Yes, with STL file export.

>> **Community:** www.blendernetwork.org/

>> **User level (above or below Tinkercad):** Above.

Figure 22-8 shows a typical Blender screenshot.

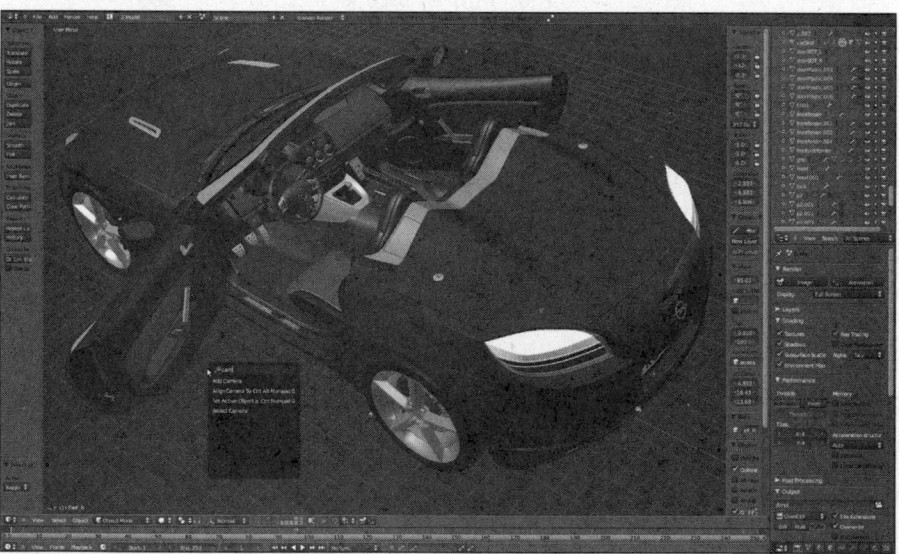

FIGURE 22-8: A typical Blender screenshot.

Credit: www.blender.org.

Index

About the Author

Shaun C. Bryant is an Autodesk Certified Professional with 30 years of industry experience using Autodesk software, including AutoCAD, Revit, and Tinkercad. Shaun gained his skillset while working as a consultant, trainer, manager, and user. He has a varied background, comprised of 18 years as a CAD and FM consultant/trainer; 3 years in sales, pre-sales, and business development; and 9 years as a CAD manager/user.

Shaun is also a published author on Lynda.com and an instructor on LinkedIn Learning. He is the author of the reputable CAD blog Not Just CAD! and has been responsible for creating numerous bespoke training systems for both large and small companies all over the world.

Shaun has been speaker at numerous Autodesk events, including Autodesk University, for more than a decade. He also speaks at and manages AUGI Design Academies and AUGI CAD Camps, both in the UK and around the world.

Shaun is an Autodesk University Speaker Mentor and a member of the Autodesk Expert Elite program. He contributes regularly to the AutoCAD Influencers program.

Dedication

I would like to dedicate this book to my family, without whose support I would not be able to be where I am today. You are the reason I work hard every single day.

I would also like to dedicate my first Wiley title to all of us out there who choose to learn something new every day. Learning never stops. Just choose to learn and find something new. Don't stop, keep going.

Author's Acknowledgments

Thanks go to all the wonderful team at Wiley who has been incredibly patient with me as I write my first Wiley title. Special thanks go to Amy Fandrei and Kelly Ewing, who have helped me every step of the way, to my great friend and Tinkercad product line manager, Guillermo Melantoni, at Autodesk, and to all of the Tinkercad product team.

Publisher's Acknowledgments

Senior Acquisitions Editor: Amy Fandrei

Project Editor: Kelly Ewing

Copy Editor: Kelly Ewing

Sr. Editorial Assistant: Cherie Case

Reviewer: Sarah Guthals, PhD

Production Editor: Tamilmani Varadharaj

Cover Image: Courtesy of Shaun Bryant

Take dummies with you everywhere you go!

Whether you are excited about e-books, want more from the web, must have your mobile apps, or are swept up in social media, dummies makes everything easier.

Find us online!

dummies.com

Leverage the power

Dummies is the global leader in the reference category and one of the most trusted and highly regarded brands in the world. No longer just focused on books, customers now have access to the dummies content they need in the format they want. Together we'll craft a solution that engages your customers, stands out from the competition, and helps you meet your goals.

Advertising & Sponsorships

Connect with an engaged audience on a powerful multimedia site, and position your message alongside expert how-to content. Dummies.com is a one-stop shop for free, online information and know-how curated by a team of experts.

- Targeted ads
- Video
- Email Marketing
- Microsites
- Sweepstakes sponsorship

20 MILLION PAGE VIEWS EVERY SINGLE MONTH

15 MILLION UNIQUE VISITORS PER MONTH

43% OF ALL VISITORS ACCESS THE SITE VIA THEIR MOBILE DEVICES

700,000 NEWSLETTER SUBSCRIPTIONS TO THE INBOXES OF *300,000* UNIQUE INDIVIDUALS EVERY WEEK

# of dummies

Custom Publishing

Reach a global audience in any language by creating a solution that will differentiate you from competitors, amplify your message, and encourage customers to make a buying decision.

- Apps
- Books
- eBooks
- Video
- Audio
- Webinars

Brand Licensing & Content

Leverage the strength of the world's most popular reference brand to reach new audiences and channels of distribution.

For more information, visit dummies.com/biz

PERSONAL ENRICHMENT

9781119187790
USA $26.00
CAN $31.99
UK £19.99

9781119179030
USA $21.99
CAN $25.99
UK £16.99

9781119293354
USA $24.99
CAN $29.99
UK £17.99

9781119293347
USA $22.99
CAN $27.99
UK £16.99

9781119310068
USA $22.99
CAN $27.99
UK £16.99

9781119235606
USA $24.99
CAN $29.99
UK £17.99

9781119251163
USA $24.99
CAN $29.99
UK £17.99

9781119235491
USA $26.99
CAN $31.99
UK £19.99

9781119279952
USA $24.99
CAN $29.99
UK £17.99

9781119283133
USA $24.99
CAN $29.99
UK £17.99

9781119287117
USA $24.99
CAN $29.99
UK £16.99

9781119130246
USA $22.99
CAN $27.99
UK £16.99

PROFESSIONAL DEVELOPMENT

9781119311041
USA $24.99
CAN $29.99
UK £17.99

9781119255796
USA $39.99
CAN $47.99
UK £27.99

9781119293439
USA $26.99
CAN $31.99
UK £19.99

9781119281467
USA $26.99
CAN $31.99
UK £19.99

9781119280651
USA $29.99
CAN $35.99
UK £21.99

9781119251132
USA $24.99
CAN $29.99
UK £17.99

9781119310563
USA $34.00
CAN $41.99
UK £24.99

9781119181705
USA $29.99
CAN $35.99
UK £21.99

9781119263593
USA $26.99
CAN $31.99
UK £19.99

9781119257769
USA $29.99
CAN $35.99
UK £21.99

9781119293477
USA $26.99
CAN $31.99
UK £19.99

9781119265313
USA $24.99
CAN $29.99
UK £17.99

9781119239314
USA $29.99
CAN $35.99
UK £21.99

9781119293323
USA $29.99
CAN $35.99
UK £21.99

dummies.com

dummies
A Wiley Brand

Learning Made Easy

ACADEMIC

9781119293576
USA $19.99
CAN $23.99
UK £15.99

9781119293637
USA $19.99
CAN $23.99
UK £15.99

9781119293491
USA $19.99
CAN $23.99
UK £15.99

9781119293460
USA $19.99
CAN $23.99
UK £15.99

9781119293590
USA $19.99
CAN $23.99
UK £15.99

9781119215844
USA $26.99
CAN $31.99
UK £19.99

9781119293378
USA $22.99
CAN $27.99
UK £16.99

9781119293521
USA $19.99
CAN $23.99
UK £15.99

9781119239178
USA $18.99
CAN $22.99
UK £14.99

9781119263883
USA $26.99
CAN $31.99
UK £19.99

Available Everywhere Books Are Sold

Small books for big imaginations

9781119177173
USA $9.99
CAN $9.99
UK £8.99

9781119177272
USA $9.99
CAN $9.99
UK £8.99

9781119177241
USA $9.99
CAN $9.99
UK £8.99

9781119177210
USA $9.99
CAN $9.99
UK £8.99

9781119262657
USA $9.99
CAN $9.99
UK £6.99

9781119291336
USA $9.99
CAN $9.99
UK £6.99

9781119233527
USA $9.99
CAN $9.99
UK £6.99

9781119291220
USA $9.99
CAN $9.99
UK £6.99

9781119177302
USA $9.99
CAN $9.99
UK £8.99

Unleash Their Creativity

dummies.com

dummies
A Wiley Brand